Early Diamond Days

OSWALD DOUGHTY

Early Diamond Days

The Opening of the
Diamond Fields of
South Africa

Longmans

LONGMANS, GREEN AND CO LTD
48 Grosvenor Street, London W1
*Associated companies, branches and representatives
throughout the world*

© *Oswald Doughty 1963*
First published 1963

*Printed in Great Britain by
Richard Clay and Company, Ltd.,
Bungay, Suffolk*

Preface

The reminiscences of a pioneer on the South African Diamond Fields, lighted upon by chance in the Library of Rhodes House at Oxford, during the unusually wet summer of 1958, stimulated not only nostalgic memories of the warm sunlit shores and blue seas of the Cape, but also an interest in the early days of the South African Diamond Fields, which in turn led to the present volume.

In further visits to Rhodes House more material was collected, and in the late summer carried to Spain, where during the autumn and winter in a sunny villa near Malaga, a preliminary outline of the work was made. On my return to the Cape in the following spring, more material was obtained and the final version written. During this process I abandoned my original intention to present an authentic account of the subject almost exclusively in my own words. With such material to hand, to do so would have inevitably entailed the loss of immediacy, colour, actuality; in short, of 'life'. I have therefore incorporated into the narrative, verbatim, whatever of the diggers' reminiscences seemed to me particularly appropriate to such illumination of my theme.

Mechanization, radio, gramophone, television, speech-recorders, have made our age peculiarly that of the 'spoken' word. In the following pages, almost like some radio compère, I have called on many voices of the past to recreate for us the Early Diamond Days of South Africa.

OSWALD DOUGHTY

Kelmscott
Newlands
Cape
South Africa

Fortunes come tumbling into some men's laps.
BACON. *The Advancement of Learning*

*Lord Randolph Churchill on visiting the Diamond Fields and
seeing a parcel of diamonds:* 'All for the vanity of woman!'
A Lady in his party: 'And the depravity of man!'

Contents

Illustrations

Acknowledgements

I AM grateful to the Staff of the South African Archives, Cape Town, for information; my wife, Marcelle Doughty, for transcribing much of the material; Mrs S. Grodd for typing the MS; D. McHardy, Esq., Resident Manager of De Beers Consolidated Mines, Kimberley, for illustrations and information; W. K. Hartley, Esq., Acting Assistant General Manager, De Beers Consolidated Mines, Kimberley, for illustrations; O. W. McIntyre, Librarian, the Public Library, Kimberley, for illustrations; *Optima* for the photograph of Kimberley Mine, 1872, and to the following for permission to reproduce copyright material: Macmillan & Co. Ltd for extracts from *Impressions of South Africa* by Viscount Bryce, and the Trustees of the late Sir Lionel F. Phillips' Estate and Hutchinson & Co. Ltd for extracts from *Some Reminiscences*.

The copyright owners in the poems 'Trekkers' by Beatrice Marian Bromley from *Where the Aloe Grows*, published by Juta & Co. Ltd, South Africa, and 'A Song of a Wagon-Whip' by Samuel Cron Cronwright Schreiner from *Little Songs for South Africans* cannot be traced and any information which would make this possible would be welcomed.

1

The River Diggings

THE year 1870, marked by the outbreak of the Franco-Prussian War, was a year of depression in Europe. In South Africa, then so remote in both time and place, the general mood was similarly depressed. There was little money in the country, and those who had any held to it tenaciously. Business and credit were far from flourishing. The South Africa of those days showed little promise of the great changes soon to come.

For it was the darkness preceding the dawn. Three years before, an almost unregarded incident in a deserted corner of the country heralded South Africa's future development. Near Hopetown, a small agricultural settlement on the Orange River, some thirty miles from its junction with the Vaal, there lived a Boer farmer who occasionally brought home as playthings for his children pretty stones picked up on the banks of the river. One day in the early spring of 1866 his finds included a little white stone that looked different from the rest. It attracted no particular attention at the time, but later the mother noticed its unusual sparkle in the sunlight as the children played with it. Her casual mention of it to a neighbour, Schalk Van Niekerk, led to his seeing it and being so attracted that he offered to buy it. Laughingly refusing to take money from a friend for a mere worthless pebble, she presented it to him; and with a vague idea that it might have some value, Van Niekerk entrusted it to a travelling trader, John O'Reilly, who offered to have its nature and value determined.

Various dealers at Hopetown and elsewhere rejected it as worthless; but the Civil Commissioner at Colesberg, Lorenzo Boyes, on finding that it scratched glass, suspected it to be a diamond. Next sent (it is said, by post-cart, in an unsealed envelope) to the leading Cape mineralogist, Dr Atherston of Grahamstown, it was definitely declared to be a diamond of $21\frac{1}{4}$ carats, and valued by the Doctor and by the French Consul at Cape Town, M. Henriette, at £500. At this price the Governor of the Cape, Sir Philip Wodehouse, bought it, and, doubtless through his agency and that of M. Henriette, it appeared at the Paris Exhibition of 1867, where, however, it attracted little attention. Nor was it much noticed in South Africa.

No immediate results followed. South Africa appeared as uninterested as Paris in this new portent. Only a few odd explorers gravitated to the Hopetown district to prospect along the Orange and Vaal rivers. Ignorant of geology and mineralogy, these earliest searchers believed that diamonds must have been washed downstream from their original beds. Native superstition, more imaginative, declared that snakes with diamonds on their heads bathed in the rivers and left their diamonds on the banks. Professed geologists and diamond experts who visited the district roundly asserted that no diamond field existed there, while the more pessimistic even declared that diamonds would be found nowhere in South Africa. Nor, they said, even if they were discovered, would they repay the cost of extraction. It was in the face of such discouragement that the prospectors' first successes were achieved.

In fact, a tradition of fabulous mineral wealth in South Africa had long existed. In the days of the Dutch domination, expeditions had set out from Cape Town in quest of such treasure, but without success. An old eighteenth-century map was said to have 'Here be diamonds' written across the Griqua country. Modern authorities doubt this, declaring that if such a map exists, the inscription must have been added at a much later date. If true, however, the tradition was doubtless due to occasional native reports of diamonds and the rare appearance in Cape Town of some native or stray European traveller bringing an odd stone or two, diamond, agate, onyx, amethyst or garnet.

It is, therefore, highly probable that Van Niekerk's first interest in the white stone was more than purely aesthetic. Certainly the next occasion on which he appears is definitely commercial. In March 1869 a native shepherd in the neighbourhood picked up a fine diamond, and with some suspicion of its value for queer white men, consulted a medicine man who took it to a merchant named Gers and asked £200 for it. Gers hesitated, and the medicine man immediately ran to Van Niekerk, locally famous for his discovery of the previous diamond and for the wealth it had brought him, and demanded £400 for the stone. Van Niekerk obtained it by offering the man as equivalent, the whole of his own livestock: 500 sheep, ten oxen and a horse; a vast fortune to the delighted Griqua shepherd.

Van Niekerk then sold the stone to a dealer in Hopetown[1] for £11,200. A law suit followed, brought by a group of speculators who claimed that the stone had been found on ground over which they held a concession.

---

[1] This fact and the frequent necessity for hope led the diggers to name their camps Delport's Hope, Cawood's Hope, Good Hope, Forlorn Hope, Last Hope, etc. Kimberley's motto, *Spero meliora*, improved on these.

They lost their case, however, and the stone, a superb white diamond of 83½ carats, was bought by a firm of London dealers who sold it to the Earl of Dudley for £25,000. Before the stone left South Africa, Sir Richard Southey, Colonial Secretary to the Cape Assembly, laid it on the table of the House with the prophetic declaration: 'Gentlemen, this is the rock on which the future of South Africa will be built.' Henceforth the diamond was known as *The Star of South Africa*. Next, in May 1870, a regimental officer arrived in Maritzburg with a parcel of diamonds worth £12,000 or £15,000, entrusted to his care by a small party of diggers who had been quietly working for some months along the banks of the Vaal.

Before the diamond rush began, this region was almost uninhabited. Its beauty and its solitude in those days appealed to many who passed that way. One of them saw the Vaal as 'a broad, handsome stream, bright, broad and beautiful, flowing . . . silent and undisturbed between luxuriantly fringed banks where the sounds of Nature were alone audible'. Another observer similarly described the country during the earliest days of the prospectors' invasion, though with an evident appreciation of the new social scene then unfolding. 'No scenery', he wrote, 'is more striking than that of the Vaal River. The dreary solitude that had hitherto been untrodden, save by the foot of untamed Koronna or Griqua, was the scene of civilized activity. The unfertile hills were the habitat of hares, small buck, partridge and pheasant; the only vegetation of the kopjes is the Vaalbosch and haakdoorn, which grows profusely, covering miles of country. The river is flanked on either side by willow trees, whilst further from the water's edge, the banks are overgrown by rank vegetation, which in places forms cover for innumerable guinea-fowl. The mimosa thorn, which attains a height above all other trees and shrubbery, grows to perfection. . . . Through this scenery the mighty Vaal flows silently on till it unites with the Orange River. . . . When in flood, the roar of turbulent waters is similar to that of ocean waves breaking on a rocky shore. On the whole, scenery on the Vaal is pleasing to the eye, especially during the first weeks after the dreary journey across the arid veldt from one of the coastal towns.'

Meanwhile, public interest in the possibilities of diamonds had been aroused. A rush to the Diamond Fields followed and was soon in full swing. First came South Africans, including farmers from the Cape and Natal in their covered wagons, followed by others from farther afield. One result of this was the general peaceful behaviour of the diggers in these earliest days. 'The absence in early days of Diamond Field History of violent personal encounters, robberies, lynching and such like, which were

3

features of everyday life in the early days of Californian and Australian Gold Fields, is to be attributed to the fact that the diggers who laid the foundation of the diamond industry were all South African Colonists.' So wrote one digger, and continued: 'If all the vast crowd did not know each other personally, they knew of each other, and any man coming either to Pniel or Klipdrift, who was such an entire stranger that he could not claim acquaintance with someone among all the thousands massed together on the banks of the river, would be looked upon strangely, if not suspiciously, until he could give some good account of himself, or had, by his conduct on the fields, won the good opinion of neighbours.'

After this, one is not surprised to find the same writer commenting upon the general friendly relations among the river diggers. One feature he observed that made early Diamond Fields life 'pleasant on the banks of the Vaal was the cordiality and good understanding that existed between diggers themselves. A mutual regard for each other manifested itself all through the camps. The unlucky digger shared in the luck of his neighbours. When a man was known to be hard up after having honestly invested his bottom dollar on his claim, he would not have, if he was known to have worked as a man should, to beg for a few coppers. It had not become the rule as set forth in Scripture, to take from him that hath not even that which he hath. The man who had, did not wait to be asked for help – he gave without being asked. No man was long without money; some neighbours came forward and set him on his legs again.'

Such a description may err on the idyllic side, but it is by no means the only evidence we have of the high standard of behaviour among the early diggers by the river. 'Often', writes another of them, 'the grade and intelligence of the diggers, notwithstanding their rough mode of life to which they had adapted themselves, were equal to those of the best class of society in the colonial towns, and some of them studied to show that it is possible to cultivate the graces of life in the wilderness as well as in cities. Indeed there was not enough roughness in their demeanour, save for a certain breezy frankness in their conversation and carelessness in dress, to denote them as any other than the ordinary class of people met with elsewhere.'

Estimates of the numbers who came to the river diggings during the short two years or so of their popularity vary from 5,000 to double that number. They spread along the banks of the Vaal, here, there and everywhere, looking for the richest places. One day on one spot, the next they might be miles away down the river, trying some new fancy, perhaps only to return a day or two later to their old diggings.

Thus several diggers' camps were formed, chiefly at Pniel on the south bank of the river, and at Hebron on the opposite side. Other roving parties spread themselves along the Modder and Hartz rivers, tributaries of the Vaal. Their increase in numbers was rapid. By May 1870, 100 new diggers are said to have been working; by June, 700; by July, 1,000; a few weeks later, 2,000. Another estimate asserts that ere long, 10,000 black and white lined the banks of the Vaal.

Their habitations were necessarily primitive at this stage of development. The few who were lucky enough to have covered wagons used their covers as tents on the ground. Some brought canvas tents with them; others made reed shanties; many had no cover and slept on the ground.

As few of these earliest diggers had any previous knowledge of diamonds, much less of diamond-mining, many at first mistook crystals for diamonds, or did not recognize genuine stones when they found them. Believing hardness to be the unfailing test, and that no blow with a hammer, however heavy, could damage a true diamond, they shattered many a good stone in their ignorance. Not till later did they learn to detect diamonds by their crystallization and form.

The digging was largely haphazard. Many set up their tents or huts wherever they happened to be, and began groping in the sand; then dug down several feet, and if they found nothing, moved to another spot. But serious mining was hard work, done chiefly on high terraces above the camps. For washing, the gravel had to be carried down to the river; a difficult operation like the digging itself. For the ground was not mere mud and sand, but strewn with stones and heavy blocks of basalt. Nor did the climate entirely help the workers. On that high tableland, not only was the air unusually dry, but in 'winter', which lasted from April to August, the nights were bitterly cold, and the days unbearably hot. 'Summer', which lasted from September to March, was the wet rainy season, with frequent storms and deluges of rain.

'Diamond digging on the banks of the Vaal,' wrote one digger, 'was never very light work at any time; but those who made the first start at it, had not only to dig as they never dug before, but they had to undergo privations which they had not counted upon when they left their homes. For six months at least they had not an ounce of vegetable diet of any sort, and then upon privations of all sorts, fever set in, medical aid was not easily within reach, and the diggers had to nurse and doctor each other in turns – the nursing was kindly if roughly done. It was not only medical advice that was wanting, but there were no medical comforts either. . . . For the most part the men down with fever, as well as those in health, slept on the ground with nothing to lie upon but a rug. I don't believe that out of the six thousand first arrivals twenty had a mattress. Of course every party brought supplies, more or less, and all had made provision for being jolly, but when sickness came, and it did come in its severest forms – fever and dysentery – there was no means of coping with it. Those who came to search for diamonds had for the most part, nearly all one might say, been tenderly brought up, had been used to home comforts when in health, to have medical advice when ill, and to be gently tended and nursed when ailing. Yet with all the privations and hardships, the number who died was comparatively few.'

The means employed in the discovery of diamonds at the river were primitive. The machines for washing the gravel were of two kinds, known respectively as 'cradles' and 'cylinders'; but the principle of both was the same. The gravel was passed through two or three wire sieves of differently graded mesh in the machines, so that whatever stones the sand and gravel contained were caught in the meshes, while water was poured over them, washing the sand and gravel away. The 'cradle', as its name suggests, was mounted on rockers, and had a long handle by which it was violently rocked during washing, to help the disintegration of the contents. The 'cylinder' was similarly revolved, with the same effect. The stones left in the various sieves were then removed and carefully examined for diamonds before being thrown away.

Accidents of course would happen. Sometimes, if a claim was too close to the river, water would penetrate until it was almost one with the river itself. Torrential rains would flood camps and river, which quickly rose many feet, burying everything in a sea of water and mud. Unable to work, the depressed and shivering digger must then wait in his cold wet tent or hut until the weather allowed him to resume his search for a better fortune, or pass the time convivially with comrades who were similarly enduring the enforced idleness in the nearest canteen. The canteen indeed offered a particularly desirable refuge, when in the middle of the night a sudden storm, which might last for several days, brought the cold, rainsoaked tent down on the sleeping occupant's head, and he found himself and his belongings wrapped in a swirling pool of water. At such times the canteen proprietors reaped a rich harvest while the diggers, unable to work, passed the days there talking, drinking, playing cards, billiards and dominoes and spending their money freely. The canteens were also requisitioned when old friends met and healths must be drunk, or the discovery of a diamond celebrated.

Life by the river was certainly hard at times, but there were compensations. Even if the climate was trying in various ways, all praised it as on the whole remarkably healthy, and were surprised at the general absence of illness in the mining community, particularly as sanitary organization in the camps was for a long time inevitably most primitive. But for most, the freedom of the digger's life more than counterbalanced all deficiencies. Some, indeed, evidently idealizing their experiences in retrospect, wrote afterwards of their life by the river with an almost lyrical enthusiasm.

'A digger's life', wrote one, 'is a good life; with all its drawbacks it was a manly one, possessing the advantage of a purpose attached to it. Looking back with a *soupçon* of regret, I recall with envy, on some sleepless nights, the refreshing repose I enjoyed in my tree-encircled tent, which I had earned by open-air life and strong developing exercise. Up in the morning with the sun, and after a hasty cup of coffee, to work with a will until breakfast, then the one hour repose and the pipe of reflection, after which, down to the river to see what the cradle and sorting table might reveal. Alas! how often did careful hand and watchful eye sweep over and see nothing but rubbish! Then when the load was washed and sorted, to repose until the great heat of the day became less, when some other work was done in preparation for the morrow's layout at the cradle; then as the sun sank low and shadows lengthened, once more to the "shining river", off clothes, and a long dreamy swim in the cool water, a plunge of delight compensating for the toil of the day. At night, what amusements or occupation individuals cared for or could realize.' But despite this idyllic description, its writer remained only one year at the diggings, and imaginative nostalgia and sentiment are surely as evident in his retrospect as the actual experience on which it is based.

In a similar mood many another digger writing of his life at the river diggings records his experience; also seeing it – particularly in later years, by contrast – in a sentimental and 'poetic' light. 'The quietude of these solitary regions', wrote another in 1870, 'is now broken by the song of the happy digger as he goes forth in the morning to begin his day's labour among the huge boulders in his claim, where throughout the day, the sound of pick and shovel is heard, or perhaps the shout of a lucky digger who has just succeeded in finding a diamond.'

Of all the camps on the Vaal, Gong Gong particularly appealed by its beauty and peace to the more refined diggers, who found it a paradise, though with very few diamonds – as perhaps a 'paradise' should be. They recalled in later years the pleasant 'park-like scenery and luxuriant bush to ramble through at will', the delightful climate, freedom from snakes and mosquitoes and sickness, from the expenses and other anxieties of civilization: rent, taxes and the rest. All contributed, along with plentiful food, friends to talk to and even books to read, to make an unusually agreeable way of life. 'A man pitched his tent where he liked. . . . Such a free, unconstrained existence must often be recalled with some feelings of pleasure and regret.'

Nor was the praise of Gong Gong always due to the heightened emotions of sentimental nostalgia. One digger thus described it on the spot, in 1872, contrasting its beauty with the ugliness of the dry diggings twenty miles away: 'At sight of this charming spot, one ceased to wonder that diamond digging has fascinated all the population of the [Cape] colony. Up yonder at Dutoitspan, the search is carried on under every drawback of discomfort and ugliness. It is the hardest of labour unredeemed by any charm of the surroundings. Very very different is the scene at these older diggings on the river. The work may be even more laborious, and there are not, probably, even such conveniences of living as we have now inland. If the shaft-sinking be absent here, with the constant danger attendant upon it, there is, on the other hand, heavier work and an almost greater risk in the wet and exposure. But Gong Gong is a spot as lovely as will anywhere be found. The river bank is clothed in tall willow trees. Thickets of mimosa and other thorns, most brilliantly green, form an undergrowth almost impassable. Here and there the thick springing bushes fall back, and a grassy glade intervenes, surrounded with dense foliage. A rapid, below, makes perpetual murmur on the ear. Leaves gently flutter in the wind, and chequers of sunlight come and go. Beneath the trees, in little unexpected clearings, arranged without order, but following each man's fancy, stand the tents. They come upon one suddenly; small neat dwellings of canvas, with the cradle and sieve before them, and the housewife sorting at the sheltered table. The men are carrying loads of pebbles from the river side, by devious paths amongst the brushwood, their clothes dripping as they go. There is a sound of children's voices everywhere, calling to one another and laughing, as they play in the sunny thickets. No wonder people left their dreary homes upon the veldt, or offices in a lifeless town, to risk their chance of fortune in a spot so free and lovely. At one point, prying around – with such delight in trees and grass as only two months' stay on the "dry fields" can give a man – I came upon the quaintest scene.'

Certainly it was not always Mammon that brought the diggers to the Fields. The spirit of romance was still strong, pervading not only the higher literature of the day, but also popular novels and tales of adventure. Romance is as evident an influence as conscious patriotism in the spirit of Empire then prevalent and in the deeds it inspired. A romantic, sentimental, even 'poetic' optimism animated many of the diggers, and we are not surprised to find some, at times, describing almost in the language of poetry the pleasanter aspects of life in the river diggings.

Indeed these earliest days were the days of the amateur, and held for many a charm, a spirit of romance, which soon disappeared with the rise of the dry diggings and the consequent industrialization.

But for the present, the romantically minded digger felt a sense of adventure, the excitement of the quest, and in many cases the attraction of a new and strange environment and way of life. Nor was this all. Towards the diamonds themselves their attitude was an extraordinary combination of the romantic and the practical. 'We have all become more accustomed to diamonds nowadays,' wrote one digger, many years later, 'but forty years ago a diamond stood rather for crystallized romance than for a form of carbon worth so much per carat. It stood for the making of history, for Empire, and for unbounded wealth. We knew that wars had been waged for the possession of such gems, that neither blackest crime nor oceans of blood could dim their piercing lustre. We felt that every celebrated stone, whether shining on the breast of a lovely woman or blazing in the sceptre of a king, was a symbol of power, a nucleus of tragedy, a focus of human passion.' That something of this was felt even by the sophisticated and cynical, is implicit in the story told of Lord Randolph Churchill when visiting the Diamond Fields, and of a lady in his party. 'All for the vanity of woman,' said Lord Randolph on seeing a parcel of diamonds. 'And,' replied the lady, 'for the depravity of man!'

Among the harsher realities of their experience the worst was the fact that diamonds by the river were far from obvious. Many days of labour were fruitless; long intervals elapsed between 'finds'; many had no luck at all. But when a diamond turned up, all knew the finder's shout, and the rest rushed to see it. If it proved to be of some value, there was general rejoicing and a procession to the nearest canteen, where the lucky man had to 'stand drinks round', or be despised as a mean and selfish fellow. Many diamonds certainly were found. Within two years the value of those collected from the river was said to be some £300,000. But by 1871 there were 5,000 diggers in the region, leaving an average of only £60 each! As one of them wrote: 'Although a great many diamonds were found . . . no one appeared to become rich in consequence. As a matter of fact there were but few diggers who made anything more than a bare living out of their claims.' And from the first, 'Luck' was regarded both at the river and later at the dry diggings, as the most important element in the Diamond Fields.

9

Those who came to the river expecting that diamonds lay about waiting to be picked up, were quickly disillusioned on seeing the diggings there. On each side of the winding and difficult path skirting the river-bank were deep craters, at the bottom of which the diggers, covered with dust and sweat, were hard at work removing great boulders, clearing out sand and gravel and carrying it down to the river to be washed and examined. The faintest-hearted newcomers merely looked and departed. One such, known as 'the Dean's first victim', was said to have been brought from England to the Fields by an enthusiastic letter in *The Times*, written by the Dean of Grahamstown at the Cape. But appalled by the spectacle of arduous toil the diggings presented, the 'victim' is said to have immediately returned home, anathematizing both Dean and diggings as partners in a swindle. Another would-be digger who had walked all the way from Cape Town to within twenty miles of the Diamond Fields is said to have there met some of the faint-hearted returning home in disgust, and to have been so impressed and depressed by their stories that he went no farther but returned to Cape Town after a futile pedestrian journey of some fourteen hundred miles. Many who lived on the Diamond Fields remained there half-hearted, troubled, demoralized, ever wandering from claim to claim, undecided to go or stay.

Pniel on the south bank of the Vaal and Hebron on the north side were the first prominent centres of the mining camps by the river. Pniel was a straggling little town, barely more than a village, situated on the brow of a hill overlooking the river, which at that spot was some two hundred yards broad. The buildings, wood-and-iron save for a few more substantial ones of brick, straggled down the hill-side, while the diamond claims stretched away below, down to the Vaal. The place grew rapidly into the largest of the river centres, for it proved the most prolific in diamonds, almost every claim there yielding a satisfactory supply. One at least was said to have yielded no less than a hundred and twenty. And although small, seldom larger than 10 carats, the stones at Pniel were of good quality.

At Pniel as elsewhere on the Fields, new and numerous well-stocked stores soon appeared, for the diggers were quickly followed by eager but cautious tradesmen, shopkeepers and general merchants ready to supply all the diggers' needs, and in time much more successful financially than the great majority of the diggers themselves. Although at first the population was too temporary, too peripatetic to encourage plans for permanent buildings – for men quickly moved from place to place in search of better luck, or joined the latest 'rush' to some newly favoured spot – large tents and marquees, wood-and-iron huts and houses accommodated the commercial and professional community as it increased. First appeared shops, stores, canteens, bars, lawyers' offices, headquarters of auctioneers and diamond-buyers, places of amusement, billiard rooms and similar resorts. Later came banks, hotels and churches, all with a little more conventional dignity in their appearance. There was then no lack of supplies from the coast, and luxuries as well as necessities were obtainable – at a price! Even books, as at least one digger noted with pardonable surprise and pride. Not only so, but 'the Press' made its appearance on the Fields. Pniel produced *The Diamond News*, while Klipdrift on the opposite bank of the Vaal produced a rival, *The Diamond Field* – journals eagerly bought by the news-starved diggers.

Pniel in these early days was a centre of animation. Up and down its streets of shops and offices passed crowds of people, the bronzed, active diggers conspicuous in their usual dress of corduroy trousers, shirt, broad hat and leather belt, as they went backwards and forwards between their tents and their claims. The shops were crowded with buyers; wagons drawn by teams of oxen, mules or horses drove up every day to discharge their loads of men and of merchandise. Public sales and auctions were constantly held and well attended, being indeed one of the most popular amusements of the diggers in their leisure hours. 'The whole place', wrote one inhabitant, at that time, 'appeared a busy, well-contented community. Impossible to feel comfortable in idleness in such a place.'

'Life at Pniel', wrote a digger, 'was bright, care-free, and unconstrained to a degree. Its social centre, the principal hotel, was kept by Mrs Jardine. There the boys foregathered every Sunday and enjoyed wonderful veldt dishes. There were very few women in the camps. Men young and old called Mrs Jardine "Mother" and thought of her hotel as a home.'

Another visitor gives the following description of this 'home': 'Jardine's was the first hotel erected. It is a straggling chain of rooms, one storey of course, without windows, but abundantly supplied with doors. The walls are wood, and the roof iron. In the midst is a store and bar, never destitute of custom. On one side thereof lies a dining shed, on the other, a nondescript apartment containing beds and chairs, a table, a carpet, guns, harness, picks, baggage, heaven knows what. It may be 18 ft. by 12, and in it I have seen fourteen "first class" guests asleep. Each night the floor is laid with mattresses packed so close one cannot choose but tread on them. Beyond are two tiny compartments for married folk, divided from the bachelors by walls of torn green baize. Over the other side of the dining shed lies a room of six beds, and across the street a building with as many more.

'Cookery at Jardine's is an art reduced to its earliest elements. Roast and boiled we had, at six punctually. A numerous company sat down, of many degrees and divers nationality. The only female form was that of a buttery maiden, who carried plates and dishes. Perfect decorum ruled. There is nothing here of Australian brutality; the rowdy element does not exist. As regards costume and such matters, the absence of collars and waistcoats, the presence of a broad belt and sheath-knife at the waist, and a general dingy tone about the garments, are all one can see of distinctive signs. But it must be remembered that Pniel is a sanatorium. Invalids who can afford it come here to pick up strength, fleeing from the hot and poisonous whirlwinds of Dutoitspan for the pleasant coolness of the river.'

Pniel, until the English acquired it, was under the Dutch authorities of the Orange Free State. Its rival, Klipdrift, on the opposite side of the Vaal, was always under British rule. On the slope of a hill or kopje facing Pniel, Klipdrift was reached by any of the numerous ferry boats that charged sixpence for the crossing, and by the *pont*, a little above the ferry, which carried wagons, carts, horses, mules or oxen across, when the river was too high for passage over the *drift*, or ford, a few hundred yards above it. Klipdrift was the centre for all kinds of produce from the Transvaal which it supplied to the dealers in the camps, and the merchants of Klipdrift also did well by buying ivory, ostrich feathers and valuable skins, supplied in large quantities from the interior. Like Pniel, Klipdrift had a more settled appearance than the other camps, being among the earliest. Visitors familiar with the noise and bustle of the dry diggings in a slightly later period, rejoiced in the contrast Klipdrift presented with its quiet and peaceful streets and freedom from the irritating dust clouds that helped to make life intolerable at Dutoitspan and the 'New Rush' or 'Colesberg Kopje', soon to be as well known as Kimberley.

Other camps on the river were Hebron, twenty-five miles up stream from Klipdrift and on the same side, while twenty miles down the river from Klipdrift and also on the same side, was Cawood's Hope, which sustained the hopes of diggers for but a short time. Opposite Cawood's Hope was the beautiful Gong Gong, soon worked out of its diamonds. Some five miles farther down the river were Forlorn Hope and Delport's Hope, both found fairly satisfactory by the diggers. Other small settlements of diggers, more remote from the two larger centres, spread along the river banks. The chief drawback of these remoter places was the lack of shops and stores, necessitating frequent journeys to Pniel or Klipdrift, with only coarse and monotonous food as an alternative. 'A friend of mine,' wrote one digger, 'working at Forlorn Hope, subsisted for months, sometimes, on meat and "mealies".' Evidently Forlorn Hope deserved its depressing label.

For a time the river diggings flourished, spreading rapidly along the banks of the Vaal. If hope died in the hearts of some diggers, others came to try their luck and filled the gaps left. If one place proved a disappointment, another could always be tried.

But this too sudden blossoming bore within it the seeds of decay and dissolution. An almost inevitably migratory population, ever ready to follow some new will-o'-the-wisp rumour of more and better diamonds elsewhere, formed no solid basis for rooted communities and permanent townships. Various circumstances indeed prevented the river digger from settling for any length of time on one spot. Many claims soon became exhausted or proved barren from the first, or rumour appeared to offer better fortune elsewhere.

Disappointing too was the discovery that although many diamonds were found, very few diggers, if any, appeared to become rich as a result. Even the high total of values produced by the large number of diggers, brought to all but the very lucky few, little more than a mere subsistence, by means of which they continued, with gradually fading hopes, their wearisome, little rewarding task. What wonder that some cautious diggers after one good find, invested their newly-won capital in merchandise and turned to the less exciting but generally more profitable occupation of shopkeeper on the Fields. Without good luck, even if assisted by a little capital, the individual digger, however great his efforts, could achieve little that was worth while.

From first to last, uncertainty presided over the river diggings. Even when a region was known to be fertile, there was often extreme doubt as to the existence of a single diamond on any particular claim. One man might reap a rich harvest while his immediate neighbour found but barren ground. So the luckless spent their lives vainly hoping and searching for the magic stone which was to change their existence; the great undiscovered diamond which ever beckoned, yet ever eluded them.

Another cause of uncertainty was the fluctuating market value of the diamonds themselves when found. This value largely depended upon many unstable factors, particularly upon demand and supply. Before the Vaal field was discovered the value of all precious stones was rising in the world market, as the supply then failed to meet the increasing demands from nations of growing wealth and luxury. But upon the discovery of the South African field, dealers had panicked for a time, fearing a glut of diamonds on the market, and prices had fallen. Only when experts made reassuring prophecies, asserting that the quantity required to depress values must be far beyond anything South Africa could supply, and that any temporary excess must be quickly absorbed, were confidence and prices upheld.

With so many active causes of mental and physical unrest, it is not surprising to find the inhabitants of the earliest centres soon abandoning them for what seemed more promising spots on the river. Thus Pniel and Hebron gradually gave place to Klipdrift and Gong Gong, which were in turn deserted, particularly when a new land of promise appeared, no longer on the banks of the Vaal.

Rumours of this new field and its astonishing riches had been growing for several months, but for a time with little effect, as the diamonds there, though plentiful, were said to be inferior to those by the river. In the spring of 1871, however, some diggers on the spot had achieved such startling results that a new diamond fever broke out, and a 'new rush' followed. At the river centres whole streets of wood and canvas vanished in a night. There also came new aspirants; tyros from Britain and other lands; men and youths fascinated by tales and hopes of immense riches, and fallen under their spell.

The new and greater diamond rush had begun, and soon the river diggings were almost deserted. 'It is not the Pniel of old,' wrote one of the early diggers, pausing on his way to the new field. 'Where are the eager crowds which one short year ago thronged its busy streets? Where are the shops, stores and people? Where are the diggers? Gone to the "New Rush". Of what had been Pniel only remain half the houses, as many tents, a dilapidated street with a flea-troubled dog, a vagabondish looking mule out on the loose, an old gentleman in spectacles reading his newspaper, and a drunken Koronna. On the claims once so prized and struggled for, a few melancholy persons moved about disconsolately, and to one who knew Pniel in its glory, its present aspect was very depressing.'

The rise and fall of the river diggings has been graphically described by one digger in the following passage: 'The rapidity with which towns in the Diamond Fields sprang into and vanished out of existence can only be realized by those who were eye-witnesses of the transformation scenes of that eventful period. During 1870 and 1871 both banks of the Vaal on which diamonds were found sprang from barrenness and desolation into first, camps of canvas, then into wattle-and-daub cottages, and ultimately into what looked like permanently established towns in which there were banks, post-offices, hotels, club houses, court houses, newspaper offices, music-halls, billiard saloons, hospital and church; and before 1871 had got far into its course the whole vanished and left nothing much behind but empty sardine and canned meat tins, paper collars, broken pipes and mud walls. In 1870 and the beginning of 1871, from sixty to eighty ferry boats plied for hire on the river, and were going to and fro from dawn to midnight; by June of the same year there were but two boats and one ferryman left. In the stirring months of the period there were horses and carts running to and fro between Klipdrift and the down river diggings; by midsummer 1871 a horse and cart could not be got for love or money. The property of the diggers was . . . all "portable"; every scrap of the property was portable with the exception of the church and the bank. The bank had been portable at one stage of its existence, and so had the church. All the rest was splendidly adapted for a moving population, and when in 1871 it was known that the Du Toit Pan dry diggings were yielding diamonds without washing, the river diggers, sick of standing knee-deep in water, cradling, and being wet all the week round, moved to a man with all their belongings. The newspapers with their presses and types, the canteen-keepers with their barrels and bottles, the smith with bellows and anvil, the shoemaker with lapstone and hammer, the clock and watchmaker with all his time-keepers and jewellery, the chemist and druggist with his drugs, the doctors with their instruments, marched off in long processions for the new diggings, but all admitting whilst they were going, that they had had a good time in Klipdrift. And they *had* during the latter part of the time.'

Whereupon the writer recalled some of the happy occasions the river diggers had enjoyed: the weekly dances, concerts and public readings, the celebrations for the birthdays of every member of the Royal Family, that of the Queen including a birthday regatta and a ball, the Protestant emotions which found vent in the exploding of squibs and fireworks on Guy Fawkes' Day, along with numberless spontaneous and uncalendared festivities. 'I honestly believe', he continued, 'that nine tenths of the people who were at the river diggings in 1870 and 1871 were more happy than they ever were before or have been since. If ever there was a land of liberty – perfect liberty, religious, political, commercial, and social, it was there and then.'

Nor was this short period of enjoyment to be discounted because of the better fortune that awaited many on the new Fields: 'True it is that a great number of those who were first on the dry diggings made rapid fortunes. The Colesberg Kopje, afterwards called the Kimberley Mine, was unquestionably the richest diamondiferous locality that anyone has ever known to this day. Men who set out to work of a morning, not knowing where their dinner was to come from, became richer than any member of their family had ever been, before it was time for an eleven o'clock snack, and many a digger who left Klipdrift on the pony of shanks in 1871, was riding in his carriage in London before the close of 1872.'

Nevertheless, however regretfully, the diggers left their pleasant life by the river; the call of greater possibilities of wealth and the happiness wealth appeared to offer them, turned the scale. 'The "finds"', wrote another digger, speaking of the river diggings, 'are so small on the average, as compared with the wonderful riches daily yielded by the dry diggings, and the instances of long-continued ill-luck are so sadly numerous, that I would not advise our "new chums" to pitch their tents on the banks of the Vaal. True, the temptations to do so are great. The pleasant sight and sound of running water, the facilities for bathing, boating and fishing, the abundance of splendid trees, affording shade and firewood, and the comparative absence of dust, make a camp on the river seem a perfect elysium, when contrasted with the dry, barren, treeless waste which surrounds the dry diggings. But I think there is little doubt that the latter will continue to prove much the richest, and will, therefore, attract by far the largest proportion of the digging population of the future.'

So the writer proceeded to a summary comparison of the advantages and disadvantages of the river and dry diggings. 'The former are abundance of water-bathing, a great luxury and very conducive to the preservation of health, plenty of wood, good fishing and consequently an important addition to diet, a slight superiority in the quality of the diamonds, [the best at Kimberley had not yet been found] and more interesting sorting, owing to the immense quantity of beautiful pebbles, some of them of slight value.' The 'beautiful pebbles' included a few valuable rubies, and sapphires, many garnets but almost without value, immense quantities of beautiful agates, besides cornelians, jasper, chalcedony, while 'rock crystals of pretty shapes, clear and shiny, glitter occasionally among the bright and many-coloured pebbles, and woefully deceive the "new chum".'

The disadvantages of the river diggings he finds in 'less uniformity in success, the diamonds lying a good deal in patches, much harder work owing to the innumerable boulders, [at this time only surface diamonds were being worked at Kimberley; he would not have said this later] far less society, less life and amusement than at the dry diggings, and at the smaller camps deficient supplies of food and other necessaries and total absence of luxuries. Many of our "dried up" diggers will, of course, make frequent trips to the river for bathing – in fact, we of the dry diggings are beginning to look upon the pleasant little camps by the Vaal River as our

Scarborough and Brighton, or perhaps Harrogate and Matlock would be nearer the mark.'

So the great, short season of the river diggings soon came to its close. The different accounts of various diggers about this time help us to visualize the camps in their rapid decay. 'At Pniel and Klipdrift,' wrote one on the last day of July 1871, 'though they look very quiet and deserted in comparison with Dutoitspan and De Beers, there is still a good deal of work going on, and new claims being opened. The work is very hard, every claim being full of immense rocks and boulders, so that it takes a long time to get out a cartful of stuff for sifting.'

Four months later the same man writes: 'I found that the old diggings at Pniel and Klipdrift were nearly deserted, scarcely fifty claims being worked on both sides of the river, and the little towns presenting a striking contrast to the New Rush in everything – in their quietude and appearance of peaceful stagnation; in the large, dark boulders and bright gravel of which the claims were composed, instead of the red sand, glowing white limestone, and crumbling green trap of the New Rush; and most refreshingly, in the broad stream of the Vaal, with its rocky, trout-suggesting rapids, its deep pools, its bright green islets, and the grand shade-giving trees which fringed its banks.'

A later glimpse of the deserted river camps is given by another digger who visited Pniel shortly after the last writer, early in 1872. Standing on the brow of the hill on which Pniel stood, he described how 'a traveller looks down on such a tossed and tumbled scene as the deserted bivouac of a marauding army may present after the troops have left, and the camp followers are still packing. For the glory of Pniel has fled. . . . An observer here could stand upon the crest and survey all the sea of tents at once, the hive of men, chequer of claims, loud busy river flowing between trees, and populous heights of Klipdrift opposite. The natural scene is still before us, visible; but its red earth is bare, its pyramids of high-piled stones standing like cairns for the departed. All the slope is pocked with holes, some big and deep enough to bury the largest of our stores, some shallow and small as an infant's grave; the similitudes are lugubrious, but lesser diamond fields are more like rude and careless cemeteries than aught else I think of.

'Round each claim, big or little, is the heap of pebbles. Earth has a deep red tone. Two or three pathways, much encroached upon, wind downwards to the shingly strand. Another, wider, and bordered by piles of stone, runs parallel to the river, beneath the shade of lofty willow trees. On narrow platforms between the holes, where the digger has not been tempted to insert his pick, stands a gipsy tent, with people white or black loafing about the doorway. Here and there is a "canteen" of dirty canvas, or a plank-built "store" with roof of corrugated iron. But such habitations are rare. Rarer still is the "sorting table". Men pass up and down the path with buckets now and then. A slender stream of passengers goes down the road that leads one to the ferry. A stranger wanders with meandering and anxious step, amidst the yawning labyrinth of pitfalls. How different is this picture from the photograph. Five thousand workers made the place to swarm two years ago. And now there are not fifty claims in use.'

Nor was the scene at Klipdrift by this time less desolate. For Klipdrift, with its brick houses and stores which gave it the most stable appearance of all the camps, though but some two years old, fell as quickly as Pniel into decay. Its fallen glory was also noted and described, although more summarily than Pniel's: the 'towering Klipdrift shore, a red, burnt heap of shingles, lightly strewn with sand', the raw stumps of the many fine trees destroyed that shaded its river banks, the town's 'little square, quite empty', its one street 'sufficiently well kept, descending from the crest of the ridge lengthwise with the river, a few small canteens still at the mouth of the roadway to the pont or boats'. But there were few now to patronize them, for the population of 5,000 had dwindled to a mere 600. 'As a digging,' writes the describer, 'Klipdrift may be said to have dropped from the list. It is now to be reckoned as a seat of trade for the river camps, and as the temporary metropolis of Griqualand West. As such, an air of dignity and sedateness becomes it. There are actual gardens at Klipdrift! Yes, and neat little cottages.'

One final glimpse of the river diggings in decay was given in 1877, when the novelist Anthony Trollope visited South Africa and the Diamond Fields. 'I was taken', he wrote, 'up to Barkly [the new name of Klipdrift] "on a picnic" as people say: and a very nice picnic it was – one of the pleasantest days I had in South Africa. The object was to show me the Vaal river, and the little town which had been the capital of the diamond country before the grand discovery at Colesberg Kopje had made the town of Kimberley. There is nothing peculiar about Barkly as a South African town, except that it is already half deserted. There may be perhaps a score of houses there, most of which are much better built than those at Kimberley. They are made of rough stone, or mud and whitewash; and if I do not mistake, one of them had two storeys. There was an hotel – quite full although the place is deserted – and clustering round it were six or seven idle gentlemen all of whom were or had been connected with diamonds. . . .

'When at Barkly we got ourselves and our provisions into a boat so that we might have our picnic properly, under the trees at the other side of the river – for opposite to Barkly is to be found the luxury of trees. As we rowed down the river we saw a white man with two Kaffirs poking about his stones and gravel on a miner's rickety table under a little tent on the beach. He was a digger who had still clung to the "river" business; a Frenchman who had come to try his luck there a few days since. On the Monday previous – we were told – he had found a 13-carat white stone without a flaw. This would be enough perhaps to keep him going and almost to satisfy him for a month. Had he missed that one stone he would probably have left the place after a week. Now he would go on through days and days without finding another sparkle. I can conceive no occupation on earth more dreary – hardly any more demoralizing than this of perpetually turning over dirt in quest of a peculiar little stone which may turn up once a week or may not. I could not but think, as I watched the man, of the comparative nobility of the work of a shoemaker who by every pull at his thread is helping to keep some person's foot dry.' Trollope, who disapproved morally of diamond digging, was far from investing it with the romantic attraction it had for so many diggers, who would have loathed the thought of writing novels for a lifetime.

'After our dinner,' Trollope continued, 'we walked along the bank and found another "River" digger, though this man's claim might perhaps be removed a couple of hundred yards from the water. He was an Englishman and we stood awhile and talked to him. He had one Kaffir with him to whom he paid 7s. a week and his food, and he too had found one or two stones which he showed us – just enough to make the place tenable. He had got upon an old digging which he was clearing out lower. He had, however, in one place reached the hard stone at the bottom, in, or below, which there could be no diamonds. There was, however, a certain quantity of diamondiferous matter left, and as he had already found stones he thought that it might pay him to work through the remainder. He was a most good humoured, well-mannered man, with a pleasant fund of humour. When I asked him generally of his fortune at the diggings, he told us among other things that he had broken his shoulder bone at the diggings, which he displayed to us in order that we might see how badly the surgeon had used him. He had no pain to complain of – or weakness; but his shoulder had not been made beautiful. "And who did it?" said the gentleman who was our Amphytrion at the picnic and is himself one of the leading practitioners of the Fields. "I think it was one Dr ——," said the digger, naming our friend whom no doubt he knew. I need not say that the doctor loudly disclaimed ever having had previous acquaintance with the shoulder.

'The Kaffir was washing the dirt in a rough cradle, separating the stones from the dust, and the owner, as each sieve-full was brought to him, threw out the stones on his table and sorted them through with the eternal bit of slate or iron formed into the shape of a trowel. For the chance of a sieve-full one of our party offered him half a crown – which he took. I was glad to see it all inspected without a diamond, as had there been anything good the poor fellow's disappointment must have been great. That half-crown was probably all that he would earn during the week – all that he would earn perhaps for a month. Then there might come three or four stones in one day. I should think that the tedious despair of the vacant days could hardly be compensated by the triumph of the lucky minute. These "river" diggers have this in their favour – that the stones found near the river are more likely to be white and pure than those which are extracted from the mines. The Vaal itself in the neighbourhood of Barkly is pretty – with rocks in its bed and islands and trees on its banks. But the country around, and from thence to Kimberley, which is twenty-four miles distant, is as ugly as flatness, barrenness and sand together can make the face of the earth. . . .'

When Trollope visited the Vaal, some ten years had passed since Van Niekerk's discovery of the value of the little white stone had broken the ancient peace of the great river. Five years or more before Trollope's picnic, the river's popularity had begun to fade. Although the search there for diamonds has never entirely ceased, even to the present day, and although 'Klipdrift', never a good or important diamond centre, has blossomed into a permanent township, (the Barkly West of today,) with the discovery of the 'New Rush', the dry diggings twenty miles away, the short day of the river diggings' importance was over. Never again would it be more than an early and half-forgotten incident in the tremendously increasing race for wealth that would yet further change the face of South Africa – and of other countries as well.

2

Trek

Trekkers! slow, slow,
In the bright deep-dawn's glow –
Against the crystalled sky
Looms the white tent on high –
Patiently plodding span,
Patiently plodding man.

*

Trekkers! slow, slow,
Thro' the red sunset glow,
Patiently plodding span,
Patiently plodding man,
Slow, slow, out of the fading glow
Into the night they go.[1]

NOT far from the feverish activity of the river diggings lived Boer farmers on their solitary farms, generally remote, and enjoying the isolation and peace they valued above almost all earthly things. It was even said that a Boer farmer could not tolerate another farm within sight; but if this occurred, must trek elsewhere, finding the locality too crowded for endurance. To such, the external world beyond the confines of their farms mattered little or nothing; hardly indeed existed. Without news, seeing none but the rarest visitor or stranger save the occasional pedlar on his round, and enfolded by the vastness of the veldt, the Boer farmer knew little and cared even less about the doings of the outer world. Almost his sole earthly interests were his farm, his livestock and the weather, for drought might bring ruin.

Hitherto there had been nothing to disturb the ancient peace of the region, which offered to the rare traveller little more in general than roughly rounded hillocks rising from the level plain covered with grass and

[1] From 'Trekkers', by Beatrice Marian Bromley (1861–1925).

bush and without anything to suggest the almost fabulous riches that lay below; sometimes indeed almost on the surface.

Soon, however, this peace was to be rudely broken. Some knowledge of diamonds and of their value had spread about the country from the river diggings, and in the late summer and early autumn of 1870, the owners of several of the farms situated some twenty miles from the Vaal, found, almost if not quite by accident, diamonds on their properties.

Throughout the later months of 1870, whispers of new diamond discoveries on these Boer farms away from the river spread among the diggers along the Vaal. At first they were generally dismissed as idle gossip, or as a trick of the landowners to make money; but soon some of the river diggers, especially those who had met with little or no success, drifted over to the new grounds, where their discoveries proved so startling that a new 'rush' to them took place, not only from the Vaal, but as the news spread, from all quarters of the world – which converged upon Cape Town: a place, wrote Cecil Rhodes' brother Frank, on arriving in the spring of 1872, where 'they do nothing but drink and smoke and talk about diamonds'.

As one somewhat expansive digger asserted: 'Tidings of great joy was wired from Cape Town in all directions, and the depressed and despairing in industrial and commercial circles were soon as lively as fleas. Diamond Fields became the only talk of the colony. Everybody talked of going – merchants, lawyers, clerks, civil servants, counter-jumpers, boatmen, tradesmen and mechanics wanted to be off on the instant. They saw in their lively imaginings diamond fields glittering with diamonds like dewdrops in the waving grass, on branches of trees along the Vaal River, and covering highways and by-ways like hoar frost. But how were they to get there? Where were the Diamond Fields? How far? Whose lands were they upon? Such like were the questions – which there were few to answer.'

'How were they to get there?' was certainly not easily answered. The only railway was that from Cape Town to Wellington, 45 miles away, while the Diamond Fields were 700. The completed railway, when it came in 1885, was both inspired and largely provided by the diamonds themselves. In the meantime, apart from the difficult, dangerous and exhausting adventure undertaken by a few of the poorest on foot (some of whom permanently disappeared *en route*), several vehicles were at the disposal of the diamond seeker according to his financial ability and personal preference. The most expeditious of these were the 'mail-carts' or 'post-carts'. But as they were also the most expensive, costing £40 to the Fields, they were seldom patronized by the diamond seekers. Next came the public 'coaches' or 'passenger carts', sometimes miscalled 'wagons', drawn by teams of mules or of horses, less expensive yet still fast. Last came the 'ox-wagons' or 'bullock wagons': slow, but cheap and so most favoured by the many impecunious travellers to the Diamond Fields.

One adventurer to the Fields who reached Cape Town on 8 November 1871, found it the only place in the country with 'a wagon every week with decent speed and punctuality'. As his fare to the Fields was £12, including second class fare by train to the terminus at Wellington, these 'wagons' must have been the coaches or passenger carts. Not only the traveller, but the coach itself was carried by train to Wellington. And, as the traveller noted, The Inland Transport Company which provided the service, was about to introduce a second weekly coach immediately.

The Inland Transport Company of Cape Town was soon followed there by the Diamond Fields Transport Company which provided vehicles similar to those of its predecessor. Although the fares were the same, the routes followed by the two companies differed. The older company's coaches passed through Wellington, Ceres, Beaufort West, Victoria West and Hope Town to its terminus at Pniel in these earliest days; those of its rival diverged after Beaufort West, via Murraysburg, Richmond, Colesberg, Philippolis, Fauresmith and Jacobsdal to its terminus at Dutoitspan. Each passenger was allowed 40 lb. of luggage, excess weight being charged from 1s. to 1s. 3d. a lb.

The journey by passenger coach was uncomfortable and tedious. 'These conveyances', wrote one traveller, 'are drawn by six horses or mules, and travel at an average rate of nearly a hundred miles a day, almost always stopping the greater part of the night; so that the traveller, though fearfully jolted over rough roads during the day, till he feels there is scarcely a whole bone left in his body, will get the advantage of sleeping in a bed at night, for towns and fairly comfortable inns are very numerous along the greater part of the road. In this way the intending digger can get from Cape Town to Pniel in nine or ten days. The advantages of this system are speed, and decidedly cheapness . . . its disadvantages are that you don't see the country well, have no time to hunt, shoot, fish, prospect, or sketch, and don't get accustomed to "roughing it" in such a way as to prepare you for camp life at the diggings.'

That this journey by coach included no preparation for 'roughing it', can hardly have been the opinion of another passenger, who travelled to the Fields in a large coach carrying some fifteen persons and drawn by a train of mules: 'I shall never forget the uneasiness and misery of the experience. Travelling day and night, with very short intervals for rest and

refreshment, the journey became a horror, especially towards early morning. Packed like sardines, it was impossible to move our legs from one
position to another, and they were so cramped and painful that one felt,
many hours at a time, in absolute torture. For women it was much worse
and there were three or four very nice ladies with us. It is impossible to
describe what a shock such a journey must have been to a tender and
modest woman. Discomfort made the passengers quarrelsome; incessant
wranglings were going on which increased as we sped on our pilgrimage.
One day was very much like another. Pleasantly exciting when crossing a
river. Confoundedly less so when it rained in torrents and thundered and
lightened. The flies too were not cheerful companions. Sometimes, when
the mules got tired, or the driver wanted to give them a "blow", or when
negotiating a particularly stiff hill, the passengers would venture out and
walk, and often get wet through.'

Of all forms of transport to the Diamond Fields, preference was given by
most travellers to 'the exceedingly slow but more comfortable ox-wagon':
as one of them described it. But to judge from the accounts of many
sufferers, the ox-wagon or bullock wagon provided little enough comfort for its passengers. The fare from Cape Town ranged from £5 to
£7 10s.; meals were not included. Most of the trade with the Diamond
Fields came through Port Elizabeth, Natal, and other ports. Ox-wagons
were continually leaving Port Elizabeth for the Fields, and as they moved
very slowly, travellers by them often preferred to shorten the trek by
starting from Port Elizabeth instead of Cape Town, thus reducing the
journey by wagon from 700 miles to 400. Most of the goods-transport
from Cape Town carried the lighter merchandise.

The ox-wagon was drawn by from eight to twenty bullocks. Its average
speed was some three miles an hour, including stops to rest every five
miles or less. In this way it covered from ten to fifteen miles a day. Halts
at towns sometimes lasted three or four days. Forty days from Cape Town
to the Fields on an ox-wagon was a very quick passage; fifty to sixty days
was more usual. From Port Elizabeth, thirty days was a fast journey; forty
to fifty days a more probable one. Mules travelled more quickly than oxen,
but could draw only 3,000 lb. to the oxen's 12,000. The oxen never trotted
with a full cargo. The charge for freight, whether by mule or oxen, was
35s. for 100 lb.

Although the great covered wagons allowed the passengers much more
room than the coaches, they were little if at all better off, for the jolting of
the heavy vehicle as it lumbered along the rough, unmade roads full of
holes, ruts and hillocks, was as bad as the cramping conditions of the

lighter and better sprung, quickly moving coach. 'A bullock wagon,' wrote one disgusted traveller, 'my first and last experience of that patriarchal equipage. Like riding on a camel, or enjoying life at sea, it is a matter of practice to be comfortable in an ox-wagon. You cannot sit with ease, nor read, nor do any other thing. You cannot sleep all day; at least an Englishman cannot, and for no other occupation is there fitting room. Straight on the bullocks go, over all that comes, at one even pace, dragging by main strength. One understands somewhat of the Boer character by a short journey in this vehicle.' It is not surprising that many who employed this mode of travel complained of 'much privation and discomfort' and of 'loss of sleep'. Passengers slept in the wagon or under it, while those who had the means, escaped for a good meal and a night's rest when a hotel was at hand.

The hazards of the journey were many, and the rivers when suddenly swollen by rain, provided many dangerous experiences, such as those of one man who set out to try his luck at the Fields during an unusually wet season when all the rivers were full, with several ox-wagons packed with provisions. The oxen and their native herd got lost in a storm, and only after much riding about in the rain, did their owner find them islanded amidst the waters. The unfortunate native was never seen again and so most probably was drowned. The Vaal proved a great and dangerous obstacle. Forced to have the wagons ferried across in a miserably dilapidated pontoon full of holes which a native was caulking with clay, the traveller wisely removed his clothes before entering the boat and although the clay immediately began to drop out and the boat to sink, he regained the river bank. Coaches often overturned in the flooded rivers, some of their occupants were saved by being dragged through doors and windows, some were drowned. Deaths *en route* were not unknown. A sick woman, who died in a wagon on the way to Grahamstown to consult a doctor there, was carried on to her destination, nevertheless.

But whatever the drawbacks to travel by ox-wagon, all were outweighed by the 'freedom and fun' many found to counteract the discomforts of the journey. The slow pace of the oxen and frequent halts allowed passengers to drop behind or go before, see the country, camp out, cook their own food, get the wood and water they needed, buy their food cheaply from the farms they passed, or, wander in search of it with gun or rifle, through wild regions well stocked with game. So too, when opportunity offered, they could even take to fishing. Thus many diggers in embryo learned very pleasantly to 'rough it'; found the month or two so passed 'an amusing and useful' experience, preparing them for the camp life awaiting them at the

Fields; as one described his experience of the ox-wagon, 'a very jolly life for a month or so'.

Inevitably some passengers recorded so unusual a combination or alternation of the pleasant and unpleasant as the journey by ox-wagon provided. Thus we read of one such travelling from Port Elizabeth to Dutoitspan for fifty days at less than ten miles each day, hewing wood, drawing water, buying and cooking his food, and sleeping 'in a jolting wagon with twelve other men on a heterogeneous mass of luggage, provisions, guns, etc., which no amount of coaxing could ever make nearly level.' The picture is grim. But then, as he points out, they passed through half a dozen 'delightful towns. At some of these our wagon halted for three or four days – and then what happened? Why, of course, we swore we would once more enjoy the luxury of sitting on chairs and eating off table-cloths – many of us did, at least – and patronized hotels and billiard rooms extensively, even being sometimes effeminate enough to sleep therein, instead of on the hard ground by the "outspanned" wagon, with a couple of rugs for all bedding.'

Not all, however, found so many compensations. The weather and the season had much to do with it. Barnato, the future millionaire, forced by poverty to take the ox-wagon from Cape Town to the Fields in late August 1873, was quickly disillusioned. A wet winter was closing and the Great Karroo was flooded. The driver of his wagon forced him to walk as much as or more than he rode. The wheels stuck in the mud, and Barnato and the rest, pushing and pulling, helped the vehicle more than it helped them. Wet and cold, with clothes unchanged, he had to sleep on the muddy ground under the wagon which gave but poor protection against wind and rain. His meals consisted solely of mealies and biltong. Spring came as they advanced. The Orange River was swollen with rains, and the luggage had to be taken across in canoes by natives, while the wagon crossed at a ford. So they came to the end of their dreary and dismal journey.

Barnato's cousin David Harris, also forced by lack of means, travelled from Durban to Dutoitspan by one of the many ox-wagons heavily laden with the goods now needed by the diggers. To say that he travelled by wagon is somewhat misleading; his 'two small portmanteaus' did, but he was obliged to walk alongside the wagon, one of several that made up a baggage train. In this way he set out on the 600-mile journey, at a speed of about fourteen miles a day, with the wagons jolting, lumbering along, 'groaning under their heavy load of provisions and merchandise'. Were it not for his baggage, he said, he could have walked twice the distance in the time.

From time to time during the journey the wagons halted for two days at suitable spots where the grazing was good; whereupon Harris would leave the wagons for a time and make for the nearest farm, perhaps ten or fifteen miles ahead, with the hope of getting 'a good square meal and a sound night's rest'. Very rarely was he disappointed on these expeditions. The farmers and their wives proved most hospitable; gave of their best, even the poorest of them, their 'best' indeed ranging from coarse brown bread, mutton and coffee, to coffee with grilled chops and fried eggs, fare which Harris[1] said he enjoyed more than he did the finest menus of leading London and Paris restaurants in later years. The farmers who helped him he found unsophisticated, kind, profoundly religious, men and women who felt that in helping the needy they were 'doing good in the sight of the Lord'.

One digger has left us a detailed and spirited account of his journey from Cape Town to the Fields. Having paid £12 for the whole journey, including the train fare to Wellington, he went to the railway station – where most of Cape Town's inhabitants appeared to have gathered, whether travelling or not, to discuss diamonds – and took his seat in the train, while the 'wagon' was placed on a truck behind. It was 'a gigantic van, weighing probably four tons, with low wooden sides and a flat roof of canvas supported on iron stanchions. It is thus all awning and body. Curtains of canvas, however, hang from stanchion to stanchion, capable of buttoning down in case of rain or overheat. Under these, now rolled up, big pouches are suspended, by the four corners, full of bottles, flasks, meat tins and other objects. They oscillate and bang your miserable head to bits should you crouch up too snugly in the angle. Across the body of the wagon are fixed three seats, each calculated to bear three persons. In front sit the driver and the "leader", up to their knees in ropes and thongs and broken harness. They commonly violate the company's rule by admitting an extra passenger between them. At the back is a coupé, occupied by the guard and two travellers. Thus the full complement is 11; 9 inside and 2 behind; but 12 can be carried, and very frequently are. Add to them the driver, leader and guard, making 14 or 15. As much luggage as can be crammed therein is put into the boot, and the remainder is corded on each side of the vehicle in a miscellaneous heap. It was a comfortable reflection to me that the pile would act as a first rate buffer in the event of an overturn.'

From the same traveller we learn that when more than four horses were employed, two drivers were needed, of whom the chief, the only one called a 'driver', handled the whip, 'a monstrous instrument'. To the trekker, the

[1] Later Sir David Harris.

whip was as important for guiding and controlling the sixteen-strong team
of oxen or the teams of horses or mules, as the 'wheel' of a modern motor
car is to the driver. The following verses vividly illustrate this importance.

The great buck-wagon, our 'desert-ship',
With its four-ton heavy load,
And its rooi-bont[1] span[2] and the Wagon-Whip,
Is coming along the road,
With its whip-stick light from the bamboo-brake,
Where the eyes of the tiger gleam,
And its whirling lash from the thick tough hide
Of the sea-cow by the stream.

*

The lash was a length of the sea-cow's hide
By the broad Limpopo stream,
Or where Zambezi breaks in foam
O'er its great white falls agleam;
And the hardy Boer from the two-inch hide
Of the river-horse cut the strip,
And brei'd[3] and rolled and hammered it round
To make the Wagon-Whip.

*

The agterslag[4] tough and the voorslag[5] keen
Came from the royal koodoo[6]
With his glorious lyred horns laid back
As he bounded the forest through;
But the hunter's deadly eye ran up
The levelled, rifled gun –
And the antelope's hide was brei'd and stryk'd,[7]
And the Wagon-Whip was done.[8]

The whip's butt was a pliant reed from twelve to fifteen feet long; its
lash of plaited bullock's hide was sometimes twenty feet in length. 'It would

[1] rooi-bont – red and white.
[2] span – team of oxen and donkeys.
[3] brei – to soften skins.
[4] agterslag – the thong of a whip.
[5] voorslag – the lash of a whip.
[6] koodoo – large South African antelope.
[7] stryk – to stretch.
[8] From 'A Song of the Wagon-Whip', by Samuel Cron Cronwright Schreiner
(1863–1936).

cut the horses' backs like a knife if it were not moderated by a tag of ante-lope-skin. The "driver" takes a kind of rough precedence over the "leader", who holds the reins. To handle eight to twelve horses tests even the most experienced. The whip must guide, restrain the fractious, make the whole team pull together. In moments of difficulty the driver will lend a hand with the reins, but in general he sits with watchful eye and ready lash, counselling the "leader", swearing at him, chewing tobacco, and cracking his whip each instant. He is commonly a Boer, or a "bastard" – mulatto that is; the other is nearly always a powerful black.'

As the Transport Company did not provide meals, passengers took with them whatever was most convenient: sardines, potted meats, bread, and frequently brandy. All these necessities were stowed away in the big loose pockets of the wagon. Such personal provisions were certainly necessary, for whatever places might be able to offer a meal were fifty miles apart, and for several days at a time the passenger had no certainty of finding other food than he brought with him.[1]

Wellington reached, the wagon-trek began. 'To our allotted seats we climbed when the bugle first rang out the devoted twelve. Eight fine horses, mighty light in the matter of harness, stood ready to go at a touch. The word was given and with a furious bound and jolt, the lumbering wagon started at a gallop. Down the street, round the corner, with clang of hoof and crack of whip, shout of child and clamour of bugle – off to the Fields! Our leaders are all over the road, galloping at every angle from each other. The traces lie across their necks, and swingle-bars are tossing all about. "Keep them going!" is the cry. A jerking of the rein would be – smash. And our drivers *do* keep them going! The thirty-foot whip cracks on their hides like a rifle-shot; now here, now there, now curled up to catch the wheel horse, now let out to touch the fiery leaders, light and straight as a fly-line. The stalwart Hottentot who holds the reins is bent like a bow with the strain and struggle. The rush of wind through that burning air is almost cold about our ears. Rocking and reeling the great machine rolls on, plunging round corners, seeming to double up. In five minutes we are clear of apricot hedges, white houses, green palings, and the rest. And then, with the united efforts of driver and leader we pull up to mend our broken harness. Such a mean and shameful ending has ever a "burst" in this country. Eight horses dragging at full gallop a weight of three tons would try the best leather that ever was tanned; and that is not the quality

---

[1] Cf. *supra*, p. 27. The apparent discrepancy is doubtless explained by the different speeds of the respective vehicles, and perhaps also partly by different financial positions.

of which they make Cape fixings. I suppose one stops, on an average, every quarter of an hour on this journey, to mend or rearrange the harness.'

Harness, and wagons also, needed frequent attention. Complaints of the state of the various transport vehicles and their equipment are widespread and numerous. 'I look back', wrote Sir David Harris, 'on the ancient method of transport and the type of vehicle then in existence, and I often wonder how we reached any place at all.' Once the hired cart he travelled in had to stop in the middle of the veldt – it was a horse-drawn vehicle – because the axles had become red-hot and refused to turn. Fortunately water was near, but it took him and his driver more than an hour to bring the temperature down by bathing them. However, when the possibility of resuming the journey was achieved, he discovered that the driver, a Boer, had no grease with him, and the situation was only saved by Harris suddenly remembering that in his dressing bag was some Bond Street brilliantine, most of which he devoted to greasing the axle!

The cart in which another passenger travelled from Pniel to Dutoitspan, was one of two public conveyances which made the journey every day, taking five hours for the mere twenty miles or so, and in a period when the fifteen shillings a seat cost had probably the purchasing power of £5 to-day. Despite the *de luxe* charges, there was nothing luxurious about the cart. 'A most dreary vehicle was that in which I took my place. Paintless, coated with mud, ripped and split and bound up with thongs. Its springs enswathed in hide. Its rusty tilt in ribands. With harness of rope and leather and raw skin all intermixed, knotted together. The four plump mules inspanned looked round at it and us with plain contempt.' Nevertheless, he reluctantly climbs into his broken seat, while both whip and harness crack at the same time, the whip like the harness, fastened with string and thongs. The driver swears, and they depart, undeterred by a road riddled with holes and puddles.

Nor were defective vehicles the only danger to the traveller; defective drivers were as bad if not worse. 'About eight miles from Pniel,' wrote another diarist, 'I got a "lift" on a cart drawn by four oxen, driven by a very drunken Koranna, who frequently lashed the beasts into a full gallop, and never "outspanned" till he got to De Beer's, where we arrived about 9 p.m., my driver having fallen off the front of the wagon twice. The second time he fell close to the hoofs of the hinder oxen, and the wheel of the cart went right over his chest; but he didn't seem to mind it much, though the cart was pretty heavily laden.'

The kings of the road were the new American horse-drawn coaches, rendered superfluous by the building of the Trans-Pacific Railway, and so shipped across the Atlantic by Cobb and Co., with a capital of £10,000 to start a twice-weekly journey from Port Elizabeth to the Diamond Fields. They carried passengers and light baggage, for £12, and reached their destination in five and a half days. The mule-drawn goods wagons from Port Elizabeth to the Diamond Fields, which also took passengers, but at a cheap rate, took fifteen days for the journey. Travellers greeted the American innovation enthusiastically – not only because they found the new coaches strong and comfortable, but also because the company in some ways anticipated the methods of modern tourist agencies by arranging with the hotels *en route* for a reasonable and uniform scale of charges, and also by ensuring adequate rest for the passengers, whose general comfort and convenience were now first considered.

One valid excuse for the many decrepit and antediluvian vehicles on the roads was the sudden overwhelming demand for, and consequent shortage of transport, a deficiency exaggerated by the sudden departure to the Fields of many of the cart, coach and wagon builders themselves.

'Transport rises every day,' complained one digger to his diary, on 1 February 1872, 'in two months from 25s. to 35s. for 100 lb. and despite this monstrous rate, the press of business far transcends the resources of the [Cape] Colony. Ten times the supply of carriage available is demanded – and higher rates would willingly be paid by those without a regular service of transport drivers. One of the first merchants in South Africa told me some days ago he has a hundred wagon-loads of goods in his warehouse at Port Elizabeth without prospect of delivery, and he has great advantages over his poor rivals.' In these circumstances, the more visionary dreamed of various expedients of transport; trains of elephants – 'which may be considered poetry', wrote our diarist – of Arabian camels, and Montevidean pack mules! The less visionary cogitated traction engines, and the realists foresaw the great railway schemes that must come, and feared the heavy burden on the exchequer.

The average digger was far too practical to pay attention to the landscape through which he passed, much less to attempt to describe it – except, in some cases, when natural difficulties or accidents halted his impatient progress. Occasionally, however, one more observant, of finer culture and of literary temperament, would record his impressions.

One of the best and most interesting of these records was made by a lawyer, an Oxford graduate, who included in his account of his experiences, his journey in November 1871 from Wellington (reached by train from Cape Town) to Pniel by coach. The road to Bain's Kloof on the outskirts of Wellington he found good even in those days. The great and beautiful mountain pass much impressed him: 'Blasted here and built up there, it winds along the side of lofty granite peaks, with giddy steeps beneath, and a canopy of overhanging rocks above.' The grandeur of the scenery reminded him of the wilder parts of Scotland. 'Deep gullies lined with fern and broom, a slender stream at bottom, fretting amongst the purple rocks, dip from the road. Blue furrowed hills wind mostly away from the further brink, showing grey valleys, patched with the golden stone-crop. High overhead the bare, stern mountains tower, haunt of leopards and fierce baboons. Vultures circle round, and hawks with all sober variety of plumage build shaggy nests.' The naturalist would transfer the adjective 'fierce' rather from the baboons to the leopards; but a romantic emotion is evident throughout the description of the landscapes. Nevertheless, the varied scenery as the traveller passes through it day after day is graphically and not always unrealistically described, vitalized rather than distorted by the emotion.

Three hours from Wellington they reach the further end of the pass: 'The rude and broken landscape of the mountains has not yet subsided to the dull horror of the plain.' They change horses and lunch; then start again at half past three. 'All charm and beauty now left the landscape; scorched slopes, clothed in pebbles as a garment, rose on either hand. In the deep dells and glades there was indeed a greenish tinge of vegetation, but the upper land grew only stones. Sometimes on a plateau between two hills, the earth thrust out a harvest of low, grey bushes, brittle and sapless. The swollen floods of rain had intersected all such spots with deep *barrancas*.[1] There was neither soil nor grass; only sand and pebbles, and burnt bush and channels waterworn. Nothing lives here but snakes, and those wild animals which prey at night, and sleep in solitude the day. We heard no noise, we saw no living creature, nor any sign of man's existence for a stretch of hours. Before this little book is done, I shall have wearied my reader with descriptions of the desert. If he rise with the impression that these far famed pastures of the Cape are for the most part dreary beyond the thought of man, I shall have conveyed to him the truth. There is but one exclamation amongst all classes, nations and languages of emigrants – "What a frightful wilderness!" they cry, with something of awe in their tones.' Which again shows how far romantic suggestion can affect reality!

As the travellers proceeded, through Mitchell's Pass (or '*kloof*') to the little town of Ceres at the foot of the pass, all they saw of human life was a Hottentot on horseback leading another horse, and some poor Boer women

---

[1] *Barranca* (Spanish) – a deep break or hole made by heavy falls of rain, a ravine, a precipice.

in a cottage, sewing, who offered them coffee and, muttering something about its being for a bazaar, accepted the money – 'two times the price' – they tendered in return. Unlike Harris, this traveller found the Boers 'far from hospitable'. But he rightly admitted that in present conditions the refusal of all payment, with so many travellers requesting hospitality, would soon ruin the farmers on the transport routes.

In the early evening they reached their inn at Ceres, but at two o'clock the next morning they resumed their journey, halting three hours later for breakfast.

By this time, the company of twelve travellers, almost as various as Chaucer's pilgrims, were beginning to know one another. Two were barristers hastening to the newly constituted High Court at Klipdrift; two were Cape Town merchants setting out for diamonds, and there were also three young men on the same errand; there was a 'veteran' digger returning to the Fields from a 'spree' in Cape Town, a contractor of the transport company running the buses, a mineralogist prospecting for diamonds and gold, a woman on the way to rejoin her husband, and lastly there was the narrator, who found them 'a pleasant party'.

Walking up the next pass, as 'red, sterile and pebbly as Mitchell's', with the wagon toiling up the winding road behind them, they reached Karoo Port at half past ten that morning, and on emerging from another pass which wound its way beneath steep and rocky hills, they saw the 'desert' of the Karoo before them. 'This is no waste of sand like the Egyptian wilderness. In many parts it is found to bear a vegetation which, for the Cape, might be called tolerable. And yet there is perhaps no tract of land upon the whole earth's surface – certainly there is none I have seen in many wanderings – so horribly desolate and forbidding. Not in waves and hollows here, but one unbroken sheet of barrenness it lies. No object over six inches high, whether plant or stone, breaks that dead level, till in dim haze it fades against the low and dusty hills. At distant points a chip of crystal twinkles like a star. Beside the path, at every step, a hundred spring to light and dazzle and expire. The sun pours down in pitiless supremacy. No shadow falls here but the gloom of a passing cloud. Even the stones that clothe the land are small and shadeless. A dusty knot of prickles here and there, a sprig of heath, a tuft of camomile or sage, a thin grey arm of nameless root, a bulb like a football broken, peeling in the heat – such is the vegetation. The dry sand will not bear so poor a load as this except at distances a yard wide. Its hot yellow drowns the feeble greys and olives. Though never a breeze be blowing, faint, pale whirls of dust arise, and circle languidly and fall again. But this is the home of Morgana the Fay.

On every side you see her cruel cheats. Below the far-off hills that bound our colourless horizon, her baths lie; great lakes of shining water. Islands there are in them, which cast reflections on the surface. Trees adorn the strand and breaks of lofty cane. Mirage and deception all! The sole thing real in all this landscape is that abomination stretched before you.'

But even while the travellers gazed for a moment upon the scene, a dust storm struck their wagon as it rolled into the open country: 'An instant more, all fades from sight in a lurid tempest. The dust leaps up like a foe from ambush. It wraps you round in clouds that are palpable. Nose, ears, mouth, hair are filled at once. It penetrates your clothes, and makes an inner garment for your flesh. The horses are invisible; driver and passengers loom fantastic through the mist, and there is much coughing and swearing. Then there is a cry for water, and the 3-gallon keg is nearly drained. Such the Karoo desert and such the pleasures of travelling it.'

Nor were their trials on this second day of their journey over. When at two o'clock in the afternoon they outspanned at a lonely farm on the Karoo, the diarist, in deepening gloom ruminated: 'Surely this must be the dreariest habitation in the world. Built of mud, surrounded by a mud wall, it stands wretched, dirty and alone as a clod upon a dust-heap.' Within an hour, however, they departed; 'full of misery. Still through those eternal plains of dust, bordered by the same low hills.' Misery made him ironical: 'Crossed a ditch which on some occasions is the Patatas river; not at that moment, however. Canes and bushes lined the dry channel.' And even when at seven that evening they reached a farm for the night and had a longed-for bathe, it was 'in company with more, and more inquisitive frogs than ever before made attack upon a man of virtue. . . .'

Throughout the nine days which followed and brought him on the last to Pniel, his experiences were in general more or less a repetition of those of the first two days. Even the despised Karoo, however, on the third day yielded him 'a noble sunrise', so that he admitted: 'There is no climate where the sky-effects equal those of Cape Colony,' though he refused to describe them.

Next they passed 'five poor fellows tramping it to the promised land. They had one horse amongst them, loaded with picks and spades and home-made sieves. They were from Caledon and this their sixth day out. Thirty-five miles a day in such terrible sun and dust is good travel. They had suffered all the tortures of thirst in the Karoo, and their eager prayers were now for water. On these two deserts not a few poor fellows have succumbed. To lose the road is almost certain death, whilst the temptation towards travelling at night becomes irresistible after one day's experience of the heat. There were, and are, continual discoveries of unknown dead in this wilderness.'

Shortly afterwards they saw two sailors who had been picked up on the Karoo, unconscious and dying of thirst. They were now making bricks for 2s. a day, saving in order to resume, but more prudently, their journey to the Fields. There were few tramping the country at that season; but later, 'every road swarmed with them. Every farmer, his harvest in, every shop boy who dared a bolt, was hastening up for the cool season. I met with men who had "footed it" from Cape Town, 750 miles in 18 days; several who had done it in twenty-two; and hundreds there are who have covered the distance in twenty-four.'

At 5 a.m. on the fourth day of their journey the party met the 'down wagon' in which some found friends, and immediately the talk was of diamonds, in which a young man returning with 235 carats of good quality, naturally played a leading part. Political gossip too was exchanged: the Free State might send a commando or militia to enforce its claims over part of the Diamond Fields. Later, in the afternoon, when they were again well on their way, one passenger had a fit caused by the heat and flies, perpetual torments.

'I have said little', wrote the traveller, 'about our torments from these causes. The fact is I dread the subject. No words of mine could sketch the agonies we endured. . . . Suffice it that the sun ruled 130 degrees to 140, whilst we were packed so close as scarcely to allow movement; that we had no possible position for our legs but one; no change for our backs, nor rest for our heads. Dust blinded and stifled us. Flies! . . . We never had a cloudy day upon that journey, and we never escaped the utmost Beëlzebub could do against us.'

Nevertheless, that night they had only an hour's rest – 'the first night absolutely without bed!' The passengers' geniality noticeably declined, and complaints, particularly of swollen feet, were heard. However, coffee and a wash at 6.15 that morning improved spirits a little, but soon dust and heat made all 'open their mouths like dogs and choke and gasp alternately'. Beaufort West they found 'a pretty little village', with 'stores of surprising extent, and evidence of considerable wealth. At Beaufort the wild and naked Kaffir begins to make his appearance, children dispense with clothes, and your new driver wears an ostrich feather in his ragged hat.' Their favourable opinion of Beaufort West was doubtless also influenced by their discovery of a 'very comfortable inn' for the night.

Now, too, the country improved a little: 'pastures that looked fertile in comparison'. But soon came a new difficulty. As they crossed 'the damp bed' of a river, 'a desperate struggle' developed with the team of mules which had replaced the original horses. 'They plunged all ways at once, and the leaders turned right round in harness, putting their heads where their tails should be. We all scrambled out in a monstrous hurry. Even the lame men – we had several of them now – bounded to the earth like peas. It was an awkward place for an overturn. But the refractory animals were slewed round, and on we went.'

After 'winding through a succession of narrow plains, dusty but green, which twisted in and out in endless chain between two mountain ranges', they outspanned 'in a plain where all the burning winds of Africa appeared to rendezvous': 'a hurricane of living heat.' But later they reached 'Jackson's Farm, an extremely pretty place; fine mulberry trees enshade the door, a well filled garden lies within a hedge of roses opposite; there is a pool, spring-fed, therein, and noble trees embower its bank.'

But setting out on the next stage at five in the afternoon – without even having coffee! as they complained – 'we rode into the most violent and awful thunderstorm I have ever yet witnessed. Then I perceived how it was the rivers were so dreaded – the sluits were worn so deep, and the rocks so bare. Not twenty minutes the deluge lasted, but for that –

'The earth was all a yell, the air was all a flame.'

We were travelling through the plain that surrounds Victoria. The road had become a torrent. Again and again we had all to alight, knee-deep in mud and stream to assist the mules. At length, tired of these mere alternatives of misery, I set forth to walk, accompanied by another passenger. A tribe of jackals came sniffing round our heels, vanishing and reappearing, grey, light and noiseless as four-footed ghosts; but we reached the village safely.' At Victoria, too, they found a comfortable inn, but were there for only two hours, leaving at midnight.

The seventh and eighth days of the journey were each enlivened by a slight accident with the wagon, the second one when the wagon got stuck in a river bank. This indeed 'was perhaps the most miserable night of the journey. Every quarter of an hour our wretched doze was broken by the necessity of descending to push the wheels to hold them back – to restrain them somehow from getting into further mischief in a bank or in a hole, where they had no business on earth.' At four o'clock in the morning he resolved to walk. Many of the travellers were in bad condition by this time, with swollen ankles, limbs swollen to double size and blotched and discoloured, lame and in pain: a not unusual experience for journeys in these conditions.

Next as a fitting climax, the driver drove into a ditch, and did not know where he was; the tired mules often fell down; sometimes they fell down together; and the horses were sent to help the 'down wagon' approaching, which was also in distress. As they waited for new horses, the down wagon arrived with more friends, and greetings were interchanged. To anxious questioning as to prospects a most favourable report was given. 'Every man had a pocket full of stones, and a story yet more dazzling.' As for the fears of Free State commandos, they were absurd; President Brand was too prudent for that, they were sure! So passed the eighth and ninth days, the latter concluding with a rapid run to Hopetown and early supper and bed at the inn there. On the way they saw 'that peculiar phenomenon of the country, a "pan". This was a small one, perhaps not above an acre in extent – a circular depression in the level of the veldt, with earthy bottom and sides.'

The following day, the tenth, they reached the Orange River. 'On the further bank we found a party of wild Kaffirs, magnificent figures of men, purple black, with pleasant faces. They laughed and jested amongst themselves with that good humoured ease peculiar to the African. Every man had an excellent rifle and plenty of ammunition. I could not but read in their faces, merry and good natured as they were now, the signs of a spirit quickly roused, and dangerous while it lasted. Their foaming excitement in the dance was proof of this. But nothing could be more genial than their behaviour towards us, and towards each other, and they seemed half-scornfully surprised at the present of sixpence to the best dancer. These were Basutos, but I never after saw any of that tribe quite so wild. They were clothed, as one might say, in an ostrich feather, a riband and a bun.'

A great change in the scenery was now observed. The pale sand was gone; 'the eternal scrub shoots up to dignity.' The earth was red, with great crops of grass, tall and green, waving in the wind; and there were low trees. 'In every nook between the polished pebbles, which are heaped to the size of hills, some form of plant displays a tinge of green.'

It was half an hour past midnight when they reached the village that marked the end of the stage, but too late to arouse the sleeping inn; so they 'munched provisions and lay down round the wagon', while huge dogs slept with them when not chasing away wild beasts with furious barkings. Rising early, as usual, they set out on the last lap of their journey and just before four o'clock that afternoon, the eleventh day from Cape Town, they emerged in triumph from the trials and terrors of the wilderness, into the main street of Pniel.

3

The Dry Diggings

Scepticism as to the reality of the diamonds considerably delayed and doubtless also reduced the numbers flocking to the new Fields. Even in South Africa itself confidence grew but slowly, and some who set out for the Fields dallied on the way, half-hearted, visiting other places and so retarding their ultimate arrival by, in some cases, as much as seven months. Diamond seekers sailing into Table Bay with high hopes, and anxiously questioning the friends who met them, were given the depressing information that 'the diamond fields were played out', that many disappointed diggers were returning home in whatever vehicles they could get, while many others, unable to pay even their fares, were plodding back on foot. 'None of the Colonists had much faith in the new discovery; few outside Cape Town and Port Elizabeth were in much hurry – and the hurry in these places was not particularly stimulating, and did not go far to stimulate the courage of those on the go. When you told fellow Colonists that you were on the road to the diamond fields they either laughed at you, or with long faces hoped you would not die of fever like poor So-and-So, and so many others who had gone up; but if you did – and here their feelings were too powerful for utterance, and they left the rest to your imagination!'

But whatever the doubts and forebodings in South Africa, those in England were far greater and far worse. 'For a full year – and for more than a full year after diamond digging had been successfully going on on the banks of the Vaal,' wrote the same observer, 'the wiseacres of England had been pooh-poohing and ridiculing the reported diamond discovery in the country. Diamonds at the Cape – or anything good to come from Cape-ward – was too absurd for an Englishman born on English soil, and especially a Londoner, to swallow. They could believe in a Kaffir War breaking out or Cape wine being sour, but that there should be any natural formation in the Cape that contained diamonds of the first water was a story to tell the marines – not Englishmen.'

Even so late as 1882, twelve years after the opening of the Fields, and when the export of diamonds had reached twelve millions a year, *The*

Times of London, it is said, was still warning its readers to beware of Cape diamonds, asserting that the reports about them reaching England were misleading exaggerations. 'When I first arrived in London,' wrote the editor of a Diamond Fields newspaper in his reminiscences, 'I found that very little was known about the South African Diamond Fields and the diamond industry, which had then been established over ten years. The grossest misrepresentations appeared in the columns of the London journals, and the most influential of the morning papers were continually throwing out insinuations that were most harmful. I found that the English people were misled by the papers they read. Many, reflecting what they had gathered from their favourite papers, boldly said they didn't believe that the diamonds coming home were Cape diamonds at all, and these people kept alive the old absurd invention that the diamonds were from the Brazils, purchased and sent home by South African landowners with a view to a land swindle. Those who admitted that some diamonds might come from the Cape, made out that they were of inferior quality. . . . It was very tantalizing to hear and read all this.'

When this indignant English, or rather Scottish, South African met the editors of some of the London journals who had so offended, he got little enough satisfaction. *The Observer* refused to publish his corrections on the ground that it would show its readers it had misled them! The *Daily Telegraph* accepted them but did not publish them. *The Times* argued and hedged, while its City Editor suggested that the South African diamond market was being managed by dishonest men, and that perhaps the complainant himself was a large shareholder in it, trying to increase his profits by boosting it: a charge which was not only indignantly repudiated, but emphasized by a timely reminder that a former City Editor of the paper had in fact so feathered his nest.

*

The small companies who first came to the river and to the dry diggings were, as previously said, chiefly composed of residents from neighbouring farms; even a little later when others came from somewhat farther afield, they were mostly respectable persons: 'particularly decent and peace-loving people who had brought their families with them and treated the whole business as a prolonged picnic which might even turn out to be profitable,' one digger wrote.

This somewhat surprising presence of whole families, commented upon by several observers, was naturally almost entirely confined to the Boers, whose comparative proximity to the Fields made the journey less trying for the women and children. Nor were the families mere unavoidable impedimenta. How useful they could be, and were, many diggers bear witness. 'Children are profitable here. Some of the deepest holes are made, and largest heaps of stuff thrown out, by Dutchmen with large families. It is a pleasant sight to see mother and daughter busily picking over a sorting table, while father and sons are all hard at work digging and sifting. In such cases: "Happy is the man who has his quiver full."

'Happy also is another man whose hot lunch I see brought every day at one o'clock by a fair young wife; I envy that man. There is an Australian digger, too, working close to my claim; only he and his wife. She does all the sorting, and she has such a lucky hand for picking out diamonds that they have averaged £7 10s. od. per day since they started; and they are now going very deep, in confident hopes of finding a "big thing".'

The children working and playing about the camp must have greatly enjoyed the whole adventure, especially when, as sometimes happened, they found stones among the siftings that had been thrown aside after inadequate examination, a quite common occurrence.

Indeed the appeal of comradeship, neighbourliness and familiarity was particularly felt where, as often, whole families set out from the same village for the Fields, or when neighbours, friends and relations found each other again there. It was thus that in after years some recalled with almost poetic pleasure, those calm clear nights under the shining stars, passed at the diggings beside their camp fire, with song, dance and music, and simple refreshments of coffee and rusks, while all around, far and near, other fires glowed through the darkness. There was romance too for the young men and girls dancing together, hoping too that tomorrow or perhaps the next day the diamond would turn up which meant marriage, ease, pleasure and happiness.

That this family life made for stability and sobriety on the whole, was very evident. Mostly Boers, hard-working, stolid, solid and law-abiding, they were easy to control. 'Many of them had their families, and nearly all lived as respectably as possible. This character may still [that was later] be given to the mass of diggers. There are bad fellows amongst them, and plenty of drinking always; but no such scenes have ever been witnessed as made the Australian and Californian fields a by-word.'

As time passed and news of the genuineness of the South African Diamond Fields spread, new, larger and largely different crowds flocked to them from all corners of the world. Seamen deserted their ships at Durban, East London, Port Elizabeth and Cape Town; tradesmen shut up their shops, and all set out to make their fortunes as quickly as possible.

All kinds and classes caught the diamond fever and made for the land of promise: butchers, bakers, sailors, clerks, gamblers, labourers, loafers, doctors, carpenters, army officers and privates, schoolboys, husbands and wives. From Brazil, North America, the Dutch East Indies, Australia and elsewhere they came, in all the varieties of dress that national conventions, personal preferences and social and economic circumstances dictated. And in the great majority of cases, as with the river diggers, their ignorance of diamonds and of diamond-mining was complete.

Even the Cathedral at Grahamstown in the Eastern Province of the Cape suffered from this unholy passion for Mammon, losing its organist, its stonemason, and much of its choir. Nevertheless some of the devout regarded the discovery of diamonds and its consequences as Providential: a divine dispensation, not only to solve South Africa's then severe economic troubles, but also to secure the future by achieving the settlement and cultivation of vast regions hitherto waste and desert, but now becoming centres of busy communities. Others, however, preferring their primitive solitudes to the noisy, bustling, acquisitive crowds invading them, believed the discovery of diamonds to be a temptation of the Devil.

Nevertheless, hope, optimism, and enthusiasm, whether divine or diabolical, brought the invaders in ever increasing numbers through the hardships and rigours of their journeys. In these circumstances, the original, almost family atmosphere and higher standard of behaviour inevitably declined. Yet there is an impressive unanimity in the wide and general testimony of the diggers to the good behaviour and honesty of the crowds as a whole, and even to the superior social standing of many who came, led rather by the love of adventure or the gambler's lure than by poverty or failure in other ways of life. 'Men of all classes came – few, but some, of the lower class. The arrivals were generally from the middle, the well-to-do, and upper classes. The first who came were the best who came; they were lords, honourables and Sir Somebodies by the dozen, and amongst them the Lord-knows-who.' This last generally appears to have been more successful with diamonds than the other aristocrats who came.

'The real sprigs came with money in both pockets, and for the most part were gentlemen well trained at the "Bar" to which they found ready admittance at the Fields, and where they spent more of their time than in the claims. I don't know that any of them did much to improve the morals of the community. Truth to tell, I don't think they did; but their company was much sought-after, for over all the world there will be tuft-hunters so long as there is a tuft to hunt. The veriest democrat in creation loves the warmth of an aristocratic wing. The Prince of Wales's plume attracts more human flies than a whole barrel of treacle, wasps.' There, in his own particular idiom, the digger gives us a clear insight into at least one section of Diamond Field society.

With so many nationalities, social grades and classes, the Diamond Fields offered a colourful and animated panorama. Not the least striking element in the scene was the diggers' dress. For although we are told that the corduroy trousers, the light flannel shirt with rolled-up sleeves and without collar or tie, the wide-brimmed felt hat and broad leather 'piratical' belt with pockets for diamonds and money were all *de rigueur*, there is plenty of evidence that many men followed their own tastes in such matters, as did the non-diggers on the Fields, and that the digger who wrote 'at the diggings everyone dresses just as he damn well pleases,' was not without justification.

Not only was the pith helmet an occasional substitute for the felt hat, but gay and ornamental additions were made by many to the conventional dress. 'The colonists come out the strongest in feathers. Large ostrich feathers, worth perhaps ten shillings each out there, are frequently to be seen curling gracefully round the slouched felt hat of some stalwart young farmer from Natal or Cape Colony – wings of birds of gay plumage, shot on the way up, immense long feathers of the Kaffir Crane, all these and many more make gay their head-covers; nay, I have seen a broad strip of the soft fur of a silver jackal, or some other animal, going right round the crown of a hat.

'Red sashes, of silk and other materials, and of great length, like the Eastern "cummerbund" are very extensively worn; not only because they are ornamental, and softer and pleasanter to wear than a leather belt or strap, but because they are considered to be of some use as a preventive against diarrhoea and other disorders of the bowels. Green veils, blue veils, red and white puggarees, and divers other arrangements for coolness, shade or ornament, are also very prevalent amongst all the diggers; so that with the numerous suits of brown or yellow cords, with "white ducks" here and there, the gay colours and variegated patterns of the shirts, and the eccentric but highly ornamental character of the headgear, an assemblage of diamond diggers has in it many elements of the picturesque, and a good deal of vivid colouring.'

The 'Dutch Boers' at the Fields are described as 'industrious though somewhat sluggish, affectionate to one another, kindly, courteous, and helpful to strangers, especially to such as speak their language, keenly sensitive to ridicule or ill-treatment of any kind, and often imposed upon by keen colonial traders.'

42

An occasional detailed reference in a digger's diary or in letters, gives us a clearer and more definite insight into the kinds of 'gentlemen' and others at the Fields; as thus: 'Mr E., a wealthy and cultivated gentleman from the North Countree, dined with us. He is a hunter-mad. Having just fallen in for another fortune at home, he proposes to celebrate his luck by an eighteen-months' trip amongst the nakedest negroes, elephants, and other wild beasts of the Lake country. . . . The eldest son of one of our wealthiest bankers has been dwelling in a lonely harem some 200 miles to the northward these five years. An ex-officer of the Lancers, with many thousands a year, is living as the most trusted warrior of Sechele. Half a score of others I could mention are well-born, rich and cultivated men, suffering from like mania.'

But inevitably with the increasing numbers, the gentlemen and the gentlemanly decreased in proportion, and the effect of this was not unremarked. 'The character of the population soon changed. At first the ordinary colonist predominated – the kind of man who had hitherto led the simple life, in most cases that of a farmer. He was very often accompanied by his whole family. . . . But as the fame of the rich and ever richer finds went abroad, a cosmopolitan crowd of wastrels and adventurers poured in from the ends of the earth. However, there never was in those early days anything like the lawlessness that afterwards – as much under British as under Republican rule – prevailed on the Rand. The great stay of law and order was the individual digger, and this element of stability has always been missing at the gold fields, except in the few instances where alluvial mining has been pursued.'

James Anthony Froude visiting the Fields a year or two later, in 1874, gave a clear and colourful yet entirely realistic account of the very mixed pattern the crowds on the Fields assumed: 'diggers from America and Australia, German speculators, Fenians, traders, saloon-keepers, professional gamblers, barristers, ex-officers of the Army and Navy, younger sons of good family who have not taken a profession or have been obliged to leave; a marvellous, motley assemblage, among whom money flows like water from the amazing productiveness of the mine; and in the midst of them a hundred or so keen-eyed Jewish merchants, who have gathered like eagles over their prey, and a few thousand natives who have come to work for wages, to steal diamonds and to lay their earnings out in rifles and powder.'

Despite the frequent assertions by diggers that those at the Fields were almost incredibly law-abiding and honest, the actual facts which emerge naturally show a less ideal moral standard among many. Yet, partly under the influence of tales of the American and Australian gold fields, and perhaps partly in reaction against the idealized descriptions, unduly derogatory and sweeping generalizations soon gained world-wide currency, and retain their hold even today. The journalistic appeal of such over-charged sensationalism was too obvious to be overlooked, and such exaggerated and evidently 'literary' sketches as the following, became popular: 'As time went on the fame of the Diamond Fields spread far and wide; men of all conditions, from all countries and continents hurried to the source of wealth. Each post-cart and bullock-wagon brought its load of sordid, impecunious humanity. Rabbis, rebels, rogues and roués from Russia and the Riviera, transports from Tasmania, convicts from Cale-donia, ex-prisoners from Portland, brigands from Bulgaria, and choicest pickings of dirtiest street-corners in all Europe, many of whom were de-vout, but nearly all decidedly improper. . . . They all came here to escape grinding poverty or in many cases punishment of their crimes. Unfrocked clergymen with the air of saints and souls of sinners, who had never known the stain of work; broken, stalwart soldiers with fair moustaches and freckled faces, caring for nothing but billiards and brandy; lawyers who knew Horace well but Holloway better; and divorcees with a variegated past printed on their features. . . . It was a horde that increased and multi-plied, and would have made a fine haul for the Devil. Many well known names in literature, war, art were to the front. Sons and daughters of Thespis too, began to pop up, and some ruby-faced flatulent members of the defunct Prize Ring. About 60 per cent of the new arrivals knew as little of work as they cared for it, and consequently there was a rapid increase of crime and consumption of whisky. The police were aug-mented.'

The inexactitude of such writing, evidently ready to sacrifice truth to alliterative rhetoric, is obvious, although, within reason, doubtless small numbers of all these elements did find their way to the Fields. But that they were out of all proportion is disproved not only by the almost un-animous testimony of many diggers, but also by the actual work achieved at the diggings and the speed with which it was done.

Nevertheless, such a picture by the Devil's advocate, although enorm-ously exaggerated, is a perhaps necessary corrective to numerous scarcely less exaggerated descriptions of the diamond-seekers as crowds of such outstanding virtue that law and police were not needed. 'Taking all things into consideration,' wrote one of them, 'the Fields were perfect models of honesty. We were without police, gas, bolts or other thief-producing attributes.' And he asserts that tents, necessarily left unguarded all day (and often all night), fastened if at all with only a piece of string, knew no invaders beyond an occasional stray dog in search of food.

The same high standard is also said to have been maintained in civil matters. Despite the tension of lives anxiously searching for sudden wealth, partnerships were generally conducted with complete honesty, and as the stores that sprang up dealt only on a cash basis, credit being neither asked nor given, disputes and legal proceedings were almost impossible.[1] Nevertheless, an occasional canteen, it is admitted, would be broken into for liquor, and low idlers would hang about to buy stones stolen by native servants.

A good corrective to such pictures of exaggerated evil or goodness is the following passage: 'The character of the population has been most absurdly decried. "The Diamond Fields of South Africa", writes one flighty reporter, "have been hot-beds of rowdyism. The libertines, forgers, bird-catchers, and other outcasts of Europe have found a refuge there as in Alsatia of old. The Houndsditch Jew and the London rough reign supreme." Thousands of witnesses might be summoned, if necessary, to refute this nonsense. Libertines and forgers drift elsewhere for prey than to hot, dusty mining camps in the midst of the Karoo; though dainty folk might shrink from the roughness and grime of the diamond diggings, and weak nerves might be shaken by the boisterous exuberance of the bustling camp, the restless crowd tramping the streets, the uproarious canteens and music-halls, and the capers of motley diggers and wild Africans. . . .'

The first diggers on the Fields were forced to depend almost entirely upon themselves, and as a consequence, individualism reigned unchecked. Unheeded by any government, they rejoiced in their freedom from authority, from taxes, from all the restraints imposed by law and order; so far apparently unnecessary, as 'rows' we are told were infrequent, and each man could go his own way, unmolested. But as the numbers flocking to the Fields increased and their quality decreased, the need to impose order and peace on the community became evident, and soon Diggers' Committees were elected by the diggers themselves, to make laws and regulations for the Fields. Such was the origin of the 'miners' democracy'. But although the original unfettered individualism now largely disappeared, many of the early individualistic qualities remained, until the diggers' consequent refusal of any cooperation to meet the practical difficulties of diamond mining, brought amalgamation by business interests and the ultimate elimination of the individual digger.

One 'democratic' custom of the early period was the diggers' habit of using one another's Christian names, a practice then not favoured

[1] For a different opinion, cf. *infra*, p. 142.

45

elsewhere by educated persons, except in cases of close relationship or intimacy. The miners often added a distinguishing word to prevent confusion with other persons, drawing upon the native town, county or country of the individual whose Christian name was invoked. Thus Tom from Lancashire became 'Lanky Tom' without any reference to his appearance; 'Yorker Bill' came from New York; 'Yank Seymour' needs no explanation; Joe from Port Elizabeth became 'Betsy's Joe' – a quite misleading name to the uninitiate. Nor was the distinguishing word confined to origins. When we find a man from Cape Town named 'Snooker', the billiard room and its refreshments are clearly indicated.

Life on the Fields was certainly a test of character. Neither birth nor social position counted for much amongst the miners in general, unless other qualities went with them, as nearly all scrambled in the dirt for diamonds, the undergraduate or army captain swinging his pick beside the navvy. With the general sense of equality went that of independence: the knowledge that the poor man of today may be very rich tomorrow.

In these circumstances it was some time before any individuals could rise above the general mass. But in time, the most acute, energetic, farseeing and audacious began to outstrip the rest, until 'democracy' became plutocracy on the fields. Sir David Harris, recalling his own personal experiences on the early Diamond Fields, well described the days of the 'diggers' democracy'. 'In those memorable days, when money was easily made and as easily spent, when the flotsam and jetsam of humanity mingled with sons of titled British parents, all life was a gamble. In the lives of those early diggers, drama and comedy jostled each other alternately in the race for supremacy. A braver band of adventurers never set foot on the soil of Klondyke – they who smiled at good fortune were equally chivalrous when the dark shadows of adversity crossed their path.'

*

The Dry Diggings, the magnet which drew such crowds from all ends of the earth, was in all a tract of some sixty square miles of chiefly arid, barren country, unoccupied save by natives and an occasional Boer farm. Desolate and poverty-stricken, it gave no promise of its immediate future. Sold shortly after the discovery of diamonds there for some ten thousand pounds, twenty years later it could not have been bought for ten million! By that time the land had been proved to contain within its borders the three richest diamond mines in the world.

The sequence of events which led ultimately to this startling consummation was, in its beginning, as casual, as unsensational as were the first discoveries by the river. Jagersfontein, a farm some hundred miles south-east of Klipdrift, was the scene of the earliest of the new finds. One day in August 1870, the owner of the farm, a Boer widow, Jacoba Visser, during digging operations in dry gravel and six feet down, found a diamond of 50 carats. Upon hearing of this, her neighbours, almost in the spirit of child's play, set their native servants digging, and paid the widow £2 a month for lots twenty feet square. The diamonds found at Jagersfontein were particularly good, some of them magnificent gems, including the Excelsior, 971¾ carats, and the Reitz or Jubilee, 634 carats. Thus the total value of the diamonds found far exceeded that of the fees paid; but the stones were spread over the area in so haphazard a way that diggers' luck at Jagersfontein became almost proverbially hazardous, and consequently it never developed like other parts of the Diamond Fields.

About a month after the discovery of Jagersfontein, another Boer farmer, Adriaan Van Wyk, found diamonds on his farm Dorstfontein, at Dutoitspan (or -pond), situated half-way between the Vaal and Modder rivers, some twenty miles south-east of Pniel and Klipdrift. Van Wyk in the usual way of the farmers had built his house himself, making the mortar from the sandy ground. Thus it was, tradition declares, that his first diamonds were accidentally discovered in the walls of his home. Uninterested in his discovery, Van Wyk continued placidly farming, as before, until the news spread and brought crowds who overran the farm. Failing to check them or to obtain the 25 per cent he demanded from them, of the value of their finds, he then charged 7s. 6d. a week for each claim of thirty feet square, and not long afterwards sold the farm to The South African Exploration Company for £2,600.

From Dutoitspan where diamonds were found in the surface soil early in 1871, the invaders quickly spread to the neighbouring farm, Bultfontein, owned by Cornelius Du Plooy.[1] After some vicissitudes, including a legal action, it was finally bought by The London and South African Exploration Co., in 1876, for £6,000.

Northward, some two miles distant from Dutoitspan and Bultfontein, was the Boer farm Vooruitzigt (Foresight), where early in May 1871, diamonds were found. The place came to be known as De Beers' Rush or Old De Beers, from the name of a former owner. The Orange Free State Police were unable to stop the crowds overrunning the farm, and towards the end of the month the farmer was driven to open the field on payment of a licence fee of 10s. a month for each claim of thirty feet square.

---

[1] Some accounts assert that the discovery of diamonds was in the wall of Du Plooy's house at Bultfontein, not at Van Wyk's.

Two months after the first discovery at Vooruitzigt a second diamond bed was found on the farm. A small 'kopje' or hillock there was suspected to have diamonds, and in July 1871 four diggers from Colesberg sent a native servant to test it. When he returned with a diamond of 2 carats the diggers went there and pegged claims. The place became known as 'De Beers' New Rush', the 'New Rush', and as 'Colesberg Kopje'.

Despite the tremendously increased values of these farms later, the farmers who first sold them had no legitimate grievance. They had obtained a price far above their original value as farm land, and before its potential value as a diamond field could be more than speculative, nor could they have supplied the enormous amount of capital later needed for development. They had made good, and indeed for their world, unheard-of profits, while the purchasing companies took no small risks; risks in fact not primarily in diamonds, but in land values. For the early discovery of diamonds was so uncertain that neither buyer nor seller had any definite idea of what the land contained. Rather the purchasers speculated on the fact that diamond-hunting must almost inevitably increase the price of land, and now that digging had spread from the common property of the banks of the Vaal to privately owned ground, the companies preferred a deal in real estate as a sounder speculation than the search for elusive and problematical diamonds.

The miners along the Vaal at first turned a sceptical ear to the rumours of wonderful discoveries in the 'dry' country twenty miles away. The tendency towards incredulity was intensified by the general but mistaken belief that the diamonds were not of local origin but had been brought down from distant regions by the waters of the river, and many continued to doubt and disparage the dry diggings as long as possible, and even longer. The unsuccessful river diggers were naturally more disposed to try their luck elsewhere, and so largely led the exodus from the Vaal to the new Fields. How eager many were, the records show. Even two small boys aged five and six years, a local journal tells us, escaped from a river camp, but, discovered when well on their way, tearfully protested that the next day they would have reached the dry diggings and made their fortunes!

Each new discovery was of course immediately followed by a new 'rush' to the fortunate spot. The following description clearly reveals the mixture of serious fortune-hunting and 'sport' which strongly appealed to many of the better types of digger in these earliest days. 'Whenever it was rumoured or asserted that diamonds had been discovered in a certain locality, at once there would be a wild rush to the attractive spot. It was a strange sight to witness the motley crowd on their road to a new rush . . .

away they "scooted", all sorts and conditions of men, helter-skelter across the veldt, most of them on ponies, horses and donkeys, also conveyances of varied descriptions, gigs, traps, chaises, Cape carts, lorry carts, sanitary carts, butchers' carts, costers' carts, even water carts. Many were pedestrians whose only worldly possessions were what they stood in. Arrived on the chosen ground, claims would be pegged out for miles round, and on these sacred spots could be seen proud owners, happy enough with their castles in the air, as they patronized itinerant vendors of liquors and solids, or disposed of their pegged claims, as many of these last were purchased by speculators on the ground. I have scrambled to many rushes, but have never been to one that has turned out successful. Glorious fun it was, however, galloping over the boundless veldt with a lot of jolly fellows, the cool, delightful air, as exhilarating as champagne, stimulating the freshness of a youthful heart, and the vast blue expanse of multi-coloured country, purple, brown and gold, fronting you, as illimitable in extent as the beautiful sky, looking like a garden of opals, pearls and turquoises, or as the chances of fortune were to your mind in the new El Dorado.'

About the dry diggings the white tents appeared and increased even more quickly than at the river. On their outskirts, over the fields and about the kopjes, were grouped the wagons, horses, mules, bullocks, all the inevitable accompaniment of an embryo mining camp, while beyond were the native huts made of wood, dirty canvas or mud. Some of the natives, indeed, slept in holes dug out of the hillside.

Speed of settlement was followed in the leading camps by equally speedy development. Within a few months the mining camp at Du Toit's Pan had become 'Dutoitspan'. Cecil Rhodes, arriving there from Bloemfontein, sent his mother the following description: 'Fancy an immense plain with right in its centre a mass of white tents and iron stores, and on one side of it, all mixed up with the camp, mounds of lime like ant-hills; the country round is all flat, with just thorn trees here and there: and you have some idea of Dutoitspan, the first spot where dry digging for diamonds was begun.'

Another visitor, reaching Dutoitspan about this time, wrote: 'One afternoon in the distance we caught sight of the diamond fields. People gazed with the same interest and excitement as those who see the outline of an unknown land. Many a heart beat faster as the Diamond City of the Plains became less and less indistinct, and those whose everything depended on the success of their expedition watched this ghost-like series of tents grow whiter and whiter as they outlined clearer. These were anxious times for those who had imagination and ambition, and hardly a word was said.

... Nearer and nearer we came. Canvas shelters were everywhere, and as the coach got into one of the roads leading directly to Dutoitspan, the only wooden buildings seen were made of packing cases, though dismal-looking iron shanties intermingled with mud-heaps, wells and washing apparatus were on view by the score. However, on we went; tents got more numerous, less lilywhite; and unwashed diggers popped their heads out to see us pass. Naked Kaffirs and dogs appeared in plenty, acclaimed the mules and passengers as if the precious lot was Lord Sanger's Circus before the flood. The driver, livening up the tired mules, showing his gleaming teeth and looking supremely happy, drove up the Main Street of Dutoits-pan in what he considered fine style.

'It was about three in the afternoon and the place was full of people. Niggers and negresses of different tribes were walking in the roadway, diggers in woollen shirts and sombrero hats were standing without the canteens or drinking inside, and Coolies arrayed in white turbans and linen suits were ringing bells outside the eating houses. There were numerous medium-sized timbered buildings and a few large ones. Although it was the principal thoroughfare, many small bell and wood-framed canvas tents lined either side of the Regent Street of Dutoitspan. . . . I noticed, lying on a bale of chaff, the figure of a man dressed in the ordinary attire of a digger – felt hat, top boots, corduroy breeches and coat.'

Another description overlooks none of the grimmer aspects. The 'attractive spot' was certainly far from attractive to sight, touch and smell, perhaps even to taste. Leaving Pniel on 20 November 1871 to return to Dutoitspan, already disgusted with the springless and patched old cart and broken and decayed harness attached to the four stout mules that carried him along, the digger surveyed all with increasing dismay as they proceeded, lumbering through the deep and gaping holes that covered the road. Leaving the deep, red, dense sand round Pniel that the mules could hardly drag the cart over, they came to a region of thorny bushland. For the rest, we must turn to the digger's own words or lose the immediacy and intensity, the lugubrious clarity of vision they express.

'After mounting the slope, traversing the table-land, and risking one's neck in the further descent, the red sand vanishes, and the eternal plains ensue. Across them cuts a very broad track, mud-coloured, broken with wheelmarks, the road to the fields! About a mile beyond Pniel, in a hollow, stands the famed canteen belonging to "Job". It is a tent most roughly shaped. Job made it himself, I believe, and he is not equal to the other patriarch, apparently, in tent-making. The pole and woodwork are mere branches of a tree; the furniture is a plank resting on two barrels; barrels and roots are set around for seats. In a simplicity that does credit to his heart, Job exposes the sleeping accommodation to public criticism in the shape of half-a-dozen sacks and an old kaross or sheepskin.' Soon, 'the road was lined with bones and half-dry carcases. Here is the animal world's Gehenna. Always take for granted in the scenery of the Diamond Fields a hedge of bones and horns and rotting bodies, along each side of the path.' Flies that made life a terror naturally accompanied such phenomena.

'The nearer we drew to our journey's end, the more busy became the road. Carts passed by every five minutes, many of them handsome vehicles, and handsomely horsed. Empty wagons lumbered by, on the homeward journey. There was no chaff. Passers-by paid no more attention to each other than in London streets. Yet many of them were colonial born, arrived within very few weeks from some distant farm, where a strange face is the rarest of all chances. . . .' Similar descriptions are left by others, such as the famous Barney Barnato who noticed the carts, coaches, wagons and pedestrians in increasing numbers as he neared the Fields; the single tents standing upright by the roadside; the men who passed them, walking away from the Fields dejectedly, in ragged clothes – failures, unable to pay their fares back to their homes.

So the traveller, still pursuing his way to Dutoitspan, reached the 'New Rush' (soon to be known as Kimberley). After dropping half the passengers, they drove on through the same camp chaos, and, some three hundred yards away on the left, passed the Old De Beers, bounded by a real mountain chain of siftings. A few bushes at intervals bordered the path, still lined with the carcases and skeletons of oxen. 'Mostly they lie just in the shape they fell in, with limbs outtossed, and head extended. Some have been picked clean by dog and bird, but their bones still hang together; others have dried up as they lay, no one having taken the trouble to skin them; the bones of some are scattered in queer dissection, head and forequarters here, hind legs and spine two yards away. Our noses gave proof that the waste of animal life has not yet ceased, nor are the scavengers active.' A mile and a half beyond the New Rush, the driver raised his whip to point out Dutoitspan, 'another city of canvas, lying low, and on that account all visible at once. . . .'

As 'at New Rush, the extreme outskirts of the town are occupied with wagons and solitary tents. These become thicker set and larger. A flagpole, with the representation of a black horse, dominates them. Right in front are the hills of siftings, higher than those we had seen, and more fully occupied with sorters. Turning sharp round to the right by these, one crosses a deep worn sluit and enters the upper street. It is of excellent width, bordered by neat wooden stores and "frame houses". . . . Passing several wide roads, lined only with tents at present, but busy with plank and tool, we reach the market square. This is a space handsome without extravagance, surrounded with stores. I think there are but two canvas houses in the square. . . . All the rest are plank, and not a vacant corner could be had under a price of £20 the foot. Few of the traders there will sell at twice the price. The Briton will say it is no great boast for a capital, that its main streets should be lined with timber houses; but . . . a timber house is just the most expensive thing in all the country. Speedy warehousing for their goods, a start before the rivals, and a roof to shelter customers, were the objects that these *fore-treking* tradesmen had in view. They could not wait, they cannot wait now, for bricks to be made, houses built and seasoned. At any cost they got up timber dwellings from the Eastern Province, and never since have they found time to plan a house of brick.'

Another description of the scene happily supplements those of others, and incidentally suggests sporting potentialities. 'Passing over a broad plain, covered with stunted grass and here and there a little thornbush, we rapidly neared the camp. We were barely half a mile distant from the nearest tents, when I saw four springbok grazing, and got so near to them that I risked a couple of shots with my revolver, but missed them. Then we got to the "Pan" from which the camp takes its name, a large, shallow depression in the ground, which will apparently be full of water in rainy weather. Cattle were grazing all around, nigger men and women of all tribes and colours busy drawing water from two dirty wells, or washing clothes at two dirtier dams, while on a slight rise of ground beyond the Pan stood tents and wagons of every description, and farther up yet rose the huge mounds of earth and gravel thrown up by the diamond seekers, above which a dense permanent cloud of fine dust showed that they were all busy at work "dry-sifting".'

The farm Dorstfontein on which Dutoitspan stood consisted of some 6,500 acres, of which, it appeared later, only fifteen acres or less yielded diamonds. It had been bought from the Orange Free State Government in 1860 by a Boer farmer, Paulus Du Toit. The 'Pan', described by one writer as 'an oasis in the dreary landscape and generally known as Dutoitspan', was in fact a large pond, a depression in the ground, about a quarter of a mile long and half as broad. The scenery around the Pan was 'flat, a broad expanse of "veldt" or prairie, with stunted growth of scrub, and here and there a mimosa or thornbush, but at a distance varying from five to twelve miles run ranges of picturesque hills, many of them well wooded'.

In the wet season the Pan served as a reservoir, and Du Toit used it to water his cattle. On the side towards Pniel, (twenty-five miles away northwards) it had a sloping ridge or long 'kopje', and the diamonds which attracted the attention of the world to it in 1870, were found near the top. Once the news leaked out, 'it was not a rush but a stampede', and the poor bewildered farmer was overwhelmed as he watched in amazement the endless flood of carts, wagons, horse and foot invaders, as they surged onto his land, caring nothing about the landlord or his interests as they gaily measured out their claims before setting to work with pick and shovel.

The main 'town', called by some enthusiasts the 'City of the Pan' (now Beaconsfield), lay between the claims and the Pan itself, and at this early stage of its development consisted of hundreds of diggers' tents covering the veldt above the claims towards De Beers and Pniel. People noticed later how comparatively spacious it was compared with the rising New Rush, where diggers wished to be as near as possible to their claims, in the 'Great Hole'. 'Large and picturesque tents, marquees and buildings of every possible material being charmingly grouped round the large, open market square from which streets, mostly of canvas, radiate in all directions.'

Writing to a friend in August 1871, a digger thus describes the environment at the Field: 'Of course we live in tents, and they are of every size and shape imaginable, and, with a few exceptions, pitched together all anyhow, or higgledy piggledy; but the effect is far from unpicturesque. Many of the Dutch Boers live in their wagons, erecting cooking sheds, and ovens close to them, and generally showing themselves keenly alive to comfort. Though we have largely marquees, corrugated-iron houses and even brick erections are beginning to be made. There are stores, canteens, and billiard rooms, and they all do a roaring trade. Claims are spreading in all directions, threatening to push away the tents and encroach upon the road. I need hardly say we have no gas, and on a dark night, evening calls on friends in distant parts of the huge, straggling camp are fraught with many dangers. One instant you narrowly escape falling into a 15-foot deep claim; the next you are almost impaled on the horns of a bullock – and there are hundreds lying by the wagons at night; then you come upon huge rocks and boulders, and just as you see the light glimmering in your friend's tent, you fall over a sleeping donkey.' Not all the new arrivals found Dutoitspan 'picturesque'. Some were 'disappointed to find a primitive camp', despite the diggers living 'happily' in their tents.

Work at these dry diggings was at first much easier than by the river; there were no big boulders, no water was needed for washing, and dry

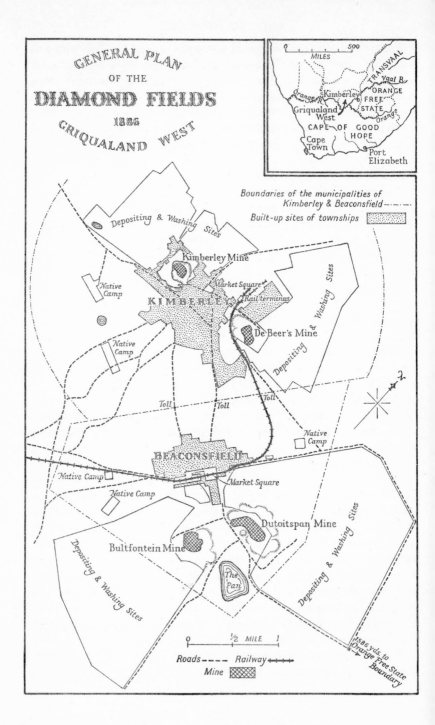

GENERAL PLAN OF THE DIAMOND FIELDS 1886 GRIQUALAND WEST

land was preferred by the miners to standing knee-deep in the river, with flooding of their claim an ever-present danger. These early diggers of 1870 needed only a pick and shovel, for they dug no farther than eighteen inches or two feet down until they reached the limestone stratum, when, believing that the diamondiferous earth went no deeper, they abandoned their claims and sought others, which, of course, they treated in the same way.

Theory played no part in the exploration of the Diamond Fields; the sight of diamonds lying on or near the surface was the only test accepted by the experienced digger in these earliest days. It was in this way that Dutoitspan and the other diggings were discovered.

The following account is doubtless typical of many. 'Satisfied by ocular demonstration [of the presence of diamonds] or relying on reports which he believes trustworthy, the digger proceeds to work in monstrous haste. Rushing to the spot of which the news has reached him, he measures out a space which he conceives to be 30 feet square, digs a shallow trench round it, and fortifies the work with a stone here and there. This done he withdraws to the ambulating canteen which has followed the earliest to the spot, and cools his brow and whets his hopes in pontic [*sic* – Pontac?] and gingerbeer, "pickaxe", or some such compound. Thence returning to his claim, if an energetic fellow, he sets to work off-hand, digging and picking, whilst a mate puts up the sorting-table in a convenient spot. The third of the party – for diggers should go in triplets – or a black fellow in his service, riddles the stuff thrown out. So they work steadily on till the authorities – an elected committee in former times, the nearest inspector now – comes to survey the kopje, and receive applications for claims. When the lines are rectified by this official, and his full 30 feet square allotted to every one, it generally happens that a digger finds himself some yards away from the spot where he has begun to dig, perhaps to "find"; sometimes his boundaries will be moved to an immense distance, and numbers of those who have arrived late will be pushed off the hillock altogether.'

At that time, before the rush to Colesberg Kopje, 'the Pan' was the camp which yielded the largest stones, many of them over 100 carats. The area worked was large; not less than half a square mile was completely covered by claims, all joining one another: 'at first sight, a chaotic mass of irregularly shaped holes of various depths, and endless whitish mounds of various sizes.' It is not surprising that many disputes as to the ownership of diamonds took place. The general appearance of the Field was one of great activity, for each claim generally employed two Whites at least with three or four natives, all ceaselessly busy, particularly after they discovered that the best and largest diamonds lay deeper, that claims were not exhausted when two feet had been unearthed, but in fact were only just begun. Then they worked above and below ground, 'picking' the 'stuff', throwing it up, breaking, sifting and sorting it, while the natives formed a half-naked choir of barbaric songs and shouts.

Thus in 1871, diggers, now aware of diamonds in depth, again rushed to Dutoitspan to work over old abandoned claims of which the ground had been merely scratched. In 1870, claims there in a good position sold for anything from £1 to £50 each, 30 feet square, while a digger's licence cost 10s. a month. The place was popular because the rise of the New Rush (Colesberg Kopje, later Kimberley), attracted so many that claims at Dutoitspan were cheap in comparison, and although it offered no such daily and weekly certainties of "finds" as the New Rush did, very large stones were often found at Dutoitspan, and living was comparatively cheap and comfortable, since many large stores had appeared there, competition among their proprietors was keen, and the immense market supplied daily by the Boer farmers of the district offered everything by auction.

The market place and its market was naturally the centre of domestic activities at Dutoitspan. Its development was rapid, as new stores and hotels sprang up 'with mushroom-like rapidity', and at once began a 'roaring trade'. By the middle of 1871, indeed, until the New Rush eclipsed it, the Dutoitspan market had become the principal one on the Diamond Fields. There, at seven o'clock each morning, almost everything the neighbouring Boer farmers produced was displayed for sale, with many other necessities, and luxuries of many kinds.

The life of the market indeed rivalled that of the diamond mine for domination of the camp; particularly in summer when in the sudden, glowing South African dawn the farmers' wagons rumbled in with their goods, and the camp, unkempt and yawning, sprang to life. The wagons came to the market master's office, where the farmers handed in their statements of the produce they brought for sale. Then their goods were spread out on the broad tables waiting for them in the middle of the market square, while the market master, who would soon also act as auctioneer, wandered round, pocket book in hand, treading carefully as he clambered about the piles of food and the carcases lying there: cattle, sheep, game, wildebeeste, springbok and other similar species, turkeys, ducks, chickens, enormous wagon-loads of wool, hides, skins; meat, game, ostrich feathers, English vegetables in little heaps, potatoes, onions, carrots, cabbages, beetroot, many kinds of fruit, and products peculiar to Africa: 'karosses', fur coverings from leopards, hyenas, jackals, and many other animals.

The diversion of so much food and other goods from other parts of the country had caused great increases in prices and many complaints. At times food was scarce even on the Fields, and prices were always far above those in England for the same kinds of food.

So as the dawn grew and the streets filled, the preparations for the day's marketing went on, while the town crier with his bell warned the camp that at seven the market would open, and the market master began to auction the varied array spread out on the tables. Long before he began, the market square was crowded, although most of the diggers were at work on their claims. But the idlers, the proprietors of the hotels and canteens and the diggers who managed the catering for those in their tent, all had congregated early in the square to make the first examinations and decisions as to the food they would select.

The market master at Dutoitspan was, like many of those on the so uninhibited Fields, a 'character'. Perched high on a series of tables, above the crowd, he rapidly conducted his auction which he enlivened with typical auctioneer's patter. 'A bucket of potatoes was held up as I reached the spot – a common zinc bucket, holding perhaps, 12 lb. "Potatoes," he cried, "murphies, *pommes de terre*; you can't do without potatoes; come now! What shall I say to begin? Ten shillings! Oh yes! A gentleman wants a dish of potatoes for ten shillings! He's the gentleman as found a fifty carat pure white in his glove this morning! Hard fifteen – hard eighteen – hard twenty-two-and-six – thank ye! You know what a potato is; a *pomme de terre*, a murphy! Twenty-three shillings – twenty-four – twenty-five – hard twenty-seven-and-six! Come now, gentlemen, we shall have some of them New Rush chaps down on us on a knock-out if they hear tell of such prices! Hard twenty-eight shillings – twenty-nine – Goo-oo-oo! It's yours!"'

So the auctioneer continued; selling cabbages at 5s. and 6s. each, such as were fetching on the same day at the New Rush market 10s. to 11s. Then he sold onions in lots of six at 2s. 6d. each! But money, although the inspiration of life on the Fields, was also, by a curious paradox of the gambler's psychology, easily and readily dispensed, in a sense was little valued by the diggers who endured so many hardships and inconveniences to obtain it. Hope, chiefly camouflaged as 'Luck', was the explanation – the 'fortune round the corner' or rather 'in tomorrow's shovel-full'.

The prices then paid are not without interest for many today: whole springboks (all prices here are of this same day) fetched 7s. to 8s., being 'fine' animals; a sheep, wool and all, fetched 8s. to 10s. Average prices for Boer meal, then cheap, were 42s. for 200 lb.; Kaffir corn, 25s. for 200 lb.;

maize meal 30s.; ducks and fowls 30s. each; eggs 3s. 6d. a dozen; butter 2s. 6d. to 5s. per lb.; Cape brandy 10s. 6d. a gallon; dried peaches 1s.; wood £3 a wagon-load; forage for horses varied from 10d. to 2s. 6d. a 4-lb. bundle. Mutton at the butcher's was 3d. per lb., beef 4d.

But the prices on the Fields varied greatly at different times according to scarcity of produce and proportionate increase or decrease of demand. This probably accounts for the often great difference in prices as given by various diggers. Thus another account tells of lemons 'pretty cheap' at 10s. a hundred; little shrivelled cabbages 1s. each, 'good sized onions about sixpence', sheep and oxen 'cheap' at 3s. 6d. to 4s. each. The auction which lasted some two and a half hours, fetched prices which shocked the diggers from England.

The continual uncertainty of prices from day to day discouraged the farmers who never knew until the day was over, what their profits were. There were no warehouses at the Fields then, so that the market was quite at the mercy of chance arrivals. Flooded rivers meant a shortage and higher prices; a subsidence of the waters brought generally a reduction in price. Nor was this all. The extremely high prices of some things were also due to the fact that the sudden rush of people to the Fields had placed a strain upon the resources of the country beyond anything that had been foreseen. Although all possible supplies were sent to the Fields, the supply ran lamentably short of the demand. Sowing in the Free State and Transvaal began in time on a scale that was intended to meet the new requirements, but the results were not yet ready for the market. Nor was this the sole reason for the differences in price between Dutoitspan and the New Rush where things were so much dearer. At Dutoitspan, we are told, few were rich enough or careless enough to leave their claims in the hands of natives while the owners (as at the New Rush) went out of the town to meet the farmers' wagons before they arrived at the camp, and readily paid enormous prices rather than take the risks of the general public auction.

These circumstances explain the often great differences in reports of prices. One report, which gives us more information, incidentally, on the price of drinks, and in general agrees with the prices for many things already quoted, mentions that a 3 to 4 lb. loaf cost 1s., that a reputed quart bottle of English beer cost 2s. 6d. (some say 5s.), draught ale 6d. a glass, drinks at hotels and bars 6d. and upwards, and Cape Brandy 8s. to 9s. a gallon, somewhat cheaper than the price quoted elsewhere. Wood, very scarce and dear at £2 to £3 a wagon-load, was reserved for the wealthy: the rest made their fires of dried bullock dung which the diggers and their natives went out into the veldt to find and brought back in sacks. They found it an excellent substitute for wood, making good fires.

The market also supplied the miners' general requirements, both new and second-hand. The second-hand market was very active, for miners who left because they had failed, and also those who went away because they had been successful, sold their equipment before leaving, and this was quickly bought by the ever increasing stream of new-comers. In such circumstances trade on the Fields flourished, and the report that traders on the whole made far more money than the diggers was no doubt true. The prices for miners' tools, etc., new, and probably imported from England, were apparently not excessive. A very well-made, strong tent, ten feet long, seven feet broad and nine feet high cost £8 10s., spades and pickaxes 7s. 6d. to 10s., buckets about 7s., a good sieve about £2 10s., a new sorting table £3, but one could always be bought at the daily auctions for half the price, while table and sieve if made by the digger himself would cost only some £3 in all. A frame house for three persons, that is one made of canvas stretched over wood, cost from £7 10s. to £8 10s.; at auction, though less easy to find, much less.

The auctions held on Saturday afternoons were almost a social function, for as it was a half-holiday, the diggers also attended in large numbers, and it was then that the largest sales of tents, tools, fancy goods and general merchandise took place. The demand for the fancy goods was great and constant, for the diggers were ever ready to buy whatever took their fancy, and their demand for natural ivory and peacock feathers is said to have sent up the price of both to an extravagant degree.

The greatest drawback on the Fields in the region of supplies was the lack of water and its consequent high price. This was keenly felt at Dutoitspan. Although there were two 'dams' (artificial rainwater holes), the water there was hardly fit for washing clothes, while the one or two wells existing at that time are described as 'always besieged by a crowd of male and female natives in every variety of costume – from native innocence to a suit of "store-clothes".' From these wells muddy water was extracted at a rate of about a half-tumbler a minute. Gradually one or two private wells were sunk to meet the need, and we read of occasional supplies of good water at 3d. for two buckets; but a shortage would come with a consequent rise in price to 1s. a bucket.

The effect of this water shortage upon the camp hygiene was inevitably disastrous, and was ruefully emphasized by several sufferers. Generally, we are told, the Dutoitspan diggers were forced to be dirty, were unable to wash their hands and face every day, while a bath, unless like the plutocrats one took it in soda water, meant a twenty-five-mile journey to the Vaal river, one which as many diggers as could, made as often as possible.

Describing the unhappy effect of the waterless region upon the marketing crowd at Dutoitspan, one of them writes: 'They form a throng as rough to view as one will meet in any country. Water at 1s. 6d. the "half-arm" is legibly written on their grimy faces. I had not here to learn how conventional are our notions upon the subject of washing. When men have urged on me the vital necessity of a morning tub for the mere preservation of existence, I have said, "Go you to the Egyptian desert, as I have done, and learn that tubbing is a luxury and nothing more." As such I have always used and enjoyed it, knowing that man *can* exist, and comfortably too, upon one mere damping in the week. It is but a matter of getting through the first half hour of the day. The frowsy feeling passes off in that brief space, and one enjoys the succeeding hours as happily as if shampooed in a Turkish bath before breakfast. But if I had entertained any doubts at all upon this point, ten minutes' visit to the market place would have convinced me. Scores, if not hundreds of these men, were moving evidences of the fact. They laughed, and talked, and walked about, and bid, and carried off their purchases, as like to comfortable housekeepers as need be; and none had washed his face for an indeterminate time. Two senses assured me of this truth – the eye and the nose.'

A few, however, were more fortunate, as another digger thankfully records, even while asserting that 'Dutoitspan diggers are dirty perforce. Washing of hands and face is a luxury not to be indulged in every day. Fortunately for us, the chairman of the Committee here – a most excellent and kindly old gentleman – sends a wagon some six miles weekly for a large supply of water, and allows us to put a little cask on his wagon; so we have enough for all purposes with economy and are thankful accordingly.'

But this unhappy situation at the camp was rectified in a comparatively short time. Private exploiters were not slow to profit by the general need, for the sinking of private wells attracted a crowd of urgent clientele. We read of one with 200 'members' each paying 4s. a month for a daily allowance of four buckets; and this became a generally accepted method of distribution as the private wells increased in number. How soon the distress of the camp in this matter was relieved is shown by an entry in a digger's diary, under the date 17 July 1871: 'Wells are becoming numerous, and water consequently plentiful, so that we can now indulge freely and frequently in copious ablutions.' But that was probably an overstatement at that time. Surely too, when we consider the many needs and often high prices at the Fields, we must doubt if the following summary, surprising at least, is not too optimistic: 'I think I may venture to affirm that, if a man keeps aloof from dissipation and eschews luxuries, he may live here for about 10s. per week comfortably.'

That *comfortably*, in view of the conditions, is perhaps even more surprising than the ten shillings a week; yet there is plenty of evidence that as Dutoitspan progressed, many found the life there one of particular contentment. 'Very well pleased with the life here so far. It is a hardworking, quiet, peaceful life. How enjoyable are the evening's rest and the night's sound sleep! A club is being formed here, and musical and other entertainments are getting more frequent; but I do not think anything will tempt me out of my snug little tent. I hope it won't get much colder though.'

Undoubtedly one source of contentment among the diggers was the speedy growth of Dutoitspan, followed by not less speedy development. Within a few months the mining camp had become the proud 'City of the Pan' with its central square from which streets radiated, with its market place and shops, hotels, canteens rapidly rising in wood and iron and soon even in brick, while the canvas city still sheltered most of the mining population. In September 1871 the decline of the river diggings and the victory of the dry camps was unconsciously symbolized by the removal of the leading Klipdrift journal, *The Diamond News*, to the 'City of the Pan'. 'Klip Drift,' a digger recorded in his diary on 3 September, 'will now surely cease to be the "Metropolis of the Diamond Fields". The principal newspaper of the Diggings, *The Diamond News*, has moved all its offices down here, and will be published here in future. The "City of the Pan" rejoices greatly thereat.' Later, *The Diamond Field* moved to Kimberley. Before the close of the year the new town had not only its offices, stores, and hotels, but also a hospital, two churches and a theatre, besides billiard rooms, dance halls, canteens and similar resorts.

There was plenty of well paid work for artisans and also for labourers. Skilled, industrious, sober men could do very well at the camps. For such there were always plenty of openings. Carpenters, for example, could make £2 a day or more making wooden houses, or the sieves for the mines, or doing repairs at hotels. Blacksmiths became prosperous, repairing wagons, and tent-makers did almost as well, while butchers, bakers and confectioners were making their fortunes with greater rapidity and certainty than many of their customers. Any kind of 'handyman' too, could be sure of a job, and of good pay. Engineers, of course, made far more money than the rest, being badly needed for sinking wells and for various mining operations.

Doctors, especially those with good qualifications, were few, and so, much needed. They could, if they wished, work a claim while engaged in their professional duties. So too could solicitors and barristers later, when courts were created, for at first they had little to do. Only after mechanization and commercialization did the lawyers get their very good share of diamond profits.

Nor were the arts unrepresented even in these earliest days. Not until later when theatres had been built did many actors and actresses and their companies often pay even flying visits to the Fields, which could, however, from the first, boast of two photographers and the need of more. And in addition to all these there were dentists, watchmakers, jewellers, two hairdressers and a matrimonial agent.

'No one who is willing to work, and has been long enough at the fields to be known among a good many diggers as being honest and steady, need fear poverty; for even should he exhaust his own little resources before he finds anything remunerative in his claim, he will be sure to find plenty of chances of working good claims for richer diggers "on shares".' For such work there were various opportunities. Thus a man might become a substitute for the owner of a claim absent in England or elsewhere, who would gladly give a third or even a half share of the finds made by his substitute while working as such. Similarly, a man might work one claim for the owner of two, or even obtain and work a new claim as nominal owner for some rich man who already had both the claims legally allowed him. In such cases the substitute, whose name was on the licence, would receive a good share of the profits and also have all his expenses paid.

Then too, the excitement and the lure of the undiscovered diamonds were ever present, and, if it ever wearied, could always be renewed by merely taking one's spade and walking away to some other spot in the vicinity to start a new rush. We can follow one such in his records as he leaves his regular claim for a short time and sets out with his pick, shovel and sieves, on foot to prospect in various places, but as it happens with no luck. Nevertheless others soon arrived as news that prospecting was being done there went round, and the digger, after seeing some thirty or forty claims marked out by the new-comers, walked back to Dutoitspan, compensating himself for his bad fortune by 'feeling rather proud of having created a new rush'.

Satisfaction in the stability and prosperity of the camp breathes through many a record of the time, such as this: 'The camp continues to be most peaceful and orderly; nowhere could person and property be more secure. Store keepers and hotel keepers, doctors, dentists, chemists, jewellers, are all reaping rich harvests, most of them working claims in addition to their ordinary business. Money is very plentiful in the camp. Large raffles, for instance a hundred or more members at 10s., are got up frequently at one or two days' notice. Dutoitspan is eminently prosperous.'

Naturally the somewhat self-conscious pride of the Dutoitspan diggers increased with the growing prosperity of the camp as hotels and bars and billiard rooms multiplied, and even 'a large American bowling alley' appeared; an ambitious venture by an hotel keeper which won general approval. Nevertheless, at this very time, an occasional voice expressed very qualified disapproval of Dutoitspan as a centre of social peace, honesty and civilization. Thus young David Harris, arriving in this same year 1871, was 'disappointed to find a primitive camp'. He noted the absence of substantial buildings, the light wooden-frame houses with walls of canvas like those of the hotel bedrooms; the houseless natives lying out in the open air under what miserable covering they could find. 'The personal belongings of travellers were not safe,' he wrote, so contradicting the many who found the diamond camps almost ideally honest, 'and it was a common occurrence for the baggage of newcomers to be stolen during the night, made easy by the cutting of the outside canvas with a penknife. In the twinkling of an eye the intruders were able to make their departure with the loot.' Harris's detail is certainly convincing, despite the unconsciously opposing evidence of another digger who found in the casually heaped piles of merchandise in the market square an unintentional, but as such even particularly striking, evidence of the honesty of the Dutoitspan public. That the diggers were in general an honest society we need not doubt, but in the presence of so many claims that vice and dishonesty were almost non-existent there, it is well to note other evidence which restores one's sense of probability and of proportion.

At any rate, on 8 July 1871, at least one resident in the camp contemplated with evident satisfaction, as a final proof of the higher altitudes of civilization now attained in Dutoitspan, the foundation of a social club of distinction: a 'well conducted club where gentlemen may see all the latest home and colonial papers, or select a novel from a small but rapidly increasing library. With these attractions, combined with the pleasant society one is sure to meet there, one may be sure of passing a comfortable home-like evening at the Zingari Club.'

By this time, indeed, social distinctions and even animosities due to them had developed among the diggers, despite their early boasts of a Diamond

Fields democracy. 'I perceived', wrote one of them, describing an excited diggers' meeting: 'that two classes, antagonistic to each other, were face to face. There was the digger, bleared and grimy, with loud voice, strong arm, and aggressive individuality. There was also the younger man, scarce less grimy, as strong of arm, and as loud-voiced on occasion, but bearing always that *cachet* in tone and manner which marks the gentleman, or person of society. There is a *jeunesse dorée* of Dutoitspan, though it be not so prominent as that of New Rush. These classes were evidently opposing one another, and the cheers of one were always chorused by the ironical laughter of the adversary.'

Like this writer, many were very conscious of the presence of aristocrats and 'gentlemen' in the camps, and like him made more or less invidious comparisons in this respect between one camp and another. The rapidly rising New Rush was jealously and rightly regarded by Dutoitspan as a dangerous rival for supremacy on the Fields. Thus in July 1871 claims at the 'City of the Pan' had risen in price to £10 or even £20 readily paid for those in good positions, 'but at De Beer's [New Rush], where the diggers are mostly men of capital employing large parties of natives and consequently getting through much more work than we can, £100 is considered quite a moderate price for a good claim.'

In such circumstances, the diggers of Dutoitspan could only assert a general superiority of tone, of social quality, to counterbalance the plutocrats at the New Rush, a superiority they found not only in the general standards of life at Dutoitspan, but even in the very streets. 'The approaches of Dutoitspan are more orderly than those of New Rush. There is, indeed, in all that camp, something of the staid and decent which befits the elder sister, though elder she be by but six months. The diggings do not intrude upon the town; the streets, and not the main street only, are broader and more regular. . . . But it is also to be noticed that the appearance and manners of our comrades at the "Pan" differ from those prevalent at New Rush. Our Dutoitspan digger is comparatively quiet and reserved; neither fashion nor inclination, as a rule, necessitate champagne for his morning beverage. He does not *often* fight, blusters scarcely at all, and pursues the snug little game in hand with an abiding recollection that the first object of a digger should be to make a fortune, not to spend one. Perhaps it will scarcely be needful to say after this that signs of poverty are more frequent here than at the other digging, and that a smaller percentage of the people are gentlemen by birth and education.'

Another writer gives us an interesting critical examination of the different classes at Dutoitspan. 'We have many types of diggers here, your work-

ing man who is disgusted to see how soon gentlemen learn to handle pick
and shovel, speaks to them with surly insolence, and tries to pick quarrels;
your other sort of working man – nature's gentleman – honest, intelligent,
kindly and civil. The latter type, I am happy to say, by far the most plentiful. Your bar-room loafer, who spends all his time, as long as he has money,
in the tents where are grog and billiards, and is great at imparting "colonial
information" to "new chums". He will take a fit now and then and work
for an hour or two, but soon you shall see him back for another "tot" of
"Cape smoke" [brandy] or "Hennessy's French". Your swell, in polished
top boots, spotless breeches, trim-fitting jacket and shapely felt hat with
feathers in it. Your old Australian or Californian, looking the very typical
digger, with broad-leaved hat, thick, loose flannel shirt, red sash, cord
trousers, and huge waterproof sea boots; and your digger who dresses in a
colonial suit of plain brown corduroy, and works hard, and is brown as to
his hands and face and tattered as to his clothes, but yet whom no one can
possibly take for anything but a gentleman.'

But the summit of aristocracy and gentility at the Fields was achieved by
a then comparatively new camp, 'Old De Beer's' later assimilated by New
Rush as it developed into Kimberley. For 'De Beer's is rather an aristocratic camp, many gentlemen blessed with wives and families have en-
camped here, and made themselves comparatively comfortable, and the
English element predominates pleasingly over the Dutch or Boer. Well-
dressed gentlemen and well-dressed ladies too, may be seen cantering over
the veldt on well-groomed horses; the tents are more like marquees,
covered generally with a wide awning as an additional protection against
the hot rays of the sun. Kaffir servants are numerous, horses, mules and
oxen plentiful, and the whole place here has a thoroughly "well-to-do" air.'

Nevertheless, despite such portentous rivals, Dutoitspan continued to
grow, appreciatively watched by some of its residents, as, in the words of
one of them, it 'slowly gathered the rudiments of civilized existence'. The
Dutch, noted for their religious fervour, built their wood and canvas
church amidst rejoicing, and a long discussed school for girls was opened.
'It will', wrote the same observer, 'teach children lessons never learnt before in a land but lately a savage wilderness.' And soon he rejoiced on seeing
in the main street at five o'clock in the afternoon, 'a crowd of little maidens,
armed with slate and book, pour homeward to their tents, chattering gaily,
in Dutch for the most part'. For the Dutch much more than the English
and the others from abroad, were the ones to bring their families with them
to the Fields. 'Heaven knows, this camp is not a place for modest women,
and much less for half-grown girls and boys; however, since here they are,

it is well they should have schooling, and the diamond fields will have effected not the least of their good results in teaching some proportion of the savage Boer children to read and write – accomplishments almost unknown, as I have every reason to believe, amongst women of this district.' That the Boers, even of so remote a part of South Africa, were so illiterate as this is surely doubtful, for they were all devoted Bible readers and churchgoers, and no doubt, like many of the poor in England, at least derived a surprising literacy and culture from such humble but exalted foundations.

From the doorway of Benning and Martin's hotel, one gained a general view of Dutoitspan. 'Feeling as nearly lonesome as an old traveller can, I stood by the outer door and watched the crowd. Up the broad street was a range of stores, larger than those at New Rush. Out in the roadway their goods were piled, in a manner that told well for the public honesty. It would be waste of time to catalogue the articles exposed. Suffice it, there are but two shopkeepers in all the town who even affect a speciality; these are a watchmaker and a bookseller, or rather library keeper. But the watchmaker is one of our preachers and also deals in cutlery, while the librarian sells all things beneath the sun, including fruit and eggs. The larger tradesmen possess the utmost universality of stocks, and some of them defy the customer to pose them, so far as necessaries of dress, food, drink, and shelter go. At this end of the town your view is bounded by a tumultuous crowd of tents, and the little mountain range of sortings over all. In the other direction are more large warehouses, and the street ends abruptly in the open veldt, for the tent-dwelling population clings close to the digging from which the roadway trends further and further on this side. A blazing sun poured its whitest and strongest light upon the scene. The footsteps of the ceaseless crowd, the trampling of horses and the whirl of wheels, threw up the sand in clouds of finest dust; a noise of eager voices and loud laughter filled one's ears; and over all the shrill Kaffir shouts predominated.'

With which realistically convincing description we take leave of Dutoitspan as the earliest important dry digging and an individual entity in the complex of the Diamond Fields.

4

The 'New Rush': The Mine

'THERE is a "new rush" close by here,' a Dutoitspan digger wrote in his diary near the close of June 1871, 'between this and De Beers on the Bultfontein land. I believe it is turning out well though the diggers are trying to keep their finds quiet.' But the riches of this new rush could not be 'kept quiet'. A few days later, the diarist wrote: 'We have a "new rush" only about a mile from De Beers, where the precious gems seem to be wonderfully plentiful, it being no uncommon thing for one party to find from two to six good gems a day. I believe the largest yet found there is 45 carats. Claims taken out there at the beginning of the rush [a month earlier], are now worth £100 each. A friend of mine saw last Tuesday a 20, a 10, and a 5 carat (about) turned out on one sorting table in half an hour. One man found seven diamonds there last Saturday. The report is now confirmed that a diamond of 175 carats was found about ten days ago – that £33,000 has been offered for it, and the lucky finder is a poor Englishman who never had £20 of his own.' Such were the stories flying about the Fields from the mid-year 1871.

Meanwhile, the earliest prospectors on the new Field were exploring and seizing every inch of the ground. In the following account by one of them, despite the sober realism, we also feel the excitement, the touch of 'romance' that goes with it. The writer having already explored the place and marked off one claim, his 'burrow', had then gone for the necessary tools, and hurriedly returned: 'When I reached the kopje, men were swarming over it like ants over a heap of sugar. But I noticed with delight that my burrow and the area immediately surrounding it were still unappropriated. Accordingly I got in my pegs, enclosing a square with sides measuring approximately thirty-one feet six inches, the burrow being exactly in the middle. Then I fell to the ground panting from exhaustion.

'I remained on my claim until darkness fell. One by one I watched the prospectors depart; I was not going to risk being dispossessed of my burrow, so stuck to my post as long as a human being was in sight. . . . The stars were still shining; there was, in fact, no hint of dawn in the sky when

I reached my claim next morning. I was first in the field, having reached my destination some time even before the fire was lit in the next camp. I brought with me a pick, a small circular sieve, a piece of plank about eighteen inches square for use as a sorting table, and a small iron "scraper" – an instrument used in the sorting of sifted gravel.

'Day soon began to break, so I filled my sieve and separated the sand from the gravel, placing the latter in a heap on the plank. There was not enough light for sorting; I sat on a tussock and watched the east grow white. But the morning was chill; so I sprang up and went to work with the pick, uprooting the grass and bushes. Day waxed and a few men appeared. When I thought the light was strong enough, I crouched down and began sorting the gravel on the board. With the scraper I separated a small handful from the heap, and spread it out so that every individual pebble became visible. These would be swept off the board and the former process repeated. Before I got half way through the heap my heart leapt to my throat, and I almost swooned with ecstasy – there, in the middle of the spread-out gravel glittered a diamond. It was very small, not much more than half a carat in weight, still it was most indubitably a diamond!'

Meanwhile, all around were others frantically digging up the ground. Often, as diamonds were unearthed, excited shouts were heard, while others ran to the spot with loud 'hurrahs', to see the latest find, before returning with renewed hope and enthusiasm to their own claims. On the third day a Government official came to make a general survey and verify and register names of owners and boundaries. Some rogues falsely asserted their prior occupation of claims, but the other diggers joined to denounce and expel them.

Something of the excitement of those early days at the New Rush can still be recaptured in many records of the time. 'In giving you a brief account of the incidents of the past three weeks [August 1871], I must first notice this astonishing wealth which is being developed at the New Rush beyond De Beers. Though it has as yet scarcely been worked a month, fortunes have already been made there.'

'Have you ever read those tales where they find some wonderfully big diamonds?' young Cecil Rhodes wrote to his mother, from the New Rush, in the spring of 1872. 'Well! on this kopje I should think nearly every day they find a diamond over fifty carats.'

And as more and more diamonds appeared and new crowds arrived, competition in the purchase of claims began and prices bounded daily, even hourly. Nor were the prices of claims affected by the fact that many of the New Rush diamonds were far from perfect. Even Cecil Rhodes, while praising the mine, complained of them: 'Almost all have a slightly yellow tinge, and are getting quite unsaleable. Diamond buyers now give only £4 per carat for yellow stones of any size or shape; that is, a 70 carat would not fetch more than £280.' They had also 'a nasty habit of suddenly splitting all over. You must not, however, think that every diamond one finds is a beauty, the great proportion are nothing but splints – but still even of these you very seldom find one that is not worth five shillings.' Indeed, he concluded, if only a fair price for diamonds continued, his fortune would be made.

Rhodes's description is unwittingly corroborated by other diggers who emphasize the frequent inferiority of the diamonds at New Rush: 'Of a very inferior description, and not to be spoken of in the same breath with those found at the river, being principally chips, or fractured shapeless lumps, not of great value. Some good stones were dug out, it is true, but in general the diamonds of the New Rush were burnt-up things, upon which very little reliance could be placed, and I have seen some taken out which, on first discovery, looked well shaped, valuable gems, but which split and cracked all over after a short exposure to light and air.' Nevertheless: 'In this extraordinary spot, diamonds (of a sort) were said to be found by the handful; diamond digging was no longer a wearying mockery.'

Thus, despite the vaunted superiority of the diamonds by the river and at the older camps, many there regarded the claims at New Rush with jealous eyes, and the simple truth was well expressed by one who wrote: 'The old diggings at Dutoitspan and De Beers are still turning out well; but the wonderful finds of the privileged few who secured good claims at the New Rush naturally excite great envy, especially for those who, like myself, have worked hard for months and found hardly anything.'

Such were the chief reasons for the popularity of the New Rush in the earliest days of its discovery, before the presence of diamonds in depth, which were also the finest diamonds, was suspected. Until then, the New Rush was chiefly envied because diamonds there, being plentiful and near the surface, were easy to find, although claims were soon exhausted. Later, it was a very different story.

The consequent belief in the merely temporary value of a claim combined with the continual desire to acquire new ones, ultimately the belief that, to find the fortune awaiting the individual digger before another found it, *speed* was most important, greatly intensified the frantic bidding for claims and consequent immediate and extraordinary rise in their prices. With something of the intensity of mass hysteria, rivals bid against one another for claims believed to be both rich and easily worked. According to one digger, almost immediately after the discovery of New Rush, influence 'in the proper quarter' was needed even to obtain a half-claim at £1,000. Nor can there be any doubt that the wildest rumours of easy and almost infallible wealth were current, and affected, doubtless in some cases by calculation, the prices being paid. Sometimes this technique was practised in reverse, and by exaggerated tales of bad climate, danger to health, poor ground or falling prices for diamonds, a nervous owner might be persuaded to part with his claim for much less than its market value. 'Passed the day in looking at claims in the New Rush,' wrote one in early December 1871; 'Prices asked are incredible:—seven feet by four, £900; thirty feet by seven and a half, £1,500; so downwards to £350 for a quarter claim; nothing below this. I suppose £10,000 would scarcely buy the best claims of this wondrous kopje.'

Claims with good reputations, bought it might be for £20 or so originally, might now sell for anything up to £4,000. Many, too, were sold in whole or in part with the condition that over and above the purchase price, the seller must receive some specified percentage of the buyer's 'finds'. Thus speculation in the sale and purchase of claims and parts of claims became as much a business on the Fields as diamond digging itself, and many gained more by such speculation than by the spade. Not merely half and quarter claims, selling easily for £1,000 and £500 respectively, were bought and sold at the New Rush, but also fractions of claims down to one-sixteenth or about seven square yards. Thus when in 1888, upon the acquisition of the mine by De Beers, a survey was made, and the various owners of claims and part-claims were bought out, it was found that through concessions, bargains and sales, the separate holdings into which the original 430 claims had been divided came to no less than 1,600.

With claims fetching such fantastic speculative prices for the wealth they might or might not contain, the dishonest who owned apparently barren claims attempted to dispose of them to the best advantage by any trickery at their disposal. 'Salting' a claim was of course the most obvious method, which however had to be done with some care, not as in the case of one intending purchaser who, examining the claim at the bottom of the mine an hour earlier than arranged, received a shower of diamonds thrown from above on his astonished head!

In other ways, too, tricksters were sometimes caught in their own snares. Thus, at a time before the blue ground below was found to contain diamonds and when only the yellow ground above was believed of value, some owners on reaching the lowest limit of the yellow covered the blue beginning to show, with a coating of yellow, and secretly rejoicing, sold

Klipdrift seen across the River Vaal from Pniel

The Cape of Good Hope Inland Transport Company coach to the Fields

A gentleman's camp, c. 1871. Cecil Rhodes is standing third from the right, his brother Frank second from the right.

'The Star' en route for Johannesburg, c. 1872

their claims for a song, only to find that the supposed victim, digging deeper into the blue had made a bargain indeed!

The diggers' initial failure to suspect diamonds in depth at New Rush was chiefly due to their recent experience at Dutoitspan when diamonds were first found there. For as the majority of the diggers had come from the river diggings, they assumed that the diamonds would be found near the surface as they had been beside the Vaal. When, therefore, they struck a hard limestone layer at Dutoitspan, some two feet down, they mistook it for the barren bedrock they had found below the river, and believing the sprinkling of small yellowish stones with some larger ones already found near the surface to be all their claims contained, they worked over the shallow surface as quickly as possible – a man and a sorter could complete a claim in this way in a week or so – and then, abandoning their claim as exhausted, they rushed away to peg out new ones before others obtained them.

Only when competition for new claims became too keen did some more adventurous diggers turn to attack the limestone stratum below in the faint hope of finding more diamonds beneath. With pleased surprise they discovered that the apparently hard upper layer of limestone was but a thin crust covering soft and rotten ground easily split with a pick, and then crushed with a shovel. A little deeper this rotten rock was found fused with a yellowish, decomposed breccia, often resembling dried mud, which on sifting proved to contain more and better diamonds than those on the surface. This diamondiferous region they named 'the yellow ground'. And with the spreading news of this discovery, there came, of course, new rushes to the Fields.

Such were the conditions at Dutoitspan; but at the New Rush, when discovered a few months later, they found a difference, although in general the conditions and mining methods at the various places on the dry diggings were the same. But whereas at Dutoitspan the yellow ground had hardened at the top by chemical action into the limestone layer which had first discouraged the diggers from attempting to penetrate it, at the New Rush there was but little hard limestone beneath the red surface soil, as the soft yellow ground rose nearly to the surface and was covered by only a thin coating of chalk. Hence the extraordinary ease and extent of the earliest excavations at New Rush, and the immediate appearance of swarms of new prospectors with consequent soaring of prices. For the unusual number of diamonds found on and near the surface there, succeeded by far more numerous and finer stones in the deeper yellow ground which extended to some sixty feet below the surface, all made the New Rush claims the most enviable of all.

Indeed, invidious comparisons were made with the now almost deserted river diggings, for at the New Rush there was no standing knee-deep in water to remove huge and heavy boulders from a river-bed, while the frequency and quantity of diamonds far exceeded anything experienced at the Vaal. 'It was amusing', writes one, 'to witness the *sang froid* with which diamonds were collected here, when one remembered the exultant pride and importance with which a solitary "piece of luck" was announced at the river. At the latter the finder proudly raised his prize aloft, and all the neighbourhood hastened to examine it, and congratulations for the remainder of the day poured in upon the finder. At Colesberg Kopje to find every day was a matter of course, and no person considered it worth while to announce a circumstance of such frequency.' Indeed, the saying went round that diggers at the other camps, on meeting friends, asked 'Have you found anything lately?' often receiving a negative reply; but at the New Rush the question asked was 'How many have you found today?' And the answer would be anything from two or three to fifteen or more. New arrivals, we are told, meeting their friends at the Fields would enquire of them: 'Well, where are you working, old boy?' And if the reply were not 'the New Rush' but Dutoitspan or Bultfontein or some other place, the newcomer would enquire, half pityingly, half derisively as if saying 'What a poor shiftless fellow you must be': 'What? Not managed to get a claim at the New Rush?' By this time prospecting had spread far over the 'Kopje' and surrounding district, forming more 'new rushes' but with little or no success, while the worst characters among the diggers fell to fighting and illegal 'jumping' to get claims on the much coveted Kopje itself.

For the unfortunate deserving with a moral sense, the continual contemplation of the often quite undeserved good fortune of others was no small addition to their basic discontent. 'The lucky men at the New Rush are still turning out diamonds in profusion, and several moderate fortunes have been made within the last month. Good finds have been made at Dutoitspan too. We stick to our claim there, and hope that our turn may soon come.' But 'hope deferred maketh the heart sick'; what must the luckless have felt as their more fortunate friends came to show them their latest finds, or carried them off to the canteen to celebrate some such occasion. Still worse for these was the sudden, joyous departure from the Fields, generally amid the firing of rifles, of those who had 'made their pile', as in the following scene: 'A man possessing a wagon and oxen, a tent most luxuriously furnished, and good stores of provisions, etc., came out of his tent one afternoon, and, having collected all his neighbours, said: "Here, you can take all these things, I don't want to see a single one of them any more.

I have made my lot, and I'm off." And he stood calmly by, hands in pockets and pipe in mouth, while his wagon, tent and stores were rapidly vanishing. What is the "lot" which he has found has not been divulged, but it must be "a big thing".'

Of those favoured by fortune – often men who found themselves raised in a lucky moment from being almost mendicants to millionaires – many tales are told. We hear, for example, of an Irishman who, after failing to find fortune in America, reached the Diamond Fields with only thirty shillings in his pocket. After two luckless weeks there on one claim, he tramped, penniless, his sole possessions a blanket and billy can, to several other places on the Fields without the slightest success. Finally, having obtained a new claim in a new place, he found himself in the very centre of a real diamond mine, with diamonds both above and below the surface. On the adjoining claim two brothers were working with but moderate success. When separate access to the two claims became difficult, the three amalgamated. A few years later, their mine was bought by De Beers Consolidated Mines for £5,338,650. The cheque for this, drawn on the Kimberley branch of the former Cape of Good Hope Bank, and dated 18 July 1889, is said to have been the largest ever drawn in South Africa. Fate, from the very beginning, ordained that prospecting for diamonds should be a gamble, and Gambler's Luck was the spirit that brooded, for good or ill, success or failure over the Diamond Fields.

'Luck', of course, was the commonest and most exciting subject of conversation among the diggers. Even today it is perhaps one of the most intriguing though no longer exciting questions. How 'good' was this luck on the Diamond Fields? How many diggers found it 'good' – how many 'bad'? What general estimate of the success or non-success of the average digger can be made?

These, indeed, are the most difficult questions to answer with any certainty, or even feeling of certainty, so contradictory is the little evidence available. Without any definite, reliable record of the 'finds' and the finders, with but a few generalized and often contradictory opinions, rumour and stray instances of good and bad luck, the 'evidence' is too slight, too untrustworthy, for positive judgment. Nor must we forget that rumour is particularly dubious in this matter, as some diggers with few if any finds would exaggerate them either for personal vanity or, if wishing to sell a poor claim, as commercial trickery, while others, particularly lucky, would conceal their luck for fear of robbery, sometimes, indeed, leaving the Fields secretly at once or later.

Certainly, as the best claims passed into the possession of the few individuals, or later the companies, rich enough to buy and exploit them, the success which is evaluated in terms of output and value passed into fewer hands. A report and forecast for 1872 declared that not one man in five of the diggers made enough to pay his expenses, and prophesied (truly, it is said) that soon it would not pay one in ten, or even in a hundred. Later, indeed, as difficulties and expenses increased with depth before amalgamation, not one in several hundreds. A thousand pounds, even in the early days, would, we are told, be thought wealth by the diggers, and even the man who could pay for a good tent, lucky! Such were the men who paved the way for the fortunes of the millionaires, when a few years later amalgamation, mechanization, professionalism, and commercialism had superseded the 'amateurs'.

Sir David Harris gives us a characteristically sober, factual glimpse of the general situation in the early days on the Fields. 'Many diggers scraped continuously for weeks without finding anything. Others were more fortunate, particularly in the two rich mines, Kimberley and De Beers. Even here the average yield of stones did not exceed four grains to the ton of ground carried away from these areas. From the other two mines the yield was about one grain to the ton. It is worthy of note that at this particular period the value of diamonds was below 5s. per grain. The lucky diggers were those who found large stones which realized several hundred pounds, but the smaller "stuff" including chips and "bort"[1] only fetched 5s. per carat. Very few diggers made any money, a portion barely paid expenses, while the majority did not even earn sufficient to make ends meet. Diggers working in the Dutoitspan and Bultfontein mines were compelled to abandon hundreds of claims every month through not being able to pay the licence fee of 10s. per claim per month.'

Despite drawbacks, many, lucky and unlucky, who believed in 'better luck next time', could not tear themselves away from the soil which might conceal a fortune for them, perhaps to be revealed the next day, or when not, surely the day after. 'As long as there are diamonds in the ground, any man has the chance to find anything, and even if one has had no luck for months or years, who can say luck cannot change tomorrow!' The mentality was that of the gambler and the gaming-table. When down and out, many would take some other kind of work and save until they could return to the claims to take their chance again. Thus many diggers could not adapt themselves to any other kind of life, no matter what their luck. If fortunate, by staying they might be more so. The thousand might tomorrow be ten

---

[1] '*Bort.* 1622. Coarse diamonds and small fragments of good diamonds used as an abrasive.' *O.E.D.* (2 vol. edn.).

thousand, the ten thousand a hundred thousand the day after! If unfortunate, the same happy chances were *equally* possible. Hence the compelling lure for certain temperaments, and the explanation of so many unsuccessful (as well as successful) diggers continuing to plod along without leaving the Fields. The two Christian virtues of Hope and Faith certainly baited the hook for the diggers, though their object was not Christian virtue but Mammon.

Luck was so much more conspicuous at the dry diggings than by the river, that the dwellers in Dutoitspan and in Kimberley soon looked 'contemptuously' upon the less spectacular region. Doubtless secret envy of the so much pleasanter life by the river mingled with their 'contempt'. Some, however, doubted whether on the average the balance was so heavily weighted against the river diggers. True they admitted that although some two years' digging by the river had produced diamonds worth some £300,000, 'all circumstances considered, an astonishing figure', yet that would soon be merely a monthly average at the dry diggings. Nevertheless, although the river diggings did not provide handfuls of gems each day, neither did the dry diggings, where the really lucky could be counted on one hand. Even the most enthusiastic of the old diggers on the dry diggings did not believe that except for some half dozen well-known names, any single man had got ten thousand pounds' worth of diamonds. Several claims had produced as much, twice over, but not to the same man. Of the rest, those who had made fortunes had done so not by simple digging, but either by speculating in claims, by forestalling the market or by trading with their profits.

In addition, the acquisition of even part of a good claim at Dutoitspan or Kimberley meant the payment of £500 to £1,500, which must be recovered before any profit was possible. And once a claim had acquired a good reputation, it was almost if not quite impossible for anyone to buy it whole, as the owner would never agree to that, generally indeed retaining rights to part-profits even over the portions sold. Nor were the diamonds at the dry diggings, though large and plentiful beyond those by the river, generally so pure in quality. By the river there were many compensations: 'No monstrous sum to pay there for a space of land scarce big enough to make one's grave. A strip of canvas and a packing needle, a sieve, a cradle, and a sorting board supply the diggers' stock-in-trade. He is not afraid of fever, nor is rheumatism so severe as might be expected. The stones he picks up, if not many, are probably first class. Should he find a large one, the chances are still that he finds a fortune.'

Time, however, did not support this somewhat prejudiced view of the rival attractions of the river and dry diggings. 'Luck' was to be found much oftener at the dry than by the river, and soon few diggers remained on the banks of the Vaal. There were in fact so many diamonds in the dry diggings that *many* miners, so the chief authority[1] tells us, won rich rewards. As early as November 1871, the estimate for the weekly value of the diamonds found in the Kimberley mine alone was £40,000 to £50,000, while claims which had been bought a short while before had risen from £100 to £4,000. Nevertheless, the same authority adds that such great good luck was rare, and many won little or nothing from months of hard work.

That the capricious goddess Luck presided over the diggings, all quickly realized. Industry and hard work counted for almost nothing. If from the generalizations above we turn to a few of the experiences of individual diggers, the uncertainty of personal success is even more forcibly revealed. Thus we read of three brothers each with a claim side by side. One of them, with five natives to help him, got only £12, while the other two made £2,000. Some finding a huge stone would believe themselves rich for life, only to be stunned with the shock when the stone suddenly, and without any apparent reason, split into fragments and reduced its value by half or even by much more. This splitting and exploding was an unfortunate peculiarity of South African diamonds.

The few available diggers' diaries throw a revealing light not only upon the capriciousness of fortune on the Fields, but also upon this whole aspect of their way of life. One observes also an element almost of hysteria among some, understandable in the case of those who had toiled for months without success, their extravagant hopes alternating with moods of depression. Such particularly, a false rumour would lead to rush from their claims to the new hope, from which, disappointed, they would quickly return to their original digging, knowing that there was neither more nor less reason for hope than for despair. The following clearly illustrates this aspect of the diggers' life. 'One day, as I rode in the passenger cart to Dutoitspan, a fellow passenger was a working man, and he showed me a large stone he had got that morning, weighing about 50 carats, besides another of 10, and another of 7, all before breakfast. He said: "Yesterday I was a poor man and now I am a rich one." But at that early hour of the morning he was showing symptoms of having drunk too freely; but it is not very surprising that such success should throw a man off his balance a little. These circumstances are of daily occurrence, but on the

[1] G. F. Williams: *The Diamond Mines of South Africa* (London 1902, 1 vol. edn.), p. 206. Mr Williams was General Manager of De Beers Consolidated Mines Ltd.

other hand there are many unsuccessful – it is a complete lottery. One person finds ten and even twenty stones in a day, whilst another, working not three feet from him, finds nothing.' Another digger notes that he sees a man who after working eleven months with nothing, finds his first diamond, one of $19\frac{1}{4}$ carats, 'white and flawless'.

'One day last week,' runs another entry, 'the camp rang with cheer after cheer. I went to enquire what luck, and found that two poor men, who had been working long without success had found a splendid stone of 97 carats – their fortune made in five minutes. Such circumstances make all hopeful. I saw a person last week, who told me he had just given £450 for a quarter claim, and, before night, had got diamonds enough to pay for it, and £500 over.'

The following from entries in another diary, all made in June 1871, need no general comment:

A Dutchman buys an old claim for 10s.; before dinner that day he finds a diamond of 14 carats.

Another Dutchman worked for about three weeks, never said what he found, but at the end of that time, rode away in his ox-wagon, while his servants fired off many guns. Later it was learned that he had made over £14,000, then a large sum in value.

A gentleman arrived from Pniel to work on the dry diggings, with a bag containing 255 diamonds from the river.

Four English gentlemen lately set off to tramp down to the coast, penniless, hoping to work their passage back to England. 'Hard lines! And there are plenty of broken-down loafers about the camp. But then of course it is all a lottery; so says every one.'

'An English gentleman having worked a claim for six months and found nothing, went home disgusted, giving away his claim. The man who got it, found on the same day a fine diamond of $29\frac{1}{2}$ carats before he had gone six inches deeper than his predecessor. I believe he was offered £2,500 for it. Pleasant news for the other!'

Another digger found a beautiful 10-carat stone in an old claim in similar circumstances.

'On this day, many large diamonds were found – one of 93 carats, and many between 50 and 10. The 93 was found by a Dutchman, and in the evening he and his friends held a great merry-making, firing off also many guns, crackers, etc., so that the camp was very noisy. I had an idea that they fired off a shot for each carat of the diamond, but was too lazy to count.' Six days later the same man found a 43 and a $2\frac{1}{2}$; the 43 was thought to be a piece broken off, that had originally been part of the 93. 'The 93 was sold the same day for £10,000 – a low price. The fortunate man gave a great banquet to all his friends the next day (last Sunday); much champagne was drunk, and the fun kept up fast and furious till 5 a.m. on Monday.'

A few days later another Dutchman found a 90-carat diamond, supposed by experts to be but half of an immense stone. He was offered £10,000 cash for it. Shortly afterwards he sold his claim for £40 [£400?].

Such was the diarist's record for only the first fortnight of June, and it continued similarly to the end of the month. On 2 July 'The waggons of another successful Dutchman were seen slowly "trekking" away from the camp amid the firing of many guns.' Even before the close of June another man, who had been on the Fields from the first, had collected from various diggings 730 diamonds. 'Of course he has made his fortune.' Near the close of July, 'a diamond of 124 carats was found two claims from mine. Crowds flocked from all parts of the camp as the news of this spread, and the lucky finder had to hold it up for nearly half an hour to satisfy the admiring and constantly changing crowd. I hear it was sold for £2,000. Had it been a perfect stone, of good water, it would have been worth at least ten times that amount.' This was at Dutoitspan. On the same day a stone of 120 was reported. The 124 was found in an outside claim, and in a few minutes there was a rush of excited diggers busily marking out new claims beyond it, on ground partly occupied by the tents and wagons of some Dutch families, who all received notice to quit. An hour afterwards the surveyor of the Committee was on the ground, measuring and numbering the new claims. A day or two later a stone of 104 carats was found on the claim next to that of the 124-carat stone.

The local journal, *The Diamond Field*, called attention to the discovery of diamonds in unusual circumstances. 'A native man while chopping wood near Mr Jardine's on Saturday last, picked up a very beautiful diamond of 87 carats.' Another item is of a discovery by a youth who appears to have been keeping his eyes open when he should have been praying: 'Master Kidd picked up a diamond in church during prayer time on Sunday last.' Indeed as the church, like other public buildings, was floored with gravel from the mines, the possibility of lurking diamonds must have been an incentive to church attendance rather than to actual devotion. Another notice informs the reader that after showing the reporter a beautiful diamond of 45 carats, the finder continued: 'I was not thinking of diamonds, I was looking for garnets and agates, and I had a bit of hoop iron of about four inches long that I scraped about the earth with. I had picked up some very pretty stones, and had put them in my waistcoat pocket. I then scraped a

78

little wider scope, and a bit deeper, when the corner of this blessed thing [the diamond], showed up above the earth.' 'We state', continued the excited reporter, 'that Mr Hopkins was paralysed for the moment, and was so weak that anyone might have taken the gem from him. However that may be, he would like to see anyone try it on now. Mr Hopkins was not long, we fancy, in recovering himself. He has the precious stone, and he looks as if he means to keep it.' With such weekly incitements one can see how important a part the two Diamond Field papers must have played in stimulating excitement and reviving hopes.

What stories, too, of sudden and undeserved luck went round the Fields with the same effects; such as that of the drunken Irishman who continually found diamonds on his claim. Every time he found one, it is said, he made for the canteen and remained there until he had drunk what the obliging *landlord* estimated to be the value of the diamond just found. When he had emptied his last bottle and slept off his drunken bout, he would go back to his claim to work, and after a few hours regularly return with a new find, to repeat the celebration at the canteen.

All was life, excitement, hope, activity and generally happiness on the Fields save for the poor unfortunates who began to despair, like one unlucky digger, who, after 'hearing many more instances of good luck', returned to Dutoitspan, 'as the merry bands of native labourers were singing on the way to their tents and cooking fires, and the numerous traps of lucky New Rush diggers resident at Dutoitspan were galloping gaily past me along the dusty road', while he cogitated: 'This New Rush is quite the *bête noir* of us poor outsiders. And to think that if we had only known, we [himself and his partner], might have had claims there, and that claims worth £10 to £100 a month ago are now commanding from £500 to £2,500, and good ones hardly to be bought even at that.' So the unhappy record runs, and continues in the same tone: 'We have just completed another week of hard labour, and still our ill-luck continues, exciting the astonishment and pity of our more fortunate friends. One friend averages £30 a day at New Rush. The place is a perfect Golconda; everyone is full of it.'

Unfortunately the limits of this 'Golconda' were very narrow, which enormously increased the pressure to obtain a footing there, and the fantastic increase in the price of claims. For the New Rush or Colesberg Kopje, as it was also called, was not strictly a 'kopje' at all, as some diggers remarked, but a small hill, the highest part of which was not more than thirty feet above the surrounding country; and although its extent was some 250 acres in area, of those acres only ten yielded diamonds. And even within the magic ten some claims proved barren. But the gambling spirit that animated the diggers was only more stimulated by the risks that accompanied the great prizes the New Rush appeared to offer, as day by day fresh tales of wonderful 'finds' spread. One man had made £1,500 in four days; another had found twelve stones in a single day. There were also strange combinations of the lucky and the luckless, such as the man who sold half his claim for a mere £50, and found nothing in the half he retained, while the half he had sold presented the purchaser almost immediately with over fifty diamonds, many very large and over 40 carats.

Even these few examples of the mental environment of the diggers are enough to suggest the inevitable effects of the continual thought, expectation and hope of diamonds upon the diggers' psychology. Only the mentally strongest of those already too rich to depend upon 'finds' could escape the hypnotic influence of the diamond fixation, the constant emotional tension between hope and despair. The following passage written in self-communion by a digger who had very small success in the end, clearly shows this state of mind. 'I myself know of many more instances of great good luck at this wonderful place [Kimberley]. What marvel then if we poor "outsiders" work on somewhat gloomily at our old claims at Dutoitspan! What marvel too if we spend a good deal of time in "prospecting", each hoping to discover a "new rush" as rich as that at De Beers. And truly there is much temptation to do this, for there must be more than one rich kopje in the country; and the fortunate man who discovers fresh diggings has three "prospecting claims" given him for nothing, besides the two to which every digger is entitled according to our rules; and, should diamonds be found, he would at once realize very handsome prices for his spare claims.' So individual anxiety was increased and widened, not merely over the uncertainties of the single claim, but also over the ever present possibilities that at a hundred places over the vast region, boundless wealth lay merely awaiting its discoverer. And if diamonds came but slowly to the surface of one's claim, or not at all, why not set out instead on the vast exploration of virgin soil!

*

The actual mining at this time and for some years was carried on in the most individualistic, uncooperative and amateurish way, but with such energy and by so many diggers that enormous quantities of earth were quickly removed. In all the mines the method employed was essentially the same. In general outline it consisted, of course, in the breaking of the ground with pickaxe and shovel, and the conveying of the broken ground to the surface to be sieved and for the residue to be carefully sorted for diamonds.

The breaking of the ground at this early stage of development was too simple and primitive a process to admit of modifications or require detailed consideration. The methods of conveyance, however, not only differed slightly in various claims, but changed with the passage of time and the increasing depths of the excavations.

In the earliest days the problem of raising the broken ground to the surface, to be transported by natives on foot or by carts or barrows that were driven or trundled by natives to the sieves, was solved in various ways according to circumstances and the claim-holder's preference. Some, at the beginning, before any depth was attained, made plank inclines or cut tunnels to their claims from outside the mine, along which the 'stuff' as they called the broken ground, was conveyed in sacks or buckets of rawhide or in wheelbarrows to the sieves on the surface. Although free from the heavy work of direct lifting of heavy loads out of the pit, this advantage was offset by frequent ground-slides and rock-falls in the tunnels, and by the inevitable quarrels with other diggers when the tunnels ran into others or into other diggers' pits. As the pits deepened tunnelling of course became impossible.

Many diggers employed natives to carry the sacks or buckets up knotted ropes hanging over the pit, or by 'toe-holds', small niches cut in the rock, or by ladders made of rope or of wood, set on a descending series of terraces cut in the rock, or by a similar series of rock steps, which last, however, could not be continued in any depth, as the inevitable projection of the lower steps soon threatened to cover the whole thirty-foot-square claim. Some hauled the stuff up to the surface directly by hand with a long rope, some by a windlass that drew the rope over a pulley set in a fixed pole on the surface above the claim. Diggers who worked alone thus had first to break the ground, then climb to the surface to do the lifting.

The usual daily round of the ordinary digger has been described by one of them: 'Up a little before daybreak, call the Kaffirs to light fire, cook breakfast, then off to the claim; back to the tent at midday for half an hour's rest, and a "snack" of something cold; then back to work at the claim till five, cook and eat dinner; after which, if the digger has really done an honest day's work, hotels, billiards and other dissipations will have no charms for him, and he will be glad to lie down, amuse himself with a little light reading and the never-failing pipe, and "turn in" early, say nine or ten, to enjoy a thoroughly good night's rest.

'In the summer time, as people rise earlier and get through more work by midday, and as the heat is very intense between twelve and three, many diggers indulge in a couple of hours' *siesta* in the afternoon. Visiting is very frequent among the diggers; Sunday being, of course, the great day for going from tent to tent, from camp to camp, to see friends and compare luck during the past week.'

As the year 1871 neared its close the yellow ground at the New Rush was being rapidly exhausted. In November the average depth of the diggings was fifty feet; in the first days of December it was ten feet deeper, in some cases a few feet lower. 'Fifty feet is an astonishing depth when cut in "tufaceous lime". There were and are no supports whatever to this great height of wall. Straight down as a plummet falls, a digger worked, and from the edge of the roadway one looked down upon a sheer descent.' And at this depth, between fifty and sixty feet, the yellow ground came to an end, and once again the diggers believed that no diamonds existed below in the new stratum they were entering, that in fact, 'the party was over'.

But once again they were mistaken. The new ground proved to be even more prolific and of better quality than before. Known as 'blue ground' because of its prevailing bluish colour, it was nevertheless essentially of the same material as the yellow ground above it, but much harder. Yet despite its apparent hardness it was found to decompose rapidly on exposure to the weather, and after a few weeks in the open air could be treated as the yellow ground had been – broken up and sifted. Such was the beginning of the third stage in the early development of the New Rush mine.

But seldom would the miners wait long enough for complete disintegration, hurrying for quick returns by pulverizing the ground with their shovels and mallets. This was not only hard work but also expensive through the consequent loss of many undetected diamonds. Most of the diggers were poor men who could scarcely afford to hold stocks of blue ground for long, even if they had been able to protect it from thieves. But many losses were obviously due to the great haste of the diggers to clear their claims and find others.

In time some improvements were made in these primitive ways of raising the broken ground. In 1872 many adopted the device of two grooved wheels, one fixed at the pit bottom, the other at the surface, with a rope to which two buckets were attached passing over the wheels. On turning the wheels by the handle attached to each, a full bucket could be raised while the empty one was lowered. But again there were increasing difficulties for this method with increasing depth, as only the outer claims could in time be so worked.

Thus in the following year many diggers adopted a development of the

82

method into a system of cable-transport, the buckets running on small grooved wheels up and down tautly fixed ropes running from claim to surface. These ropes were first made of hemp or rawhide, later of iron or steel; their surface ends were fastened to huge timbers fixed on platforms, of which there were three, one raised above another. The top platform held the ropes from the central claims in the mine, the lowest platform held those from the marginal claims, while the middle platform held the ropes from the intermediate claims. The buckets, too were now made of iron and steel, and on the platforms were windlasses with guide-wheels over which hauling-ropes passed. The buckets on reaching the platform were emptied into chutes which shot the contents into bags to be carted away to the depositing floors, the sieves and the sorting tables. A year later, in 1874, the man-worked windlasses were replaced by large wheels turned by horses, known as 'horse whims'.

The appearance of the New Rush or Kimberley Mine at this time was an unforgettable sight, when innumerable wire ropes stretching from all points at the bottom to all points at the top gave the impression of a vast network, some 1,000 feet long by 600 at its greatest width. 'So thickly together were these lines set', writes a leading authority, 'that the whole face of the vast pit seemed to be covered by a monstrous cobweb, shining in the moonlight as if every filament was a silver strand. Nor has any eye seen such a marvellous show of mining as was given in this grand amphitheatre, when the huge pit was sunk far below the surface level; when the encircling wreath of the chasm rose sheer and black like the walls of a deep, gloomy canyon, or the swelling round of a demon's cauldron; when a downward glance from the perch of a platform made weak heads reel; when thousands of half-naked men, dwarfed to pigmy size, were scratching the face of the pit with their puny picks like burrowing gnomes; when thousands more, all grimy and sweating and odorous, were swarming around the pit's mouth, dragging up loads of diamond-sprinkled ground and carrying off their precious sacks; when hide buckets were flying like shuttles in a loom up and down the vast warp of wires, twanging like dissonant harp-strings, with a deafening din of rattling wheels and falling ground; and where every beholder was wonder-struck at the thought that this weird creation in the heart of South Africa had been evolved by men for the sake of a few buckets of tiny white crystals to adorn the heads and hands of fanciful women.'

'The diamond mines as they became deeper,' writes another, 'presented a rather inspiring sight. The rugged sides, smouldering here and there from spontaneous combustion, due to the presence of sulphate of alumina in the shales, seemed associated with the subterranean forces expended ages before in the original upheaval. The aerial gears rapidly winding up the gem-yielding ground at all sorts of speeds and angles, and the noise of falling clods as the load reached the depositing box and was automatically tipped, added uproar to the picture. At night when work was in progress the lights below looked far distant in the depths and ranged themselves into shapes as though a decorative illumination were set out. Those accustomed to the giddy heights used to sit upon the chains connecting the bucket with the hauling wire as the safest position. Going down at night was a weird sensation, especially as the bucket swept through the quadrant that directed it over the edge of the crater to the steeper gradient beyond.'

How dangerous the journey could be, the writer himself had experienced, when, through the standing wire breaking, he fell thirty feet and rolled down the side of the crater another three hundred feet, miraculously escaping with only a few bruises. Nor did such accidents depend upon the comparatively rare event of a broken wire, as a man going down the mine by the wire could very easily be jerked off.

The next operation in diamond-mining was that of sieving: the sifting of the broken ground by means of two sieves. The first, the larger and coarser, separated the larger lumps from the rest, which in turn was passed through a finer sieve consisting of a fine copper or wire mesh set in a wooden frame some three feet long by eighteen inches broad, with the longer sides extended into two handles at one end, and at the other, ropes attaching it to two posts set in the ground, by means of which the sifter, working the sieve with a quantity of stuff on it backwards and forwards, broke most of the remaining small lumps and separated the finer from the coarser ground, which with its diamonds remained in the sieve and was transferred to the sorting table.

At the sorting table the most important and delicate of all the operations began: the finding of the diamonds buried in this residue. If the sorter was inefficient or dishonest, all the work done in the preceding operations would have been in vain. The sorting table, (expensive, and so often well replaced by a few nailed boards), was about three feet long by two feet six inches wide, perfectly smooth and with a rim running round three of its sides to prevent the stuff falling off. The sorter sat at the unrimmed side, armed with an iron scraper some six inches long by two or three inches in breadth, detached a convenient quantity of the heap of stuff on the table, spread it out before him, examined it carefully but quickly, detached the diamonds when there were any, and threw the rejected stuff away. This was done with great speed and almost mechanical regularity and skill, the sorter never hesitating over the misleading flakes of mica which gleamed even more brightly than the diamonds themselves.

To avoid eye-strain, some of the richer diggers left sorting to their native servants. But to leave sorting in this way to others, to the dishonest or careless or unskilful, was in fact the extreme of folly. Yet anything which harmed the sorter's eyesight was particularly serious. For even in the best circumstances many stones must be lost at the sorting table as well as elsewhere. 'Everyone knows well that half of the gems of moderate size are bedded in a lump, which, if it resist the riddling, will carry them safely past the sorter's eye. Large stones, when they resist the sieve, fall loose at once by their own weight, but no man can guess how many of a carat each, and under, are daily thrown beneath the table.'

There were in fact numerous ways in which diamonds, particularly the smallest, were lost. Many slipped through the meshes of sieves not fine enough to catch them; some fell from the spade as the heaps of stuff were being loaded into the cart, or from the cart during transport to the sorting-table; some by inattention, haste or accident at the table itself. An even greater cause of loss was failure to recognize diamonds when hidden in a coat of lime. But the most serious of such losses was that due to the careless rejection of the more solid masses of stuff. 'These will vary in size from the diameter of a man's fist to that of his head. Hundreds are daily thrown away, of a capacity to enwrap a thousand carat jewel – ay, or a five thousand! The roads at New Rush are lined with them like a parapet. They are built up as a wall to keep back the mountainous heaps of sifting. They are piled round tents to block out the draught, erected into cattle kraals. In short, every purpose for which rough stones are suitable, is there supplied with "lumps". This would be the most incredible of assertions to me had I not seen its truth with bodily eyes. There is not one amongst the diggers there who does not know better than most people what his building materials may perhaps contain.

'Were he so inexperienced, the first heavy shower would give him cause to suspect the truth, for he would see all the loafing population bent in earnest scrutiny of the sopped earth, and he would shortly hear of treasures picked up, perhaps at his own tent door. But no one is so ignorant. Every man knows that the fortune he is seeking may lie hidden in that dirty ball he tosses from him with a curse. And yet he tosses it.

'If a blow of the spade, a kick, and a few hasty thumps against the ground do not shatter the lump, he lets it lie. Comes heavy rain, and from out the mass dissolved rolls forth a monstrous gem, picked up, most likely, by a "masterless" Kaffir, or an idle follower of the camp, in open roadway. Or

85

long exposure to the sun will make it friable, and then some passer-by, with careless kick, will get the prize. Every day such incidents occur. The newspapers are full of them. Schemes there are always afoot for "washing out" these nodules, a process than which nothing could be simpler. It is in human nature that the men who would not pick out the treasures at their door should yet object to others picking them. The diggers of New Rush are not so greedy. I caused the question to be put to many – whether they would allow myself and partners to carry off their "lumps". Not only was permission granted, but some fellows actually offered to load the cart, if I should send it round. Anything to get rid of those "d—— lumps!" '

Nothing brings home to the modern reader more vividly than this the faith of the diggers that the next spadeful of earth would reveal the great stone that was to be their fortune, and their frantic haste to reach it without delay. Some at any rate profited from this fixed faith, for we are told that two men came from the river diggings during floods there, bringing their cradle with them to the New Rush, to wash out as much of the rejected stuff as they could carry, and in one day found thirty-three diamonds. 'The size we did not hear, but it was apparently such as to content these enterprising fellows. Next day they vanished, leaving their cradle in the veldt, and the place of them was known no more upon the fields, whether wet or dry. But to this day the lumps continue to be thrown out with rage.'

Another account sheds new light upon these rejected lumps, carted to the nearest part of the veldt by drivers who did well at a shilling or less a time. Many diamonds were found in these lumps. Some who could not afford to buy claims went round and broke up the stuff that had been dumped, and not only made a living by it, but also 'sometimes a very good one'. But already these results were influencing the ordinary diggers who were now becoming careful to break it up themselves with sledge-hammers before it was carted away.

How general among the servants and poorest whites in the camp was the examination of neglected and rejected ground is graphically revealed in the following entry in a diary, describing a scene at Bultfontein: 'One of the most ridiculous sights I ever beheld was visible this morning. The heavy rain had cut little channels through the surface of the kopje, filled the holes, and generally disturbed the face of things. A great deal of earth had been washed down towards the dam. When I rose, on a bright and cloudless morning – always, always is it bright and cloudless, always sweltering to greater and more intolerable heat, hour by hour – and stepped outside my chamber door, it was perhaps half-after five. All the space around the house was pawed with monstrous trailings. The mud had not dried. Our maid-

New Rush (Kimberley) 1871.   In the foreground, diamond sorting.

Main Street, New Rush, 1873.   To the left, Mount Ararat, a favourite
sorting place with the diggers.

Kimberley Mine 1872, with the narrow and precarious roadways between claims

Kimberley Mine 1875, showing the 'cobweb' of hoisting ropes. The roadways have vanished, and the mine has been deepened.

servants, the Australian Paddy, our black boys, and the Boer assistants of the store-keeper, were crawling about on hands and knees, looking for diamonds in the puddle. The slope of the hill, and the space around the dam below, were black with gigantic caterpillars in human form, who crept, and paddled, and raked the mud about like gutter children after a fire. On the platform round our house I did not hear that any one was successful; but I saw a lovely little gem of three and a half carats picked up by Bultfontein dam. Several others were discovered.'

The New Rush, being slightly younger than the other mines, profited in one important respect from its youth, or rather from the miners' previous experience. Almost from the first, the mine had what the others had not – roads. Unfortunately, the need for roads at the other mines had been impressed too late upon the exasperated miners who, as the digging deepened, found their claims often inaccessible or to be reached only after much exhausting and time-wasting climbing and clambering on others' ground, often to the accompaniment of emotional and uncomplimentary comments from the invaded claim-holders.

This difficulty was primarily due to the diggers' expectation of finding diamonds only near the surface of the earlier mines with the consequent lack of any incentive to deeper digging, and with the intention of thus exhausting, as they believed, their claim as quickly as possible, and then of moving to another before it was taken. Only when diamonds continued to be found at increasing depths did difficulties of access to claims appear, and by that time it was too late for effective remedies, despite the fact that not only personal access, but even the transport of the stuff to the sorting table became almost impossible.

Thus when the New Rush was discovered, the Orange Free State Inspectors, anticipating deeper digging, and mindful of the difficulties of access they had found elsewhere, quickly ordered fourteen roads, fifteen feet wide, to be made across the mine, and so, half of that width to be surrendered by claim-holders on each side. Indeed many of the first diggers to the New Rush had come partly to escape from the increasing difficulties of access in the older mines.

Unfortunately, as the pits deepened, the roads became not only increasingly important but also increasingly dangerous. In November 1871, some were already lamenting their decay: 'Fifteen feet should be their width, but few of them actually measure two-thirds of that. Greedy and reckless diggers have undermined them in every part, and landslips more or less severe have been the consequence. Some have already given way in mass, and were bridged over; nearly all were supported by causeways of plank here

G
87

and there to relieve the pressure on the edges. Not a day passed without its accident. Now a mule-cart fell over, and now a landslip crashed headlong down upon the workers underneath. . . . One of the richest roads has toppled over, parting in the middle, and left a chasm of fifty feet. This happened in the night, or some hundreds of lives would have been lost. Such as are the roads, however, New Rush was reasonably proud of them, for the elder diggings are actually made unworkable by their absence.'

A few weeks later, in December 1871, the same digger recorded an interesting bird's-eye view of the diggings, in which the increasing decay of the roads and the accidents they produced are prominent: 'I had not before visited the actual diggings of this wondrous kopje. They lie behind the white heaps which tower above the highest of the little houses. We reach their foot and turn sharply round them to the right. It would need a greater mastery of words than mine to give a just idea of the scene that opens behind that mask of soil thrown up. The ground, which was once a hill, is cut into – whereto shall I compare the labyrinth of pits? Nothing in the whole world, I think, suggests the like. Claims spread out like a fan round the hill top – so much of it as is left – a rock stripped bare. Not an inch of soil has been wasted. The fifteen feet road which law exacts between each line of claims is undermined, and poorly strengthened with trunks and branches of trees. . . . No parapet protects the wandering stranger, or the toiling neophyte. Every day there are accidents and an accident means death.

'Holding to one of the posts by which buckets are hauled up and down, you crane your neck over the edge, and look down into the gulf. You draw back in amaze, with an exclamation! There is another world down yonder, sixty feet below! The crowd is almost as great as that around you. Naked blacks, diminished to the size of children, are shovelling, picking, and loading – hundreds of them, in that cool, shadowed, subterranean world. They fill buckets with crumbling earth, and endlessly haul them up and down on pulleys. Some are swarming to the surface on rope ladders. There is an endless cry, and laugh, and ring of metal down below. Buckets rise and fall with the regularity of a machine. On the top they are detached and emptied in a heap, ready for conveyance to the sieve. There are not many claims in the best part of New Rush where sorting can be done at the pit's mouth. The white, dry earth is carted off to the outer edge, and goes to swell the monstrous piles that lie there. Upon the surface – so much as is left of it, which is but the roadways – what a swarm of busy men! They look well to do, and many are quite neat. The reason is, probably, because men have wealth here. Each of them has paid some hundreds, or it may be, thousands, for his right to dig. If he does not work himself, he puts in a trustworthy man upon the system of half profits for his capital. But the working partner must have considerable means, seeing he has all wages and expenses of the blacks to pay. This runs into money at first, but before a week is out he has, perhaps, recouped himself three or four times over. Perhaps, however, he has not.'

Ten weeks later, in mid-February 1872: 'The claims . . . are grown horribly deep and dangerous. On most roads all partitions and unworked fragments have been cut down, dividing the earth to a line's breadth, and now, on either side the narrow, broken pathway, is a sheer descent of fifty, sixty, eighty feet. The signs of the end draw closer on us. To insure possession of each inch of soil belonging to a claim, with the fortune it possibly contains, they shave the walls with scrapers. On a board let down the dizzy height, a man will stand and slice off every morsel that projects beyond the level on another's ground. Several of the roads are quite cut and gone in parts. One speculator gave £1,000 for the roadway between two claims, fifteen feet by thirty, making himself liable at the same time for a bridge, to cost £500 more. This structure is now erected, and stands upon monstrous stilts bridging the chasm. Other people have seized the idea, and such works are going on upon every hand. Several roads, also, have been condemned for cattle traffic. Accidents upon them have grown so frequent and so terrible, the inspector interfered. These also will doubtless come down in a short time. Colesberg Kopje has probably seen its best days!' However good an observer, the digger was no prophet. But seven months later, in September 1872: 'at this time, there seem to be no roads left at New Rush. They have all fallen in or been cut away.'

Certainly the complaint of accidents was no exaggeration as other records amply confirm. Even when the excavations at New Rush were merely twelve to thirty feet deep, 'to stand on the narrow walls which the jealous miners had left between claims, was a feat of dizziness and some danger.' 'Soon after I came upon the scene', wrote another, in September 1871, 'I heard a loud "hurrah" and found that a mule cart had fallen into a claim. The claim was forty feet deep, but there was a kind of shelf near the top which prevented the cart from falling farther, so that the mules and cart were only just below the surface, and plenty of diggers volunteering their help, were soon extricated. There was a nigger working at the bottom of the claim. He quite thought the cart was coming down on him, and his terrified yells afforded much amusement to his sable comrades. . . .'

Cecil Rhodes, writing in the spring of 1872, was already impressed by the frequency and seriousness of the accidents. 'The roads are the only ground that remains at the original level. The carting on the kopje is done chiefly by mules, as they are very hardy and have so few diseases. There are constantly mules, carts and all going head over heels into the mines below as there are no rails or anything on either side of the roads, nothing but one great broad chasm below. Here and there where the roads have fallen in, bridges have been put, and they are now the safest part of the kopje. . . . On each side of every road there is now a continuous chasm from top to bottom of the kopje, varying in depth from thirty to sixty feet.' Similarly, some months earlier, a correspondent's complaint appeared in a local paper, asserting that 'accidents to carts, oxen, mules, etc., are of daily occurrence'. Men fell down shafts through the soil slipping, and were killed by the fall; others were buried by the falling soil in landslides, etc., and 'A fatal accident occurred on Wednesday last. A loaded cart, drawn by mules, fell into a claim. The driver (a black boy) and one of the mules was killed. The other mule escaped uninjured.'

'Scarcely a week passed,' wrote another, 'in which it did not happen that a Scotch cart[1] and its two mules overbacked and fell fifty or sixty feet to the bottom of the mine.' Sometimes the animals escaped serious injury when the cart reached the bottom before them. To get all up again was no easy matter.

'After summer storms it was most perilous to work in claims near the reef, as avalanches of shale came down with persistent and fatal regularity. I remember six niggers were one day working in a dangerous *endroit*, when an alarm was given and hundreds of other kaffirs betook themselves out of jeopardy. The half dozen poor chaps, paralysed with fear, hesitated to take a leap of twenty feet which would have saved them from tons of shale they saw slowly shifting to annihilate them. Bit by bit the loosened ground moved, and when the main body gave way it buried them alive.' 'Reef', incidentally, was the miners' name for the funnels of shale which enclosed the yellow and blue ground, and was itself not diamondiferous. This 'reef' broke and fell when exposed to air and moisture in the open pit, and the falls were worsened by the vertical cutting of the mine by the diggers, who should have left the exposed face of the reef terraced or sloping instead of vertical.

'A big fall of rock was an awe-inspiring sight. Along the towering face at various points, little spurts of rock broke away, increasing rapidly in number and quantity during the next hour or so. The gaps between the solid

---

[1] The name in South Africa for a small two-wheeled, one-horse vehicle, used for carting soil, etc.

ground and the doomed section increased visibly, as one watched, and the gigantic body rolled over, crashed, and, like an enormous tidal wave, swept away everything in its path.'

The great havoc created by rock-falls is most vividly suggested by the following reminiscence: 'One morning, riding up to our west-end ground, I saw all our standing wires were slack. I raced up to the point of vantage, conscious of the probable cause. Hundreds of tons of ground had given way. The situation below was appalling. Most of our men had jumped down into the claims next to ours – sixty feet below. I will not describe the havoc. It took hours to get the dead and injured to the surface. . . . One miraculous escape lingers in my memory. A young fellow employed at the signal bell was paralysed with fright. His limbs refused to move. There he stood, as I reached him, pale and motionless but untouched, surrounded by enormous blocks of ground, each many tons in weight.' In the face of such evidence and that of many other diggers, it is strange that this same writer asserts: 'No lives were ever lost owing to the great falls of reef, as we were prepared for them. Men were occasionally killed or maimed by a single stone becoming dislodged above and catching them in its descent.'

To guard against big falls taking the workers by surprise, they soon invented a simple method of testing the ground. 'Directly a surface crack made its appearance, two sticks of timber, laid side by side, were placed across it, the one weighted down on the solid, the other on the suspect, section. The crack was marked by pencil lines. Observation every week at first, then more frequently, told the tale. Near the time of collapse the gauges might separate an inch in a day.'

Nor were falls of reef the only danger. 'In the diamondiferous soil itself, there were far more dangerous and generally invisible features. During the original upheaval, the volcanic mud, in cooling, moved somewhat and left burnished contacts between great masses. These were termed "greasy slides", and if one tapped one of these blocks at the base it might slip down without warning. Most of the lives lost then were due to that cause.' Similar dangers beset the digger even in making his own small tunnel as a means of access to his claim. This was dramatically revealed to one who had 'jumped' another person's claim – legitimately, as for eight days the owner had not been seen and was supposed to have left. While digging, the new owner found the body of his predecessor buried under a fall of 'stuff' from the badly constructed tunnel. We also read of persons being killed during occasional mild blasting operations.

Despite these accidents and the dilapidated state of the roads, they were continually patched and mended long after all could see their end was near, and further mending and patching impossible. Indeed before the close of 1872, when the mine resembled a great open, oval quarry, the last roads crumbled and fell to the bottom. This clearance of the ground and the new problem it presented doubtless largely inspired the series of improvements in the transport of the ground to the surface.

Cecil Rhodes, explaining the claim-holders' dilemma caused by the roads, had also looked prophetically into the future. 'The question now of course is how are the roads to be worked? Every claim-holder has an interest in them, as a portion of every man's claim is the road, and one has no idea of leaving ground, every load of which stands a fair chance of holding a diamond. . . . Some day I expect to see the kopje one big basin where once there was a large hill.'

One digger, perambulating the mine at this time, has given us a revealing panorama of the scene below: 'Further on I strike the tap road which encircles the kopje. From this, as spokes from a wheel, radiate the working roads, between the claims. The tap road winds about amongst little mountings of sifting, at the bottom of each of which stands a Kaffir working at his sieve, and on the top a group of whites and blacks at the sorting table. Climb one of them, and, as far as the eye can reach, nothing is to be seen but similar hillocks, similar Kaffirs and sorters at work. The view is bounded by the heights of the kopje, and the town lies below a swell. I declare that sight to be amongst the most astonishing in the world, but there are greater wonders over the ridge. Tracking one's way through the white, deep sand, pursued by mule-carts loaded and empty, stolidly driven aside by oxen, hustled by blacks perspiring beneath buckets and sacks of "stuff", one pushes resolutely on to the "roads". It matters little which of these radii you take. I would recommend one about the middle, which gives a view on either side. Climb the reef or rock at its nearer end, and look around. I have once told, I think, what manner of sight it is. But in the month of my absence there have been changes astonishing.

'Ten thousand people are at work, like ants, on a space barely six acres, as I judge. Deep from the bowels of the earth comes the sound of their industry. The laughter and shouting and screamed directions of the Kaffirs re-echo from wall to wall, and reach the bewildered ear in a shrilly chorus. The clank of metal, the creak of pulleys, and the hoarser voices of white overseers make clamorous accompaniment.' Such was the general appearance of the New Rush in the first weeks of 1872.

A month or two later, young Cecil Rhodes evidently felt something of this fascination, as well as the practical possibilities presented by 'the richest diamond mine the world ever produced', as he described it. 'Imagine', he wrote, 'a small round hill, at its very highest part only thirty feet above the level of the surrounding country, about a hundred and eighty yards broad and two hundred and twenty long; all round it a mass of white tents, and then beyond them a flat, level country for miles and miles, with here and there a gentle rise. . . . I should like you to have a peep at the kopje from my tent door at the present moment. It is like an immense number of ant heaps covered with black ants, as thick as can be, the latter represented by human beings; when you understand that there are about six hundred claims on the kopje and each claim is generally split into four, and on each bit there are about six blacks and whites working, it gives a total of about 10,000 [sic] working every day on a piece of ground 180 yards by 220.'

But within a month or so of the discovery of the New Rush, its doom and that of the other romantic-amateur mining camps on the Fields was threatening. Even the change in 1874 from manual windlasses to horse-powered ones was ominous of the not far distant day, a year later, when the horses were replaced and men displaced, by steam winding-machines. Nor was this the first attempt to replace man-power by that of steam at the Fields. In July 1871, only a month or so after the beginning of the rush to the kopje, some American engineers at the New Rush set up a large, steam driven, revolving cylindrical sieve, said to be able to dispose of thirty cartloads a day, to sift all the ground to a depth of thirty feet in a thirty-foot-square claim in three weeks. An interested and somewhat uneasy crowd of diggers and natives watched it pouring out an incessant stream of sifted stuff onto the sorting table where six men were kept busy sorting it. The excitement it created did not, however, last long. Unsatisfactory in some way – probably the mesh proved too fragile to withstand the knocking and friction of the fragments of rock – it soon disappeared. Yet it was an omen of the application, four years later, of modern mining methods to the Fields.

James Anthony Froude wrote of his visit to Kimberley in 1874: 'I reached at last the famous mine itself. I wish I had time to describe it. The spot itself is a geological miracle. Twenty millions' worth of diamonds have been dug out of it in the last ten years, and no one knows how many more may be left. The town is like a squalid Wimbledon camp. Bohemians of all nations are gathered there like vultures about a carcase. They may be the germ of a great future colony, or the diamonds may give out to-morrow, and they may disappear like a locust swarm. It is impossible to say.'

For Trollope, the famous novelist, visiting the mine in 1877, it was 'one of the most remarkable spots on the face of the earth'.[1] He gave a very practical and detailed account of it. Almost his sole touch of romance comes from some tale told him, that the discovery of diamonds on the kopje was due to a lady's having accidentally turned some up with her parasol.

'The New Rush, the Colesberg Kopje . . . and the Kimberley mine are one and the same place. It is now within the town of Kimberley – which has in fact got itself built around the hill to supply the wants of the mining population. . . . The Colesberg hill is in fact hardly a hill at all – what little summit may once have entitled it to the name having been cut off. On reaching the spot by one of the streets from the square you see no hill but are called upon to rise over a mound, which is circular and looks to be no more than the debris of the mine though it is in fact the remainder of the slight natural ascent. It is but a few feet high and on getting to the top you look down into a huge hole. This is the Kimberley mine. You immediately feel that it is the largest and most complete hole ever made by human agency. . . .

'You stand upon the marge and there, suddenly, beneath your feet lies the entirety of the Kimberley mine, so open, so manifest, and so uncovered that if your eyes were good enough you might examine the separate operations of each of the three or four thousand human beings who are at work there. It looks to be so steep down that there can be no way to the bottom other than the aerial contrivances which I will presently endeavour to explain. It is as though you were looking into a vast bowl, the sides of which are smooth as should be the sides of a bowl, while round the bottom are various marvellous incrustations among which ants are working with all the usual energy of the ant-tribe. And these incrustations are not simply at the bottom, but come up the curves and slopes of the bowl irregularly – half way up perhaps in one place, while on another side they are confined quite to the lower deep.

'The pit is 230 feet deep, nearly circular, though after a while the eye becomes aware of the fact that it is oblong. At the top the diameter is about three hundred yards of which 250 cover what is technically called "blue" – meaning diamondiferous soil. Near the surface and for some way down, the sides are light brown. . . . Below this everything is blue, all the constructions in the pit having been made out of some blue matter which at first sight would seem to have been carried down for the purpose. But there are

[1] The 'Big Hole' Kimberley Diamond Mine was discovered in 1871, has a surface area of 38 acres and a perimeter of 1 mile. Work there finally ceased in 1914, at a depth of 3,610 feet. The total of (known) diamonds produced was 14,504,566 carats.

other colours on the wall which give a peculiar picturesqueness to the mines. The top edge as you look at it with your back to the setting sun is red with the gravel of the upper reef, while below, in places, the beating of rain and running of water has produced peculiar hues, all of which are a delight to the eye.'

Although we are told that steam power was introduced two years before Trollope's visit to Kimberley, it must have made very little or no headway in the interval, for although he gives a detailed account of the transport methods at the mine, mentioning the horses turning the windlasses, and the buckets, now 'large iron cylinders which sit easily upon wheels running in the wires as they ascend and descend and bring up their loads, half a cart load at each journey,' he makes no mention of steam power. The sight of the innumerable wire ropes descending from the pit's rim to the bottom of the mine with the buckets gliding up and down fascinated Trollope as it did most persons who saw them. 'The buckets are always scudding through the air. They drop down and creep up not altogether noiselessly but with a gentle trembling sound which mixes itself pleasantly with the murmur from the voices below. And the wires seem to be the strings of some wonderful harp – aerial or perhaps infernal.' None but Trollope appears to have ever doubted that the noise ascending from the great hole was infernal.

Looking down into the great hole from the top, Trollope found in the maze of claims and parts of claims with their divisions and sub-divisions, the 'most peculiar' aspect of the mine: 'Could a person see the sight without having heard any word of explanation, it would be impossible, I think, to conceive the meaning of all those straight cut narrow dikes, of those mud walls all at right angles to each other, of those square separate pits, and again of those square upstanding blocks, looking like houses without doors or windows. You can see that nothing on earth was ever less level than the bottom of the bowl – and that the black ants [the natives] in traversing it, as they are always doing, go up and down almost at every step, jumping here on to a narrow wall and skipping there across a deep dividing channel as though some diabolically ingenious architect had contrived a house with 500 rooms, not one of which should be on the same floor, and to and from none of which should there be a pair of stairs or a door or a window. In addition to this it must be imagined that the architect had omitted the roof in order that the wires of the harp above described might be brought into every chamber. The house has then been furnished with picks, shovels, planks, and a few barrels, populated with its black legions, and there it is for you to look at.' Descending into the mine, Trollope discovered the difficulties of clambering about from claim to claim, the discomfort of the great heat and other drawbacks which he summarized in the terse comment: 'The work of going up and down is hard, everything is dirty, and the place below is not nearly so interesting as it is above.'

Finally, even Trollope struck for a moment the usual romantic note: 'I must add also that a visitor to Kimberley should if possible take an opportunity of looking down upon the mine by moonlight. It is a weird and wonderful sight, and may almost be called sublime in its peculiar strangeness.'

5

Kimberley

FOUR years before Trollope visited the New Rush, it had attained the dignity of civic status and had changed its name to Kimberley in honour of the British Secretary for the Colonies, the Earl of Kimberley, who declared that he could neither pronounce nor spell 'Vooruitzigt', and that 'New Rush' was too undignified for anything within Queen Victoria's dominions. Thus on 5 June 1873 a proclamation appeared, declaring: 'The encampment and town heretofore known as De Beers New Rush, the Colesberg Kopje No. 2, or Vooruitzigt, shall henceforth be and be designated the town of Kimberley.'

Only two years before it had been a haphazard assemblage of tents on the great plateau, 4,000 feet above sea-level, which filled the angle formed by the Vaal and Orange rivers. Yet from the very beginning, it had shown extraordinary vitality.

The environment of the new town, the plain on which it stood, made very different impressions upon different observers. In 1872 one described 'a spot about a mile outside the Colesberg Kopje camp in the direction of Dutoitspan', as 'a fine, level piece of plain, where green grass was growing, pink and yellow flowers dotting it here and there, grasshoppers and locusts leaping, strange little birds singing, gemmed butterflies flitting all around. Up on yonder rising ground shine the white tents of the Colesberg Kopje; there, beyond, those confused white and grey heaps of gravel mark the rich claims where dozens of diamonds are found daily; down on the other side is Old De Beers, with its thick "business quarter", its straggling tents, its numerous big shady trees, while beyond yon farther ridge, but concealed by it from our view, lies the wondrous "City of the Pan".'

Five years later, Trollope, gloomily surveying this same scene, found it no such Midsummer Night's Dream as the previous writer. 'I do not think', wrote Trollope, 'that there is a tree to be seen within five miles of the town. When I was there I doubt whether there was a blade of grass within twenty miles, unless what might be found on the very marge of the low water of the Vaal river. Everything was brown, as though the dusty, dry, uncovered,

97

ugly earth never knew the blessing of verdure. To ascertain that the roots of grass were remaining one had to search the ground.' But Trollope, who saw in diamond mining only the wicked worship of Mammon, and the mines as the Devil's dominion, saw almost everything on the Fields with jaundiced eyes.

Twenty years after Trollope, Viscount Bryce, more objective, found the same scene of the country round not attractive: 'Save on the East, where there rises a line of hills just high enough to catch the lovely lights of evening and give colour and variety to the landscape, the prospect is monotonous in every direction. Like the ocean, this vast plain is so flat that you cannot see how vast it is. Except in the environs of the town it is unbroken by tree or house, and in part of these environs the masses of bluish-grey mine refuse that strew the ground give a dismal and even squalid air to the foreground of the view.' Indeed it reminded Bryce of Wigan and the Black Country; but without their smoke or sulphurous fumes in the air, or cinders on the ground, or the coal dust thickening the mud and blackening the roads, as in England; 'some squalor one must have, but here the enlightened activity of the Company [De Beers] and the settlers has done its best to mitigate these evils by the planting of trees and orchards, by the taste which many of the private houses show, and by the provision here and there of open spaces for games.' For by that time, the early, amateur days of the Diamond Fields were over.

That first confused encampment on the fabulous Kopje in 1871, gave no promise of the methodical development that was in time to follow. 'There was at first no orderly arrangement; each pitched his camp wherever he listed. How eventually streets and market square came to be laid out is more than I can explain.' Yet they did come, and with extraordinary speed. 'I would not like to guess at the number of people and tents surrounding the mine three months after the latter was rushed, but the tents alone must have figured to many thousands.'

So the camp grew; more rapidly than its rivals because of its greater riches and of its central position among them, until in time Old De Beers fused with the New Rush, and Dutoitspan two miles away extended its link of straggling houses along the connecting roadway, as Kimberley was born. Between the various camps 'the roads, at sundown especially, are crowded with vehicles of every description, and drawn by all kinds of cattle, while innumerable diggers and buyers, the latter always on horseback, many of the former on foot, in every variety of costume, and niggers in no costume at all, add to the animation of the scene.'

As at Dutoitspan but even more quickly, a business-centre took shape in the camp, and with surprising speed shopkeepers, hotel and canteen proprietors, workmen, tradesmen and even some professional men, especially solicitors, arrived to meet the needs of the rapidly increasing population. Many of these businessmen indeed also took to diamond digging or buying, as additional and more exciting sources of income than their more humdrum occupation, though by no means always as profitable. Sometimes, on the other hand, disappointed diggers, abandoning their search for diamonds, would join the ranks of the businessmen.

Like the diggers, who at first lived in tents or wagons, these camp-followers first set up their stores, offices, hotels and canteens in tents. But tents were often blown away in windstorms, leaving their occupants and contents exposed to the weather. The region, however, offered neither timber nor bricks suitable for building, and all such supplies, having to be brought 500 miles by ox-wagon from the coast, were for long unobtainable. Consequently wood and brick buildings were comparatively slow in making their appearance on the Fields, nor were such expensive, permanent buildings contemplated before the permanent nature of the diamond supply was established.

Nevertheless, the unsatisfactory tents soon gave way to the less fragile frame house, a square wooden framework with a pitched roof, the whole covered with canvas. Next, corrugated iron, the best material available, superseded the canvas, thus creating the iron house, which, being light and strongly riveted, could be moved by a few strong natives if the digger decided to change his claim and his address. Next, as confidence in the future of the mine grew, small sun-dried, local bricks were built into the walls of these houses, and the ceilings boarded beneath the iron roof. Many of these and similar houses still exist, and with their thick non-conducting walls and wood ceilings, thanks also to the shuttered windows, maintain a moderate temperature throughout the year.

At the close of 1871 there was no brick house at the New Rush; but when Lionel Phillips[1] arrived in 1875, Joseph Robinson[1], diamond-buyer and claim-owner, owned the only one then in existence. Yet not until 1880 did brick buildings definitely challenge the ugly but convenient corrugated iron. From then onwards many such buildings appeared. But in 1871 and for some time afterwards, conditions were as in the following passage: 'The buildings in Kimberley's business centres were distinctly good, though made of wood and corrugated iron, and there was an important, substantial look about them, quite wanting in Dutoitspan structures. Outside the town proper, nine-tenths of the dwellings were common roped

[1] Afterwards Sir.

99

tents, and the remainder were frame houses with canvas stretched over them. Many of the newcomers had not any shelter to cover them and camped under the starry canopy, thus dispensing with candles.'

Trollope, even six years later, was less complacent about the appearance of Kimberley. Although he made his habitual somewhat prejudiced and caustic comments upon the town, he at the same time recognized its many difficulties. 'I cannot say', he wrote, 'that Kimberley is an alluring town – perhaps as little so as any town that I have ever visited. There are places to which men are attracted by the desire of gain which seem to be so repulsive that no gain can compensate the miseries incidental to such an habitation. . . . The town is built of corrugated iron. It is probably the most hideous [material] that has yet come to man's hands – but it is the most portable and therefore in many localities the cheapest – in some localities the only material possible.[1] It is difficult to conceive the existence of a town in which every plank used has to be dragged five hundred miles by oxen; but such has been the case at Kimberley. Nor can bricks be made which will stand the weather, because bricks require to be burned and cannot well be burned without fuel. Fuel at Kimberley is so expensive a luxury that two thoughts have to be given to the boiling of a kettle. Sun-burned bricks are used and form the walls of which the corrugated iron is the inside casing; but sun-burned bricks will not stand the weather and can only be used when they are cased.

'Lath and plaster for ceilings there is little or none. The rooms are generally covered with canvas which can be easily carried. But a canvas ceiling does not remain long clean, or even rectilinear. The invincible dust settles upon it and bulges it, and the stain of dust comes through it. Wooden floors are absolutely necessary for comfort and cleanliness; but at Kimberley it will cost £40 to floor a moderate room. The consequence is that even people who are doing well with their diamonds live in comfortless houses, always meaning to pack up and run after this year, or next year, or perhaps the year after next. But if they have done ill with their diamonds they remain till they may do better; and if they have done well, then there falls upon them the *Auri sacra fames.*'

Nevertheless, whether Trollope was objective or prejudiced, the diggers, indifferent to the horrors which had so affected him, went, and generally happily, on their way; hope gilded their vision and stimulated their energies. As early as October 1871 a digger listed numerous offices and similar

[1] It is also the roofing which still best withstands the heavy rainfalls, the effects of the extreme changes of temperature in the African climate, and the sudden wind storms.

business places, some twenty hotels and bars, half a dozen billiard rooms and many shops. The stores, canteens, billiard rooms flaunted flags of all colours, with the red, white and blue predominating: national birds, beasts and emblems floating in the wind, familiar signs such as the 'Harp of Erin', 'Auld Lang Syne' and 'The Cat and Fiddle', arousing nostalgic emotions in various individuals. Some canteens, in place of a national flag, flaunted brightly coloured handkerchiefs. 'With its vast population, streets of shops and miles upon miles of canvas homes, the Colesberg Kopje presents a most imposing and interesting sight. A veritable city sprung up like Aladdin's palace, in a night, and at this time filled with wealth, and flourishing.'

There was little attempt at first to make regular roads except for the main business street. The diggers moved their tents or 'tin houses' to whatever places they desired, without any difficulty from authority. But as the town grew, ground became more valuable and legal claims to possession more sharply considered. Pavements were added to the principal streets, and after 1874 street watering was financed. Projecting roofs to give a little shade were extended into verandas (or 'stoeps'), porticoes and little gardens were added to some houses, and fruit trees, vines and flowers planted. 'A busy, thriving town with regular streets, handsome buildings of every material except stone,' was the surely romanticized impression of the New Rush after three months of existence, given by one resident, who added with more accuracy 'and an immense encampment of tents and wagons all round the kopje'.

The best description of the place, however, is that by the writer whose account of Dutoitspan has already been quoted in a previous chapter. Approaching the New Rush on his way to Dutoitspan, he gives us with graphic detail the whole panorama as he draws nearer and nearer to the camp: 'On a sudden the driver pointed with his whip – "New Rush!" he said calmly, and flicked the wheeler's neck. We looked out in great excitement. Far off on a low swell that reached our horizon, appeared a broken crest, faintly white against the sky. No towers or pinnacles, such as one dreams of in a fairy city. Only a white sheen of tents along the ridge. A few yards more the sight was lost, behind a dip in the plain apparently so level. Another rise, and it was seen again, defined more clearly. So on, lost and regained alternately, with every glimpse more dingy and more broken, until the pale grey mounds of "sorted stuff" came into view. Then lonely little camps occurred, consisting perhaps of a family wagon with two or three gipsy tents around, and little heaps of whitey soil; the whole encircled with a six inch ditch, and a fence, may be, of thorns. These are mostly occupied by Boers, who carry their stuff home for wives and children to "sort". Further on are more pretentious dwellings, houses of canvas stretched on wooden framework, with neat windows cut in them, bound with coloured braid or ribbands round the edge. Many of them stand upon a pavement of nodules thrown from the sieve, about the size of marbles or under; it is not very rare to pick up a diamond under one's feet on these platforms.

'The mounds of "sortings" are now close by, thronged with busy men, black and white. Our road, however, is still the veldt. Wherever no tent stands, nor hole is dug, nor heap of sand conceals the soil, the thin, dry grass appears, with trefoil leaves of cassia, and vetch-like golden flowers. It is thus even in the busiest street, where houses are of wood or metal. One never can forget that all this great town has no longer history than of three months, nor expects to exist for twelve months more. Ruins it has in plenty, however; poor old broken tents, rusted and rotted sieves, holes abandoned. At every step one kicks aside the bones of oxen. Vile smells assail the nose. An utter recklessness of decency is one of those camp features which most speedily impress the visitor.

'Through the straggling purlieus of the place we trot with crack of whip and warning shout. The roadway swarms with naked Kaffir and brawny white man. Dressed in corduroy or shoddy, high-booted, bare as to arms and breast, with beard of any length upon their chins, girt with a butcher's knife on belt of leather – one could not readily believe that amongst these bronzed fellows might be found creditable representatives of every profession.

'The roadway grows snowy white. Our wheels sink in "diamondiferous sand", brought from a depth of fifty feet. Piled upon either hand, it narrows the road to the last inch. We seem to be in a cutting ten feet deep. Above us on each side, the sieves are endlessly at work, throwing a cloud of poisonous dust upon the wind. Screened from the merciless sun by an old umbrella, sits the master of the claim, "sorting". His arm goes regularly to and fro. Our view is bounded by the close horizon of these artificial hills, save, here and there, the mound falls back to give a "canteen" place for plying trade. The work of diamond digging is all going on within ten yards of us. The "claims", the pits whence comes the "stuff", lie on the right, shielded by the barrier of their own produce. The treasure-bearing sand is borne past us each moment, in screaming bullock dray, and mule cart, and sack and bucket of the Kaffir. It goes to those solitary tents outside. The vehicles are pushed half up the hill to let us by.

'We approach the business quarter. Banks lower. The excavated road becomes a street. Wooden houses show themselves, all hung about with miscellaneous goods. Broadcloth and snowy *puggarees* are seen. Thicker and thicker stand the tents; closer presses the throng. A din of shouts and laughter fills the air. We pass large drinking shops full of people; negroes go by in merry gangs. One stares amazed at such a crush of dwellings, such a busy, noisy host. One more sharp turn, and the market square opens before us, with Main Street on the right. An anti-climax ridiculous. Brimful with astonishment, one reaches this point of view, and all the wonder disappears. It was the confusion, the "jam" of dwellings that so amazed us new-comers. Market Square and Main Street are as regular as mathematics can make them. The former is an immense expanse, set round with buildings, wooden, metal and canvas. Great gaps intervene amongst them, for the instinct of trade does not approve the situation chosen for its centre. Main Street is the favourite site. Here are great warehouses one story high, pretty frame tents of "diamond koopers", neat canteens, and luncheon bars.

'There are glass windows in abundance set in the walls of plank and iron; well-dressed people form one half of the crowd; the street is thronged with passenger carts, many of them really handsome vehicles, with fine horses. Perhaps all this fixed order and arrangement is more justly marvellous than the pell-mell outside; but it does not so much impress the visitor. The oldest of these big stores has not three months' existence yet, but the blistering sun and grinding dust of Africa have given them an ancient rusty look. There is little of the "camp" visible as one glances up and down the street; but behind, within arm's length of their neat back windows, the jumble of tent, and hole, and Kaffir shed, and cart, and tethered horse, and rubbish heap, spreads out again. At the upper end those white mounds bar the view, with the busy, seething population upon them and behind.'

This almost naïve note of astonishment, even of fascination, at the speed and size of Kimberley's development is continually repeated in the records of the time. 'Although Dutoitspan is still a large place', writes a correspondent in *The Natal Mercury*, 'its proportions are not now nearly so great as the enormous encampment around the Colesberg, which increases in size daily. It would be extremely difficult to form an estimate of the population, as the tents are so scattered, but it is really a wonderful place. . . . Indeed I know of nothing so calculated to cause astonishment – supposing one to be in ignorance of what had already occurred at the Diamond Fields – as, after travelling through the barren, sandy track which surrounds these inland diggings, to come into view, instantaneously, as it were, of the neighbourhood of Dutoitspan, a large city springing out of the desert. At night the scene is even more surprising – the encampment seems larger still, the lights appearing to extend for miles. Standing between De Beers and the Colesberg, at night, with lights on either side, the scene is exactly like that observed at a certain point in Hyde Park, where the long line of lights on the Bayswater Road can be seen at the same time as those at Knightsbridge.'

Even on the earlier writer's next visit some weeks later, the fascination still persisted: 'It was near a month since I had visited a spot which daily grows in interest. Change takes place each hour. The clank of hammers only fails at sundown. The tent-makers are in themselves a host, and they never have an idle moment, except wilfully. How many new stores and offices have been erected, how many new streets designed and partly occupied, how many fresh koopers set up business, fresh diggers come, old diggers gone, how many Kaffirs tramped in, how many living, how many dead, no one knew or cared. I have visited the Colesberg Kopje often enough to have recovered the first feeling of amazement. I can now find my way a little, nor wander hours amongst the crowded tents, seeking the main street. But every visit impresses one more strongly with the size of the camp and the energy of its population. I remember to have laughed with scorn when people estimated the inhabitants at 20,000 souls. I think now that calculation much beneath the mark. It is a forest, a labyrinth of tent-poles, and a billowy sea of canvas. To seek therein for any one person, or any one tent is more hopeless than to wander through the streets of London on that same errand. Roads everywhere, of every fashion and repute, from the broad street lined with iron stores, and pretty canvas houses, to the scrubby path between Kaffir huts. Every road is of deep red sand, and between the tents, be the interval never so narrow, stands the everlasting heap of snow-white lime, the sifting. The low brush has not been removed, and it throws out a feeble yellow flower here and there. Pretentious canteens or low drinking tents meet the eye at every step. . . .'

As at Dutoitspan, the centre of commercial activity was the Market Square, a huge quadrangle. The diggers found it a fine sight when dozens of wagons, mostly drawn by long teams of oxen, drew up in the square each morning, ready for the market. Some carried the produce from the different farms; some were loaded with game, generally shot on the flats beyond the Boshof hills, ten miles away to the north-east. Almost daily the wagons brought hundreds of springbok at a shilling each; and blesbok and wildebeest at half-a-crown. Some wagons bore loads of firewood; some, building and mining material and household utensils. Many of the wagons were covered with dust and mud and bore all the signs of having travelled hundreds of miles over bad roads. All presented a striking appearance as they stood in orderly ranks in the great square.

About the wagons the drivers gathered in little groups, discussing market prospects and incidents of their journey, while nearby, playing about in the dust, were the little black children who were engaged to lead the oxen while on trek. Then came a mixed throng, diggers, their families, merchants, dealers and the rest of the camp-followers, to explore and price the piles of goods awaiting purchase. Inevitably, with so many attractions, the Market Square became a centre of local gossip, where news, rumours, marvellous tales of 'finds', of good and of bad luck went round, where engagements and bargains were made and information exchanged among friends.

Trollope, who apparently saw the square only when it was empty, was not moved by it to depart from his tacit motto of *nil admirari*; in Kimberley's proudly presented Market Square he found nothing either to astonish him or to admire. 'The town of Kimberley', he wrote, 'is chiefly notable for a large square – as large perhaps as Russell Square. One or two of the inhabitants asked me whether I was not impressed by the grandeur of its dimensions so as to feel that there was something of sublimity attached to it! "I thought it very ugly at first," said one lady who had been brought out from England to make her residence among the diamonds – "but I have looked at it now till I have to own its magnificence." I could not but say that corrugated iron would never become magnificent in my eyes. In Kimberley there are two buildings with a storey above the ground, and one of these is in the square. This is its only magnificence. There is no pavement. The roadway is all dust and holes. There is a market place in the midst which certainly is not magnificent. Around are the corrugated iron shops of the ordinary dealers in provisions. An uglier place I do not know how to imagine. When I was called upon to admire it I was lost in wonder; but acknowledged it was well that necessity should produce such results.' Less critical than Trollope was a cultured digger, who on seeing the Market Square some years before discreetly described it as 'a space handsome without extravagance, surrounded with stores'.

As at Dutoitspan, the Market Square of Kimberley was a popular place of assembly, and here also the Saturday auctions were almost social occasions to which flocked most of the population, white and black. A leading attraction, as in the rival town, was the offer of diggers' second-hand equipment, sold by successful and unsuccessful diggers on departure, in joy or sorrow, and readily bought by hopeful new-comers. The few revolvers offered and the few bids made for them, were regarded as an additional proof of the essentially law-abiding nature of the camp as a whole – as no doubt they were.

Kimberley too had its oratorical auctioneer whose patter was a principal allurement for the crowd. He was imaginative also; he would, for example, sell a second-hand spade or pickaxe by recommending it as one that had turned up a specially marvellous diamond the week before. Doubtless the former owner had departed – in joy presumably – and so in any case could not be questioned. But such public oratory was thirsty work, requiring frequent pauses while the necessary refreshment was brought to him from a neighbouring hotel.

'A noted "card", capable and racy', with a fund of amusing anecdotes with which he enlivened the bidding, he was the most popular auctioneer on the Fields and an outstanding figure. Nor was he less impressive in appearance: 'immaculate in his attire, a real Beau Brummel', he was known as 'the Bond Street Swell'. 'His curly hair shone from its treatment with pomade, and his beard was always trimmed painstakingly. His boots fitted him like the proverbial glove, and he was really proud of his small and well-shaped feet. So intent was he on retaining their shape that he always put his slippers on with the aid of a shoehorn.' Many of the auctioneers followed other businesses such as diamond-buying or canteen-keeping, and held auctions only twice a week.

The varying population estimates made by diggers were inevitably uncertain, especially as during these early months on the Fields much of the population was in a state of flux. Probably the most correct early estimate for all the camps is that of 10,000 to 12,000 whites with two or three times as many natives, making a maximum total of some 40,000. A later leading authority increases this to 50,000, and another, fairly recent, concludes that the total for all the camps was most probably about 60,000, of which 20,000 were white, including 2,500 independent claim holders, and the rest natives.

As the diggings deepened and mechanization gradually replaced manual labour, widespread prosperity ceased for a time as the population temporarily declined. In 1876 the population of Kimberley was estimated at 8,000 whites and 12,000 to 15,000 natives. Dutoitspan and Bultfontein would add perhaps a total of 6,000 to this figure. Trollope gives the official census of Kimberley in 1877 as 13,590, making the town, he records, then the second largest in South Africa. With the addition of Dutoitspan and Bultfontein, already practically suburbs of Kimberley, the total population was 18,000, including 10,000 non-white. The native influx to the Fields during the first seven years is said to have been as high as 30,000 each year; but natives seldom remained there more than a few months.

With the rapid growth of riches in Kimberley the early 'democracy' of the Fields soon began to break up. Some acquired great wealth and rose high above the mass of diggers, forming the Kimberley *élite*. The man who could light his pipe with bank notes was not to be one of the mob. One sign of increasing 'respectability' was that, among the gossiping groups in the market square, some were beginning to wear coats, and on Sundays, even *black* ones.

'The amount of money in these camps is something beyond belief. No one comes to make a purchase without a pile of bank-notes; and this short time I have been here I have seen more ready money than the whole eleven years I have been in Natal. The great difficulty people seem to have is to find something to purchase with their money. Yesterday, a man with all the appearance of a day labourer, came into my store intoxicated, and asked for a bottle of pickles. I served him and said the price was 2s. 6d. He replied: "Who the —— asked you how much it was?" untied a dirty handkerchief, and disclosed a bundle of bank-notes as large as a pudding basin, value from £5 to £50 each. He chucked them down, saying, "There, take your choice out of them, and if you don't like that lot, I've got plenty more."' Such was the early Kimberley.

'Conviviality', wrote an envious digger of Dutoitspan, after visiting Kimberley, 'reigns rampant. There is an incredible plenty of money and no means of spending it legitimately. The hospitality of the Colesberg Kopje! It is irresistible, using if necessary, *les voies de fait*.[1] How the inhabitants exist I cannot comprehend; how they execute such wonderful works is simply beyond human speculating. They do not seem to die so much more frequently than at Dutoitspan, but "live" about a thousand per cent above our standard.'

The effect of sudden and unexpected wealth upon some was disastrous, leading only to drink, poverty and ruin. Others were merely made ridiculous by it. Thus we read of 'a very decent, gentlemanly young fellow who became intensely affected, cut nearly all his acquaintance not equally lucky, became extravagant in dress, gambling and drinking, and in his general demeanour affected the "haw-haw" swell to a ridiculous extent'. Some, born gentlemen, became so used to the freedom of the Fields that on the voyage to England they preferred to go second class, as being jollier than the first. Others, however, 'evidently no better than farm labourers, with the loutish appearance, manners and talk of a ploughboy, despite the fine clothes their new wealth bought, and in which they looked singularly ill at ease, booked "first", and seemed miserable among the ladies and gentlemen. They were driven to drinking, reckless gambling, sometimes to the society of common sailors – fish out of water – money in plenty but no manners. But there

---

[1] Blows, physical force, violence.

were many with minds strong enough to bear sudden reverses or accessions of fortune with perfect equanimity.'

The rich man in his tent is thus described: 'In some space of clearer ground, on the outskirts of the camp, stands a lordly dwelling of canvas, lined with baize, its roof of reed or protected by a "fly". Around it are smaller tents, the offices, the dining-room, and such like. This is the abode of a Leviathan, one of the lucky fellows of the world. Here, if you can claim the privilege of entrance, will be offered to you every luxury procurable on the fields. Fine horses dwell in the stable there, and eat nothing but fodder at 2s. a bundle of four pounds. A "cart" of exquisite construction, snowy of tilt, resplendent of paint, stands beneath its awning. A coolie cook, clad in tunic and turban, pursues the study of his art, with Kaffir assistance, in the tent near-by.

'The owner of the whole, most likely, will show you carelessly the current coin of his quick fortune. From an empty tobacco jar, or something of that capacity, he will pour you out a half-pint or so of gems. "These", he exclaims, "I keep, paying my expenses with the worthless stuff." Amongst the spoil you will discover monstrous stars of stone, twenty, forty, sixty carat weight, or double of that maybe. In the glittering pile so roughly pushed about and spread by anything that comes handy, a pipe, a butcher's knife, the bottom of a tumbler, or the big, brown fist of your host, will be seen countless little gems, glass-white, from five carats to the half of one, worth more than any of those great cubes and octahedrons. He declares he will sell any of them at his own price, but is not anxious to do so.

' "Look at that," saith your Leviathan, pushing out a stone literally as big as a throstle's egg, "there is a sixty-five carat, as bright as a yellow comet. What will those villains" – it is a mild translation, villains! – "give me for that? Two pounds ten to three pounds the carat! Because they say it's coloured! I'll tell you what I shall do. I'm only waiting till this or that takes place, then I go home, I get them yellow fellows cut, and off I go to Turkey, to India, to China, to Timbuctoo. *There*, wherever it may be, I get just £10,000 for that sixty-five carat, and £5,000 for that, and £1,000 a-piece for that lot of twenty over there, and so on, and so on; and what will you take to drink?"

'In one such group of tents, which is shared amongst three successful diggers, I have seen certainly a pint of finds reserved. The foolish fellows had kept them in hopes of a better market, and now they cannot get one-third of the price which they refused six months ago. These, of course, are over and above the cost of their expenses, both in working and in a style of life somewhat verging on extravagance.'

The striking contrasts between rich and poor were closely observed by the generality of diggers. The rich obtained so far as possible whatever comforts of civilization were attainable at the Fields: a spacious, well-furnished tent with shady trees around it, a luxurious couch, good and abundant food, a servant to do the cooking. They need not dig, as such men had one or more claims at the rich diggings and a trustworthy person to supervise the work.

The daily round of such patricians was far different from that of the working diggers. 'Elegantly dressed, mounted on a thoroughbred horse, he canters merely from one camp to another, hears the reports of diamonds found for him, sits down at a table now and then to amuse himself for half an hour by sorting, rides back at evening to his tent or town hotel, enjoys an excellent repast, washed down by the wines and ales of Europe, goes to call on a few friends in the evening – when the result of mutual enquiries is that a few bags containing from half a dozen to fifteen diamonds are thrown carelessly from one to another of the gay party and shown as the results of the day's or week's work. He smokes the best Havannahs, lounges into a billiard room, reads a novel, or finds a thousand other ways of amusing himself, and turns in about midnight, to lie on a soft bed till his black boy brings him coffee in the morning. . . . There are many such, and generally the richest are the most fortunate, partly, of course, because they employ the greatest amount of labour, and get through the most ground.' And, he might have added, buy the best claims.

In contrast, the poor and unlucky knew only the harshest aspects of the Fields. 'With the earliest dawn, or even sooner, he rises from the hard ground, or from one or two wretched buckskins on which he has been lying – in a poor, shaky little tent affording hardly any protection against wind or rain. He cooks his own rough food with the dung fuel he has gathered himself, eats hastily, then hurries to his claim. Sometimes shivering beneath the cutting winds and pelting rains, at others scorched or melting beneath the burning sun, still he works on manfully, for he cannot afford to employ any Kaffirs. Deeper and deeper he burrows into the very bowels of the earth, load after load of "stuff" he painfully gets to the top of his claim; wearily, mechanically, month after month he goes through the monotonous work of sorting tablefuls of the same dry stuff – with never the sparkle of a diamond to cheer him – hope fading, struggling wife and children at home – the poor but certain job he had left there – but "luck must turn", so drudges on – ill for lack of food and through exposure – storm, tent down, damage, food and goods spoiled, flooded claim and no work possible that day – and perhaps after long months of misery and seeing rich men grow richer, he sells his claim and turns homeward, only to learn soon after, that his successor who bought his claim for a few shillings or a couple of pounds, has at once found large diamonds almost daily. This is not exaggerated sentiment; such cases are only too frequent.'

It is not surprising, after such animosity to the rich digger and sympathy for the poor, to find that the writer himself had but little success on the Fields. Nevertheless, he rightly asserts that the fate of most diggers lay between the extremes of rich and poor, and that in general the diggers were 'a merry good-tempered, hopeful lot, full of fun and frolic'.

Kimberley, the rival camps admitted with some envy, was not only richer, but also – and largely as a consequence – gayer, brighter, livelier than the rest. 'Dutoitspan was quite insignificant when compared with the life, vigour and movement in Kimberley.' Little wonder then that Kimberley became *the* social centre of the Diamond Fields. Certainly, if we may trust the recollections of many, diamond digging was not without gay interludes, nor were they infrequent. Although doubtless to some extent beglamoured by distance and nostalgia, such memories are often too precise, too detailed for disbelief. When full allowance has been made for exaggeration, a solid and sometimes amusing residue of social junketings remains beyond question.

'The memory of the past of Kimberley recalls many gaieties, brilliant entertainments, public banquets, personages of high rank and distinction worth remembering, and being brought to memory bring into sad and mournful contrast the life in Kimberley now with the life in the Fields then. Take for instance Kimberley in the Lieutenant-Governor's time. There was not a day in the week nor in the year, Sundays barely excepted, when there was not something going on in the way of recreation. The Lieutenant-Governor himself entertained most liberally. At his residence there were banquets, at homes, and evening parties, and His Excellency and Mrs Southey did all in their power to make Diamond Fields life enjoyable.'

Sir Richard Southey, who had come to South Africa as a boy, had farmed there, fought in the wars against native tribes and risen to high official positions at the Cape, was a great favourite with all races and types at the Fields, including the natives themselves. Upon Southey's appointment as Lieutenant-Governor in 1873, preparations to welcome him upon his arrival in Kimberley were organized with the most generous enthusiasm. 'When the day was fixed for the Lieutenant-Governor's arrival on the Diamond Fields, arrangements were made for his reception upon the best possible scale under prevailing circumstances. In the first place, of course, the people must not wait to welcome him after he had arrived in the town.

In accordance with South African custom, he must be met somewhere on the road outside the town itself. . . . The honour done to the arrival is measured by the distance which people ride or drive out to give him his first cheer – the most enthusiastic invariably going as an advance guard some miles further out than the main body. . . .

'Alexandersfontein was settled upon as the grand rendez-vous where people were to welcome their Lieutenant-Governor. Every diamond merchant and citizen of renown kept his vehicle – "turn-out" it was called; no matter what the shape of the vehicle, breed or condition of team, it was a "turn-out". To drive anything or ride anything in the way of a nag that hadn't a bit of "blood" in him and was not in full flesh and clean of leg, was to be voted a moke yourself. Mr X was the squire of Kimberley – or at any rate, he was cock of the Kimberley walk so far as turn-outs were concerned. "No Baron or Squire, or Knight of the Shire", ever drove a finer turn-out than he. His vehicle was the pride of the road, and his pair of well-bred high-steppers went their pace as if they knew that they were the pets of a millionaire, as I dare say they did. Mr X's noble turn-out, it was arranged, should bring in the Lieutenant-Governor and his lady, the Secretary to Government, and his private secretary, from Alexandersfontein, into which equipage they were to change at that spot from their travelling vehicle.

'His Excellency was expected at four in the afternoon. At two o'clock Kimberley was all hustle and bustle, and by three o'clock the horsemen were in their saddles, drivers in their seats cracking their whips, and the vehicles were loaded up. Beauty and fashion were both there, for Beauty, in the early days was conspicuous whenever the citizens were *en fête*. There was an abundant supply of "that other sex, the tender, the fair", at the period of which I am writing. It was the land of Liberty and of liberties too. There was beauty in every social rank and there *were* ranks – tip-tops, second-rates, the rut and lower depths still. And when there was a general turn-out, all were represented.

'At three-thirty, the road was crowded. Every inch of it was covered with well mounted horsemen and well laden vehicles, and by four o'clock, when His Excellency arrived, before or behind him was one living mass of people. There had been an advance guard to bring him in, as a number of his oldest friends had gone many a mile beyond Alexandersfontein to get the first shake of the hand and to give him the first welcome. He was received at Alexandersfontein with such cheering, loud and hearty, as might have been, and, I was told at the time, *was*, heard at Bultfontein. Then the run into town was done at a splitting pace, the people cheering as they went. In the evening there were fireworks in the Market Square. The square was fairly packed with people, and the Lieutenant-Governor and Mrs Southey, who were present, met with good wishes from every one. The last display of fireworks was a blazer, for the people in charge of the rockets, the Roman candles and Catherine wheels, had placed the box containing the bulk of the stock under the platform from whence the display took place; a spark fell into the box, and the whole was ignited, and blazed, crackled, fizzed, and went off together. No harm came of it, and the fun of the thing gave people something to talk about as a wind-up.' Evidently, 'those were the days' in Kimberley.

Nor was the enthusiasm less when Sir Henry Barkly, the Governor of the Cape, visited Klipdrift. Upon his arrival the horses of his carriage were unharnessed, and the carriage with the Governor inside was dragged by diggers amidst cheering crowds to the place where addresses and speeches were made, and after Sir Henry had been 'victimized by orators' as one sardonic spectator remarked, the National Anthem and 'Rule Britannia' were sung. In his honour, a ball was held and a diamond – 'a little one', says the same witness – was presented to him, while Klipdrift, a name he disliked as undignified, was renamed Barkly West.

Dutoitspan, not to be quite outdone by Kimberley, also had its great occasions, such as the Bachelors' Ball described by a local journal, when the happy dancers made merry at the Masonic Hotel, from nine o'clock in the evening until four the next morning. 'Music good, arrangements excellent and liberal' and 'certainly no want of ladies'. Indeed, as many diggers did not dance, some thought there were too many ladies. Nevertheless, the reporter was appreciative, though perhaps a trifle patronizing. 'To the credit of the digging community, let it be recorded that so far as my observation went, there was not a case of anyone taking a little too much. This is saying a great deal, because there was a *buffet* where liquors of all sorts were to be had the whole evening for the asking. Thus, something like sixty bottles of Hennessy [French brandy] were disposed of, about fifty dozen of soda water and everything in proportion. There was no supper, but substantial refreshment for all. The bachelors at Colesberg Kopje will have to return the compliment.'

Another ball at Dutoitspan appears to have been conducted with similar *éclat*. 'The ball came off on Thursday last and was a grand success. Above 150 persons were present, of whom quite one half were ladies. The costumes were as *ravissant* as could be desired. The gentlemen, too, were nearly all in evening dress, and an uninformed spectator would scarcely have believed he was looking on an assemblage of diggers. The spacious area of Parker's new Masonic Hotel afforded a broad floor for the dancers.

A good band was in attendance, and the supper was really first-rate – far beyond my anticipations of the highest culinary art at Dutoitspan. One trivial detail slightly marred the *tout ensemble* of the tastefully laid-out supper table. Our candlesticks were all simply empty bottles, and the labels had not been removed. *Voilà tout.*' *Voilà tout* indeed!

The spirit of festivity spread even as far as Hopetown; but without the wealth and amenities of Dutoitspan and Kimberley its ball was perforce on a less ambitious scale. Nevertheless, it was in its way impressive. 'Quite a score of ladies were present, mostly in evening dress; the modest cut of their robes seemed almost ugly, and quite antiquated to the European eye. But the beauty of one sex and the courtesy of the other, were most creditable to Hopetown. We danced in a room 20 ft. by 15, and had supper in a closet, whilst beer and other liquids were retailed in a corner cupboard. Our band consisted of five concertinas, all of a row; the musicians had been kept up all the day in close confinement, our stewards relieving one another in guarding them. The excitement promised would infallibly have driven them to drink if free.'

After such occasions, the mere dinners, and '*déjeuners à la fourchette*' given to President Brand and the Executive Council of the Orange Free State in August 1871, when 'addresses expressive of mutual confidence' were exchanged between the visitors and the Diggers' Committees, seem hardly worthy of notice!

*

The following description of a sadly contrasting 'social occasion' illuminates another aspect of the diggers' existence: 'I saw a striking funeral . . . leading the procession were two gentlemen in black, clergy of some denomination, I presume, one of whom wore a green wide-awake. Followed, a mule cart, jolting, creaking, and complaining. In it a nigger, stock-whip in hand, upright, swearing at his animals in a shrill *sotto voce*. The cart contained a coffin, built out of packing cases; a railway rug covered it, and a kaross of jackal-skin spread underneath. But the jolting of the vehicle had thrown these palls half out, and they trailed behind. Then followed the friends of the deceased, a promising young fellow from Natal, I heard. They were fifty-two in number, and had plainly tried to make a mourning show. The failure was conspicuous – none got further in that direction than a black coat, evidently borrowed from a man of different size. Yet, for all their rolled-up sleeves, broad belts, and homely corduroys, these big fellows seemed to be as hearty in their mourning as any coach-borne, sable folks at home. All but two small diamond buyers, koopers, as they are called. They walked along, smiling and whispering and nudging one another. . . .'

In the earliest 'tin shanty' days of the Fields, before the visits from professional actors and musicians, the diggers, who were far from exacting critics, did the best they could by turning amateur performers themselves.

At Dutoitspan an Amateur Dramatic Society arose and a Theatre Royal was built. There was in fact nothing 'Royal' about it, for it consisted of a square, corrugated-iron affair, all pit and stalls, and without corridors, boxes or gallery. These deficiencies were, however, more than compensated for in the opinion of some, as a bar ran the whole length of one side of the building, so that the noise made by the bar's frequenters 'often mingled with the heroine's lamentations or the denunciations of the villain', while on rainy days, nothing could be heard but the shattering rain on the 'tin roof'. The theatre inevitably appealed to all the socially inclined of all classes, and became as much a centre at which widely differing and often dubious types congregated as were the theatres of the day in England. 'Here the fair ladies of Kimberley could rustle their dresses, display their jewels, diffuse scents, show their charms and tantalisingly tickle the amorous proclivities of the dude digger or dealer.'

At Kimberley the Lanyon Theatre was doubtless similar to that at Dutoitspan. Nor was it long before occasional touring theatrical companies from Europe visited the Fields and were enthusiastically welcomed. One actor who turned up at the Fields was engaged by Barney Barnato at £60 a week to give recitations. But these made little appeal to the audience and were soon abandoned for Shakespeare's plays. But the most popular and long-remembered visit was that made by the London negro performers known everywhere as 'Christy's Minstrels'.

The valiant attempts of the amateurs to diversify the routine of camp life by presenting plays, seem to have provoked more personal interest and amusement than the professional performances. Farces and burlesques were very popular, and were often given by the amateurs, whose attempts were well attended, 'not, probably for merit, but for lack of amusement'.

Often the amusement that was most effective was remote from the immediate business of the play. Sometimes, and at its most successful, it arose unintentionally and spontaneously when sudden personal disputes broke out between one of the actors and some loud-voiced and uncomplimentary critic in the audience. Then the aggrieved actor would momentarily abandon his part and make suitable retorts in kind.

Even more exciting scenes are suggested by one witness's recollection of the following incident which occurred during an amateur performance of a farce. After the play the actors were to remain and enjoy a specially appetizing supper on the stage, at which the *pièce de résistance* was to be a fat stuffed duck, upon which the thoughts of the company were already fixed. Unfortunately, the volunteer pianist who took the place of an orchestra arrived in a hilariously Bacchic condition, and instead of playing a suitable overture, played popular songs in which the delighted audience enthusiastically joined. Exhilarated by the enthusiasm, the pianist, forgetting his rôle as orchestra, continued his performance for a good half-hour, while the wrath of the performers behind the curtain steadily increased. Finally the President of the Dramatic Society rushed forward, cursed the pianist and locked his piano. Shortly afterwards one actor was still so angry when he appeared that he forgot his words; whereupon his partner, whose nerves had also been frayed, seized the hidden duck and threw it at him to the great delight of the audience. This, perhaps the most impressive of all the performances of the time, remained undimmed after many years in the diggers' memories.

The price of seats at the theatres was low, 2s. 6d. and 3s. 6d. or 4s. for reserved places.

Concerts too were frequent, especially amateur ones, and were also popular. Some amateurs, we are told, sang a few songs, read comic pieces from Dickens and others, filling a room with 'a gratified audience'. 'We are not without amusements in this camp. From many a tent may be heard at night sounds of music and of song, while travelling concert companies and amateur Christy's frequently honour us with their presence. Nor do they go away empty, for diggers are an open-handed race.' Nor was music the sole charm, for 'there were beautiful young ladies in low dresses in the reserved seats'.

The following description of one of the methods of advertising amusements in addition to the conventional notices in hotels, canteens and billiard rooms, reveals something also of the variety of these diversions. 'A grinning nigger boy perambulated the claims, bearing a board, on which was very roughly written an announcement that a good band would play that evening at Turner's Billiard Rooms, coupled with the great attractions of "Marionettes and Punch" and "Rogers the Ballad Artiste". The little darkey called the attention of the busy miners to his progress amongst them by a very loud drumming on an old biscuit tin.' A circus also visited Dutoitspan, with a huge round tent that dominated all the rest. Impromptu concerts were often made by the diggers singing choruses and solos in the hotels.

The most popular of all songs was 'The Diggers' Song', which must have originated at the river diggings, as the reference to the 'cradle', used there but not at the dry diggings, shows:

> Six months ago to the Fields I came,
>   I was a heavy swell,
> My clothes were brushed, my boots the same,
>   My coat it fitted well;
> I wore a collar then of course,
>   Alas, that day's gone past;
> And stockings too my feet did grace,
>   Oh dear! I've seen my last.
> *Chorus* Rocking at the cradle, sifting all the day,
>   That's the life we diggers lead.
> Rocking at the cradle, sifting all the day,
>   That's the life for me!

*

> Bad luck, however, cannot last,
>   A turn must come some day,
> A ninety carat would change the past,
>   And make the future gay.
> May every digger's luck be this
>   Who to these fields has come,
> And take back health, and wealth and bliss
>   To those he's left at home.
> *Chorus* Rocking at the cradle, sifting all the day,
>   That's the life we diggers lead.
> Rocking at the cradle, sifting all the day,
>   That's the life for me!

It is improbable that lyrical inspiration among the diggers rose higher than this.

Nor did the serious and anxious business of searching for diamonds entirely prevent sport. As in England, the week-end holiday from Saturday midday until Monday morning was observed on the Fields, and at those times many were attracted by the flowers, birds and bigger game out on the veldt, and by the pleasures of walking, riding and shooting. 'Plovers often come quite near the tent,' wrote one digger, 'so that I can shoot one or two for a meal. A few miles further, bigger game may be found.' Others would go as far as the Vaal river for the refreshment of a bathe and often also for fishing. To camp in the shade of the willows on the river bank for a day or two made a delightful and restful change from the noise, dust and dryness of the dry diggings.

With so large a preponderance of English among the diggers, cricket inevitably became the chief outdoor game. Many were excellent cricketers, and many matches were arranged between rival teams such as the 'Home and Colonial', 'Natal and the Old Colony', 'De Beers and Dutoitspan', etc. Other competitive sports were also popular and frequent, including shooting matches, running and walking matches, and the usual athletic sports-meetings. Football, too, held its own.

Perhaps the amusement which appealed to the largest number of the population of the Fields was that of horse-racing. In 1872 a racecourse was established, and as Kimberley in particular increased in wealth and consequently in its support of local sport, the fame of its races and of its high stakes, the biggest in South Africa, brought large crowds of the racing fraternity to Kimberley from many distant regions. The local Turf Club regularly offered a prize of £1,500. The leading training centres then were at Colesberg and Cradock, and as there was no railway yet available, the horses often walked long distances, sometimes being led 300 or 400 miles before reaching the Diamond Fields. There were many popular owners, genuine sportsmen, 'the embodiment of all the good qualities' associated with the sport. But like all racecourses Kimberley's was not without spectators of less exalted moral standards.

Nor did the rough practical jokers among the diggers fail to obtain amusement from the love of racing, as for example when two diggers held a race between their two horses to see which was the better, before an interested and cheering crowd. When the race was over and the dispute thus resolved, a practical joker, a well-known sportsman, watching, who had secretly disguised a race-horse and harnessed it to his ordinary little cart, offered the winner 100 to 1 that his own poor shaggy cart-horse would beat the winner's. The bet was accepted, the race run, and lost of course, by the previous winner, who is also said to have lost £100 by it. Such are the occasional glimpses we get of practical joking in the camps.

The 'boys' were in some ways the masculine counterparts of the 'gay ladies'; but they were not all gay. They were, in fact, a floating company of men of all social standings, flotsam and jetsam of the Diamond Fields, ruined by idleness, drink, gambling, women, drifting and loafing about the camp, maintaining a precarious, often dishonest existence. The better born, less ready in general to descend to trickery or dishonesty, usually fared the worst.

Among such elements practical jokes were common. One, for example, was played upon an old man who had fallen in love with a barmaid at Benning and Martin's Bar. Persuading the barmaid to pretend a nocturnal elopement with the infatuated lover, the jokers substituted for her a youth in disguise. Only when the elopement was achieved, did the 'lady' reveal his identity, as the 'lovers' drove along the road.

Another form of particularly practical joke – as it brought considerable profit to the perpetrator – was that played upon the whole community when in August 1871 a fortune-teller arrived at the Fields and became 'the latest novelty'. From morning to night both Dutch and English and the rest thronged his tent at Dutoitspan. At a charge of 5s. he claimed to be able to give each inquirer accurate information as to where diamonds would be found on his claim, or, otherwise, not found, and was said to be making £25 to £30 a day in this way. Some whom he warned: 'You will never find a diamond if you stop here all your life!' are said to have immediately inspanned their oxen and driven away from the Fields in hopeless dejection. When he told another, 'You will get six diamonds out of that claim within a week,' and at the end of the time was confronted by the disappointed, angry and abusive man, who said he had been deceived, the fortune-teller astutely replied: 'Well, six diamonds have come out of that claim, and if you haven't got them, your natives have!' That the man returned, searched the natives and found six prophetical diamonds on them, is less likely to be true than the first part of the tale.

A more innocent diversion at the Fields was the arrival of a children's merry-go-round or roundabout. A middle-aged Dutchman, who had never seen one before, is said to have been so delighted with an experimental ride on one of its wooden horses that he remained there for the rest of the day at a cost of 30s.

Such was the way of life in Kimberley. Its strangely mixed crowds from all classes and countries gave extraordinary variety, colour and vivacity to its multifarious activities, whether at work or play.

Next to diamond-digging in importance, and often far more profitable, was diamond-buying. Almost immediately a local diamond market sprang up with several diamond merchants occupying canvas and iron offices, buying stones from the diggers and shipping them to Europe. Later, diamond brokers appeared, some diggers employing them to value and sell their finds. These brokers also acted at times as agents between dealers. Some diamond buyers were accredited agents for leading diamond firms in Europe with large financial resources.

The buyers themselves were of various classes, widely differing in wealth, social importance, and in some cases, in esteem. The highest rank consisted of large buyers, established persons with good houses and offices, who dealt only in diamonds and were of sound reputation. For good stones they would make liberal advances. The most dignified remained in their offices throughout business hours, never going out to find buyers as the humbler dealers did. Aristocrats of the diamond market, they affected a somewhat dashing style of dress, such as a velvet jacket, white cord or buckskin breeches, long, tight-fitting, highly polished boots and glittering spurs. They wore white waistcoats, elaborate ties, and adorned their hats with ostrich feathers, red silk puggarees or green veils. Each carried a handsome courier-bag slung at his side. The grandees of the second rank, also with large sums of money at command and ready to pay cash, did not disdain to ride about the camps at times, or even to make business visits to hotels and canteens. Some, it was said, were not averse to a deal in stolen diamonds if reliable intermediaries had made it sufficiently 'safe'. These men had the pick of the market, and when a loud shout from the diggers proclaimed the finding of a specially good stone, some would be quickly on the spot with cash offers, sometimes quite large ones.

In their offices or at the mines, as the case might be, the buyers would examine the diamonds offered to them under a strong magnifying glass for flaws in texture or colour, and then ask the digger his price. The established ritual or technique in diamond buying was for the buyer, on hearing the digger's price, to laugh contemptuously and offer half, which would in turn be rejected. If no *via media* was found, the digger would take his diamond to other dealers in turn and, of course, accept the best offer, which sometimes meant returning to a previous buyer, who again might not be willing to repeat the offer he had made at first. In these circumstances, the buyers made very large profits – particularly the richer men, who, being able to pay better prices than their poorer rivals, got the best stones.

The lowest class of diamond buyers were known by the rather contemptuous name of 'diamond koopers', or, more commonly, by the yet more contemptuous name of 'kopje-wallopers'. Too poor to buy an office they perambulated the mines in search of sellers on the spot. The stones they could afford to buy were, of course, only the smaller and cheaper ones. Such at least were the kopje-wallopers' beginnings, but many were so successful that before long they graduated into the highest ranks of the diamond-buying hierarchy. One responsible writer, well acquainted with the Fields, wrote: 'Jew diamond buyers called "kopje-wallopers" went the rounds of the sorting tables daily, buying small parcels of stones. Most of them developed into merchants, magnates and millionaires, many of whom added to their legitimate business that of Illicit Diamond Buying, and encouraged natives and low whites to do the stealing and take the risks, while they piled up wealth in safety.' But not all kopje-wallopers were dishonest, nor were they all Jews. They were, in fact, a mixed bag. Some were 'respectable' but poor; others poor but not 'respectable'.

'There were so far no laws regulating the diamond trade, so a swarm of itinerant diamond-buyers were let loose on the community. Many of these were young men who were averse to manual labour, but whose business instincts were acute. "Kopje-wallopers" was the generic term by which such dealers were known. The equipment of a kopje-walloper consisted of a cheque book, a wallet – known as a "poverty-bag" – a set of scales, a magnifying glass, and a persuasive tongue. In the course of a morning, one's sorting table might be visited by a dozen of them. Naturally enough they tried to make the best bargain circumstances permitted, but on the whole their dealings appeared to be fair enough.'

A more charitable view of the kopje-walloper, after revealing some of the dangers to which they were exposed, including attacks by savage dogs, which might also chase them into the wells, pitfalls and precipices that surrounded them, concluded: 'I do not see any reason to indulge the scorn these eager and industrious fellows raise. Their gains may be large and their veracity weak, but they have a desperately hard life, toiling from claim to claim in the sun, bargaining, perspiring and forced to take a drink with every vendor. The lower of their class are often maltreated and robbed, with or without cause.'

Various kopje-wallopers have described their experiences, and their reminiscences show how primitive their requirements were. 'The tent was set up nearer Colesberg Kopje than Dutoitspan; we had a home, and no habitation was visible within a mile of ours. Inside was a large, empty packing case, which held a common kettle, three tin cups, and a few cooking utensils, a loaf of bread, sugar and some coffee. We had, too, a spade, a couple of green woollen blankets, two small portmanteaux containing our clothes, and some firewood – and that was all. Outside we made a fire, boiled the water and soon were enjoying bread and coffee. We talked over our prospects, and found that after paying for diamond dealing licences, we would have six or seven pounds between us, and two pairs of diamond scales.'

To one at least of these two partners his first day as a kopje-walloper was more interesting than profitable: 'I put my permit in my pocket, and started out for Dutoitspan. . . . I betook myself to different mounds of débris, on the top of which were claim-holders, seated each in front of a rough table, piled with carbonaceous earth brought from the mine to them by Kaffirs, which the former sorted over, picking out any diamonds they could see. How carelessly and hastily this sorting was done is attested by the fact that for years after, a number of men made their living, and sometimes more, by débris washing. Upon each mound I saw, I climbed and accosted the workers. They were Englishmen, Irishmen, Scotchmen, Africanders, Germans, etc. Many Britishers were army and University men, and they were labelled "gentlemen" as plainly as an 18-carat gold ring is hall-marked. They did not, they could not, know the anxiety and uneasiness I felt, but in every case they treated me as if I were their equal – and not a kopje-walloper. . . .

'After wandering on that sun-scorching day, I thought I ought to strike a blow of some kind. In front of me I saw a raw and whiskered Africander sorting away in a dreamy manner. I approached him and asked if he had anything to sell. He sorrowfully shook his head, and said "only that", showing me a small splint of a diamond. I knew nothing of its value, and the digger about as much; but after haggling and bargaining, I bought the chip for 35s. Then, giving him a decided assurance in the future to accord him my distinguished patronage, I, in some excitement, hurried back to the Main Street of Dutoitspan, at the end of which was a diamond office owned by an elderly man called K. I entered bravely enough, and threw the splinter on the blotting pad in front of him. He picked it up with a pair of pliers, and said, "How much?" "Three pound ten," I replied, wondering if I had asked too little. He examined it for a minute, and said, turning his spectacled eyes up to my anxious face: "I don't think it is a diamond at all. See here," he continued, laying it on a heavy brass diamond weight, and poising another in his hand, "See here." With that, he struck it a blow, and the "diamond" went to pieces. It was like hurling a rock at my heart, and I left the office a sadder and poorer man.'

Such was the danger of loss through deceptive appearance. Nor was this danger solely that of false diamonds being mistaken for genuine ones. Real diamonds themselves could be disastrously deceptive, as the following entry from a digger's diary shows: 'My partner in a diamond speculation had given £250 for a perfect gem of 15½ carats. It split last night! This is our second misadventure of the sort. We bought another dear gazelle, 9½ carats some time back. After lying in the safe at Bultfontein two months, it split, and we sold it at a loss of £40.'

A Jewish kopje-walloper thus describes an inferior class of diamond buyers: 'Talking to the diggers could be seen quite a number of men, mostly young, dressed in semi-European style. A very few of them appeared well bred, but most of them postured like pilfering tinkers who had got their best clothes out of pawn. They were, as a rule, smoking large cigars. Driving up the Main Street I had noticed the selfsame species of gentlemen standing in front of their framed canvas habitations, Abraham, Isaac and Jacob, recovering from celestial sleep and gone in for earthly diamond-buying "At the very highest prices for the European market". They looked as if they had come from the Sublime East – of London. . . . . The diamond-buyers were plying their trade, and from their numerous offices diggers came forth cramming bundles of banknotes into their pockets and ducking away from Jacob's or Isaac's office with: "You'll give me another chance, Mr S", or "Don't forget to let me have the first look next week", haunting their ears.'

Another, after being an unlucky digger, had taken to kopje-walloping almost by accident. On abandoning his luckless claim, he had been glad to find a job in a general store, whose owner was also an amateur diamond buyer, like most of the owners of stores, hotels and canteens. From him the assistant learned the technique of diamond buying, and after a time, having borrowed £100 from the store-keeper, he set out as a kopje-walloper, with the £100 and a small pair of diamond scales in his pocket, to roam the Fields for buyers. With the store-keeper he had made an agreement – to be confirmed if satisfactory after one month's trial – to give the man a first option to buy all the diamonds he acquired on the Fields, with a half-share of all profits. The first week brought a total profit of £9, to be halved; the first month £60, which meant £30 for each. 'Fairly well,' he described his first year's profit of £400 for himself, and with that he abandoned kopje-walloping and became a respectable and dignified diamond buyer, with a canvas and wooden frame office, twelve feet long and eight feet broad.

Diamond buying was, of course, widespread; for anyone with a few pounds could turn to it, if only casually, as a sideline. Indeed a multiplicity of vocations or of avocations was by no means uncommon on the Fields. One diamond buyer, for example, was also the proprietor of a well-known hotel in Cape Town, while another combined diamond-buying with the functions of dissenting minister, dentist, watchmaker, jeweller, and homoeopathic chemist.

The latest class to arise on the Fields was the diamond broker. He, of course, only appeared when diamond-buying there had become a large and wealthy business. These brokers made fair profits without having, or risking, any capital of their own. Their method was to make the acquaintance of the leading buyers on the Fields, to find out which of them offered the best prices, and then to sell to them for a small commission diamonds entrusted to the broker for that purpose. Such men had, of course, to be well-known and trustworthy persons before they could find clients.

There were also a few diamond auctions on the Fields, but Cape Town was the principal place in Africa for them. There each of the leading auctioneers held two sales of diamonds a week. Their audience was almost entirely composed of local merchants, individuals who dabbled a little in diamonds in addition to their main business. The average sale at these auctions, held six times a week, was £2,000 or more. One digger noted during a fortnight's stay in Cape Town that £20,189 16s. 3d. was the total of diamonds sold there during the two weeks, and also that very few of those sold left the city, particularly as this was a time of falling prices in London, the fall, in fact, being due to an over-supply from South Africa.

But in the crowded streets of Kimberley, life never flagged. 'The Main Street was alive with people and a wondrous place to see. Everybody appeared prosperous, and the fat foreigners who owned many of the stores, stroked their capacious stomachs as they stood in their premises, and seemed glad to be alive. The canteens too were crowded with merry visitors, and all was life and jollity. On rare occasions a well-dressed young English-woman could be seen tripping up the street, and then would bars, shops and tents be practically deserted for a look at the White Lady, who, proud and conscious of her rarity in these parts, hid her supreme satisfaction in an affected indignant demureness which penetrated the men's souls, and made her personality all the more alluring.'

The first arrival of femininity, at least of 'respectable' femininity, at the Fields was for so masculine a population a major event; and when the news that the first white lady, a certain Mrs F—, was coming went round, excitement rose high and preparations for an impressive welcome were made. As she approached the diggers crowded to see her, standing on carts and wagons and mine dumps and cheering wildly as she passed. Despite this boisterous reception Mrs F— was treated with the usual courtesy demanded by the chivalric tradition of the age towards women, and the shy though rough miners gave this 'first white woman on the diamond fields, admiration and respect, almost as if she had been a supernatural being'.

The period of feminine vacuum, although Barnato's biographer describes it as 'years', must in fact have been of extremely short duration, for as early as 22 July 1871 a digger noted in his diary: 'Ladies, I am happy to say, are adding to our civilization by their graceful presence; and it is no uncommon thing to see faces – aye, and costumes too – walking and riding through the camp that would do no discredit to Kensington Gardens or "The Row".' The way paved by Mrs F— was quickly followed by other women, generally the wives of diggers, English or American, at whom the general masculine public discreetly gaped as they saw them in the street. 'When a well-dressed woman walked along the street, heads were thrust out of every window, and men gathered in the doorways of the bars and shops to gaze at the unfamiliar spectacle.' Even Trollope's gloom in Kimberley was relieved some years later by the pretty women he met there: 'In all Kimberley and its surroundings there was nothing pretty to meet the eye – except, indeed, women's faces, which were as bright there as elsewhere. It was a matter of infinite regret to me that faces so bright should be made to look out on a world so ugly.' Characteristically he did not pause to remember that less bright faces often looked out upon more beautiful and elegant surroundings.

From the first days of the camps, coloured and native women had appeared, attracted by the opportunities of obtaining money, honestly or otherwise. The later arrival of the respectable, middle-class, white ladies made the rougher men shy; but the crowds of white prostitutes who soon followed as the wealth and the sex famine at the Fields became known, had a precisely opposite effect. Earlier, the coloured women from Cape Town and the native women who had preceded the coming of the white, had exhilarated in no uncertain manner the spirits of the more bohemian and irresponsible white men at the camps. But the coming of the white prostitutes put their dusky rivals in the shade.

At first, lacking assurance, the white ones put up quietly at inns, assumed mysterious airs, made a pretence of respectability, and invented unconvincing pretexts for their presence, before gravitating to the gambling saloons and bars where men congregated. The later ones, however, made no pretence of virtue but flaunted their profession before the crowd. The most famous was 'The Blonde Venus', as she was called on arriving with much dash, splash and glitter. To the watching crowd she threw a general invitation to meet her that night in a certain canteen, an invitation which she repeated throughout the day to the individuals she encountered as she went about Kimberley. That evening, of course, the canteen was crowded to the doors with an excited, pushing, squirming, struggling mob of men, some of whom, hoping to impress the lady, had donned evening dress, while all fought to get as near her as they could. The Blonde Venus, as well able to manage the situation as she had been on her arrival that morning, calmly mounted a champagne case and sweetly offered herself for auction for that one night. The bidding is said to have started at £5 and a case of champagne, followed by £6 and a barrel of brandy, and by other bids up to £20 and two cases of champagne, until she was finally (at least for that night) acquired by a Dutch diamond merchant, at a cost of £25 and three cases of champagne. The dubiously fortunate gentleman and his acquisition were accompanied to the domestic tent by a yelling crowd of disappointed rivals who shortly afterwards bodily lifted and removed the tent over the heads of the couple.

The arrival of large numbers of white prostitutes at Kimberley, many of them of the lowest type, drawn solely by the lust for gold or, what was the same thing, diamonds, produced a deterioration in the general moral standard, which, as wealth and population increased, fell to yet lower levels. Sudden changes in the value of diamonds, due to a glut in the market or to other purely local circumstances, had effects even more sordid than those due to 'better times'; for unfortunate women, losing their suddenly impoverished masters and at bay, would sell themselves to the uncivilized natives for a stolen diamond or gold coin. At such times too, many women of the kind sought relief in drink, while those who fell into the lowest depths of poverty, disease and despair could look for no attention, much less assistance, from the careless, unheeding crowds passing on their way to work or play. Many diggers cared little or nothing for the sordid aspects of life developing in Kimberley. Indeed Cecil Rhodes is said to have known nothing of the harpies and bullies then assembling there.

As Kimberley developed, and theatres, bars, canteens and similar places of amusement increased, white women of various nationalities, manners and morals found new, in some cases even complementary occupations. They attracted by their wit and charms rather than by their wisdom, the fascinated clientele that clustered round them, particularly when presiding over their bottle-studded counters, 'filling the customers' glasses and their own pockets'. 'Yes,' one replied from the witness-box to the magistrate's question, 'certainly I have a share in the business; I am Mr X's sleeping partner.' One of the most popular resorts was a bar next to the Lanyon Theatre, where the proprietor's two pretty and respectable daughters nightly attracted by their charm, good nature, and good looks an appreciative and respectful crowd.

The Diamond Fields presented many excuses and opportunities for convivial drinking, and none of them was neglected. When you found a diamond you drank with your friends for joy; when you found none, you drank with them for consolation. 'Drink', wrote Sir Lionel Phillips, 'was rather a curse, and most of us consumed more than was good for us.' 'The only way to avoid invitations to drink,' wrote another, 'is to say "I'm going to see what my Kaffirs are about." '

Lack of water and the dry, dusty environment favoured and perhaps excused excessive drinking – though excuses were not regarded as necessary – and the number of hotels, bars and canteens was, for a population of that size, enormous. For every 100 tents or so there would be two or three drinking saloons with their regular daily and nightly clientele.

The comment of one observer, himself not subject to the undue influence of Bacchus, vividly illuminates this aspect of life in Kimberley. 'The enormous profits made by hotels and canteens, and the increase of drunkenness, are not to be wondered at, considering the hardships of summer work at the dry diggings. I tried the effect, during the day, of two or three long drinks of ginger beer, but found my thirst so little allayed thereby, that I was tempted to accuse our canteen keepers of putting salt into all the liquids they supply to the thirsty diggers.'

The very names of these saloons: The Hard Times, The Perfect Cure, The Red Light, The Blue Posts, The London, breathe something of the bright, breezy, humorous, adventurous, self-confident yet not ungenerous social spirit of the masses at that time in England. The canteens, which provided only drinks, neither board nor lodging, were the easiest kind of commercial venture for the 'small man', being cheaper, simpler, and surer of making good profits. Anyone with fifty pounds could start one, all he needed besides his stock of drink being a small rough tent or canvas house, a counter – the 'bar' – and neither chairs nor tables. It is not surprising then that the number is described as 'enormous' for all were doing 'a roaring trade'.

But even canteen-keeping in the early Kimberley had its drawbacks. There were incursions of drunken roughs, angry scenes with indignant patrons protesting their sobriety when refused further drink, dead drunks on the floor. In such circumstances proprietors and barmen 'kept a heavy stick handy and laid it on vigorously' when drinkers who had 'had enough' clamoured for more. Many of the canteens, especially those on the outskirts of the camp, were much frequented by natives, who spent their wages or the reward for finding a diamond, on 'Cape Smoke' (brandy), drinking and chattering at the bar or buying a whole bottle and withdrawing to some corner to discuss it with friends. The general regulation aginst serving drink to natives without a written permission from their masters was ignored, for the natives were also an important source of profits. Equally ignored was the regulation ordering the closing of all canteens and hotels at ten o'clock on Sunday evenings.

The drink sold in these places was generally more remarkable for the quantity absorbed than for its quality. 'Cape Smoke' was popular, and a particularly successful digger here and there is said to have celebrated his success by drinking champagne out of a bucket. As wealth increased, prosperous diggers with even less common sense than the bucket-drinkers, publicly lit their pipes and cigarettes with five-pound notes.

Even the bad storms that swept over the Fields also encouraged the diggers' conviviality. 'When a big rain has washed us nearly all out of our tents and claims, and in a half drenched state we congregate in the hotels and canteens, many are the glasses drained to "Luck"; many the songs sung, and the merry tales related, and few, very few, are the disputes and fights.' The Dutoitspan residents prided themselves, rightly or wrongly, on being more sober than their rivals at Kimberley. 'The sudden riches of Colesberg Kopje,' wrote one, making a virtue of necessity, 'have turned a few heads, and brought the canteen-keepers some too good customers.' He also deplores 'some ludicrous and shameful examples of the effects of intoxication. One white man I saw seated in the middle of the road, leaning upon a naked Kaffir scarcely less drunk, while they both sang, shouted, threatened and laughed at the crowd that surrounded them, and passed the bottle of "Cape Smoke" freely from one to the other, till they both became "maudlin", then dead drunk, and finally lay down to sleep in the hot sun, in the middle of the road, and had to be dragged out of the way of an advancing waggon. I never saw black and white so equalized by any other medium.'

The thirsty digger entering one of these early Kimberley bars, crowded at all hours, but especially at mid-day, saw about him a crowd that as one habitué remarked, 'would make you open your eyes and close your pockets'. But the bar habitués were by no means the whole of Kimberley's residents, and the differences of opinion that developed at times rarely led to extremes, even among the wild natives. 'Liquor drinking ran to excess, as it always does in a prosperous mining camp, and the natives especially were given to drunkenness; but the wildest sprees rarely threatened danger to life, for the hot spirits were blown off in yells, chants, and dances.'

Nevertheless, the dangers due to drink were often very real and very dangerous. A false step, particularly at night, might mean death. 'An illustration is afforded, of the results of drinking "just two drains" before taking one's life in hand amongst the claims. I see a little crowd around a well, and learn how some rich fellow going past has made one false step, and tumbled downwards. He is dead, cut to pieces, before taken out.'

Night, of course, when the day's work was over was the favourite time for meeting in tents, hotels and canteens. In the darker parts of the camps particularly, the befuddled wanderer staggered amidst many dangers, not only from holes and wells, but also from stray oxen and donkeys. The donkeys indeed loved to wander round among the tents at night, eating whatever vegetables they could find; driven away by some well-aimed empty bottle, they would at once return to finish their meal.

But the centres of the camps were not plunged in darkness at night, at least not until quite late. On still, quiet nights all the camps were lit up, especially in the business part of each. One visitor expressed great surprise on finding Dutoitspan nearly as light as London was at night, and seeing how lively the camp appeared by oil-light and candle-light, as the crowds did their shopping – night shopping being then usual in Europe also. The canteens of course made the most of the night liveliness: 'Of course those substitutes for the London gin palaces are nearly as bright and radiant with light as day, and many votaries of Bacchus are flitting about, bat-like, after the shades of evening have fallen. Some have represented the diggings to be a place for deep drinking of alcoholic liquor. I can't say, taking into consideration the population and the style of living, that such is the case. We do occasionally see an old *rooi*, or a policeman, the worse for liquor, but that you must expect to see on these fields. But I maintain that the great majority are a sober, industrious, plodding set of folks; and that if they do now and then "take a drop too much", they have the sense to keep it to themselves.' In those days drinking in England was much less restrained than it is today.

That at least one portable canteen should appear whenever a new rush followed new discoveries or even rumours of such, was of course to be expected, and if the rush proved profitable, so too did the canteen. But woe to its owner and his property if the rush brought no results and the drink-seller were suspected of spreading false tales of vast secret finds in order to sell his drink to the deluded, thirsty and angry diggers.

Whatever the hardships of the diggers' lives, the spirit of fun and gaiety brought many compensations. 'The chapter of possibilities is larger at the fields than anywhere I know. Circumstance is full of fun there. Mighty uncomfortable are we all . . . sick for good food, good drink, and the pleasures of life. But nowhere are more, or more humorous, events astir, and nowhere is there heartier laughter.' Some too, of different temperament, praised their life on the Fields for far different reasons. 'Very well pleased with the life here so far. It is a hard-working, quiet, peaceful life. How enjoyable are the evening's rest and the night's sound sleep! A club is being formed here, and musical and other entertainments are getting more frequent; but I do not think anything will tempt me out of my snug little tent.'

Hotels are inevitably conspicuous targets for critics, and those of the early Diamond Fields were no exception. 'Better imagined than described, the food was greasy mutton, mealies and coffee; sugar, chiefly dead flies.' The hotels at Kimberley at this time closely resembled, but were in general not equal to, those by the river at Pniel and Klipdrift, older, established places. The more temporary structures at the dry diggings were well described by a digger as 'really big caravanserais'. Constructed of wood or of corrugated iron, they might have a separate bedroom or two, but the night accommodation was principally shakedowns consisting of one or two blankets or antelope skins spread on the floors, or for luxury the tables, of the public hotel rooms. For even such a refuge was very acceptable to be-draggled and washed-out diggers whose tents had gone down in a storm. Such were the casual, or rather 'casualty', visitors and their accommoda-tion. But the more regular patrons such as travelling merchants or rich diamond buyers, were given the *de luxe* bedrooms: 'four square yards of green baize partition, an iron bedstead and a mattress.'

The most popular and profitable part of the hotels was, of course, the bar, dispensing drinks to a ceaseless stream of miners in their working clothes 'whitened by the horrible limestone dust which dries the palate, chokes the throat, oppresses the lungs and drives men to desperation, and – the liquor bar!' At these hotel bars the general atmosphere was somewhat more private than in the canteens, and games were played for expensive rounds of drinks, or as often for a case of champagne. Lucky diggers, too, warmed by drink, would display their latest best diamonds, others with musical tendencies would burst into loud and generally inharmonious song. Argu-ments and disputes were common, but actual rows were few; indeed the disputants would often end their debates by standing drinks for all.

The daily round at these hotels included three *table d'hôte* meals a day; at 8 a.m., 1 p.m., and 6 p.m. They were taken at a long, rough deal table. Although the food was generally plentiful it lacked variety, consisting chiefly of mutton, beef, venison, stews and curries. Fresh vegetables were rare and few; the tea and coffee were milkless but in plenty; bread, white and brown, was also plentiful but of very poor quality. Prices were much as at the river hotels, though some items, particularly among the drinks, were a little higher.

The company was, of course, diverse; at the long rough table the work-stained digger in shirt sleeves, corduroy trousers and jack boots would sit beside some fashionably dressed merchant or diamond buyer, or camp clergyman, without shyness in the one or resentment in the other. Thus it was as long as the 'camp democracy' remained; all were 'free and equal' in an 'easy' atmosphere without social distinctions. So too were the impudent, bustling waiters, sworn at by the landlord and swearing back at him in return. They too were independent, probably all having shares in rich claims. Nor did they give preferential treatment to the wealthy or more important diners; all alike received prompt attention though scant civility. Nor did the prices exclude the humbler members of the community, for 2s. would buy a breakfast, a lunch or a bed; 2s. 6d. a dinner, and 1s. or 1s. 6d. a shakedown.

The most famous hotel on the Fields was 'Benning and Martin's', so named after its two proprietors: 'a hostelry far-famed wherever news of our great treasure fields has spread.' Situated near the market square, 'an edifice with lofty gable end of wood' fronting the main street, Benning and Martin's was a social centre with its dining-room, 'a really handsome apartment, as far as dimensions go', some forty feet long and thirty feet wide, with its corrugated-iron roof 'quite five and twenty feet over one's head. But the partitions, alas! are of green baize, no statelier material. Three frame doors, woefully tattered, give entrance to the bedrooms on either side. Down the middle is a long rough table, which never knew the decency of a cloth; forms border it all down its length. Here, at breakfast, dinner and tea assemble the *jeunesse dorée* of Dutoitspan, a motley but good-humoured concourse. A *nichée* of duchesses could never show such gems as the guests of this table always carry in their pockets.

'Down each side of the broad room are placed iron bedsteads, rarely untenanted by day, and sometimes doubly filled at night; but the private rooms lie beyond the green-baize walls. They are just big enough to hold two beds, with space to turn between. Wash-hand-stand or glass or luxuries of any kind we do not boast. Washing must be done *coram publico*, in the open camp behind. Other operations of the toilet you may manage with heaven's assistance, for there is no help in man at Benning and Martin's.' But the hotel had its luxuries, nevertheless; a billiard room, and twice a week smoking concerts which were well attended, the diggers coming without jackets in their shirt sleeves, while the aristocracy of the diamond buyers, those that is with offices, and also mere 'kopje-wallopers', who went about the claims buying diamonds, attended in fashionable, conventional clothes and spent their money freely. So Benning and Martin's became both by night and by day a social centre, for besides the attractions of meals, billiards and concerts, both diggers and diamond buyers congregated there in the evenings, when the hard work of mining was done and business and pleasure could be combined as diamonds were bought and sold to the accompaniment of the liquid refreshment that the climate and personal predilection encouraged.

The luncheon hour at Benning and Martin's was for the detached observer perhaps the most interesting of the day. Unwashed, often with grimy arms and faces and shirt-sleeves rolled up, the diggers came straight from their claims, while others, often with white faces and bloodshot eyes, came from the sorting tables and bore the marks of their occupational illness. Many diggers showed scars on their hands and arms, for the slightest scratch easily became infected by the poisonous sand which contained lime. Not all came for lunch; some merely wanted drink; others used the hotel as a rendezvous for meeting their friends, showing lucky 'finds' or buying and selling them.

Perhaps one reason for the popularity of Benning and Martin's was the reasonableness of its charges. The tariff for board and lodging was only 12s. 6d. a day, though few of the residents lived at the hotel. Meals cost 2s. 6d. each, drinks 6d., Boer or native brandy 3d., French brandy 9d.; Cape wines 1s. to 2s. a bottle – 'they seem to be wholesome enough, but unpalatable to a refined taste'; a digger's comment which would not apply to the best Cape wines today. Beer cost 2s. 6d. a bottle, soda-water 9d. The demands of their claims and the dangers, both social and climatic, in drinking had produced a surprising number of teetotallers in the camp.

No rules of precedence were observed at meal times, but the good nature of the guests generally prevented quarrels. For we are not allowed to forget the predominant 'gentlemanly' tone of the diners, despite their unconventional attire and appearance. 'Those whose notions of a "digging" are taken only from sketches of Australia and California, would be much astonished could they get a momentary view of our table. You will hear as good English there for the most part as anywhere in the world, and delivered with the true gentlemanly accent. Noise enough and to spare there is, but of that pleasant sort which youth and the consciousness of success well-earned, will amply excuse. Boers do not come here, and the poorer sort take luncheon at their tents or in the claim. Diamond digging is emphatically, up to this time, a "gentleman's digging". Long may it continue so.' Such was the clientele of Benning and Martin's at the close of 1871; and occasionally we get a glimpse of particular individuals dining there, often military: an ex-Captain of Dragoons, a former officer of the 16th Lancers, a late officer of the Irish Constabulary, and the son of one of the richest English diamond merchants.

Nor did bars, canteens and hotels exhaust the social amenities of the fields, especially of Kimberley, the richest camp. Coffee, chocolate and tea rooms were also popular, not less so because the 'cups which cheer but not inebriate' could be strengthened to any desired extent by the addition of several varieties of alcohol. When, however, local luxury was pushed up to the higher levels of Continental elegance, it apparently failed. The great glass and gold restaurant opened in the Main Street by a Londoner of German parentage, who considered quality before profits, soon closed. The disappointed proprietor, however, refused to sell or quit the place, and for long could be seen through the windows, a disillusioned and disappointed ghost. In contrast was the rough canteen – the most profitable of all the canteens – established in the heart of the diamond market, where every morning buyers and sellers met and discussed their affairs to the accompaniment of adequate sustenance.

Was it the intoxicating spirit – in all senses – diffused by the 'great glass and gold restaurant' in Kimberley's Main Street, before it fell on evil days, which led one to describe the town in 1873 as 'in the heyday of its glory, as were the people of the Diamond Fields. Money was plentiful, a sovereign was not deemed of more importance than a brass farthing is now. No diamond fielder outside the Malay Camp or Kaffir restaurants had any palate for Cape Beer. Without *paté foi* [sic] and Caviare, nobody that was anybody breakfasted, and to be seen drinking without finishing up with a wash-down of Champagne and a liqueur to bring the meal to a point [what "point"? one wonders] was to lose caste in Kimberley and forfeit social recognition.'

Evidently the possibilities of social disaster at the time were great for persons with weak heads, weak stomachs and weak purses. But if from this depressingly 'bright' picture of the place we turn to other soberer accounts, evidently by social 'nobodies', we find a far less exacting standard of culinary art. 'We are all pretty good cooks. We are not satisfied with plain roast and fried meat, but go in for elaborate stews, curries, puddings and cakes. Tomorrow I am going in for a big bread-baking. Very wrong to bake on Sunday; but then I have no time in the week.' On Saturday afternoons and Sundays those who must cook could be seen setting out with sacks and buckets to search the neighbouring veldt for dry dung to make their fires.

As at Dutoitspan, the cost of living at Kimberley was subject to great and sudden fluctuations, which largely depended upon transport, as there too the price of food largely depended upon adequacy of supply. Thus at times, while Kimberley was paying famine prices for food, farmers in the country round were being forced to sell their produce on the spot for very little, through lack of local customers and of transport to the Fields. No food came from native kraals. Sir Lionel Phillips tells how, during a shortage of vegetables so bad that they were almost unobtainable, he lived like the rest, chiefly on meat, tinned sausage, fish, soups, and 'compressed vegetables like cakes of tobacco, that expanded to some extent in water, and generally tasted nauseous'. He also remembered seeing thirty shillings given for a 'solitary cabbage' in the morning market.

That the supplies, and consequently the prices, of food did not quickly improve is shown by the ironical complaints of Trollope in 1877 that 'the meat was bad, the butter uneatable, vegetables a rarity – supplied indeed at the table at which I sat, but supplied at a great cost. Milk and potatoes were luxuries so costly that one sinned almost in using them. A man walking about with his pocket full of diamonds would not perhaps care for this; but even at Kimberley there are those who have fixed incomes – an unfortunate Deputy Governor or the like – to whom sugar at 2s. 6d. a pound and other equally necessary articles in the same proportion, must detract much from the honour and glory of the position. When I was there "transport", no doubt, was unusually high. Indeed, as I arrived, there were muttered threats that "transport" would be discontinued altogether unless rain would come.

'For the understanding of this it must be known that almost everything consumed at Kimberley has to be carried up from the coast, five hundred miles, by ox-waggons, and that the oxen have to feed themselves on the grasses along the road. When there has been a period of drought there are no grasses, and when there are no grasses the oxen will die instead of making progress. Periods of drought are by no means uncommon in South Africa. When I was at Kimberley there had been a period of drought for many months. There had, indeed, been no rain to speak of for more than a year. As one consequence of this the grocers were charging 2s. 6d. a pound for brown sugar. Even the chance of such a state of things militates very much against the comfort of residence.' Evidently Nature had not intended Trollope to be a diamond digger.

Yet at least one digger prided himself on having some of the comforts of civilized life: 'As evidence of civilization, I may mention that a butcher's cart calls at our tent, a Dutch boy brings some excellent sausages made by a good old *frouw* – his mother – and *The Diamond News* is brought round weekly. Our crier with the tinkling bell, summons us in the morning to market; and on Saturday afternoons to sales, meetings, etc. – for we diggers take our Saturday half-holiday like clerks and counter-jumpers in dear old London, and don't we deserve and enjoy it!'

That gambling should be popular on the Fields where all life was itself a gamble was to be expected. It was in fact very common. At a time when local government was uncertain and inefficient, some of the canteen keepers turned their places into gambling dens, and thus faro and roulette tables sprang up at once and multiplied. The principal roulette table was at Dod's Canteen at Kimberley where as a hardly needed inducement to patrons, free refreshments were provided. Another gambling canteen was The Gridiron, the usual type of eating house consisting of a wooden frame covered with canvas. Here at right angles to the central aisle were tables with benches at each side for seats, and with partitions separating the tables, where four persons played at a time, often including the proprietor. The pool there would reach nearly two thousand pounds on some nights. Play at these places would go on until two o'clock in the morning. Doctors and the more successful diggers mostly frequented the better type of gambling saloon, but amusements were still comparatively scarce, and all gambling haunts were well patronized.

Indeed the worst aspect of the gambling habit was the immediate rise of many gambling hells, ranging from the most luxurious to low shacks where Malays, Cape 'Boys', Natives, and Chinese quarrelled and killed one another over a worn and dirty pack of cards. Even in the better places suicides were frequent, and many a man entered them a wealthy person, only to leave a few hours later with nothing, unless the 'generous' proprietor lent him five pounds – of the money that an hour before had been his own – so that he might depart quietly without attracting unwelcome attention to the establishment. Occasionally, at least, the curse over the gambler was changed to a blessing, as with (Sir) David Harris, who, being dragged into Dod's by a friend one evening and at last induced to stake a pound at roulette, left as the sun rose with £1,400 in his pocket – the basis of his fortune; for very wisely he never entered a gambling hell again. His case was, of course, exceptional, for inevitably few except the proprietor's 'bank' won. But the gambling spree was of short duration, lasting only a year before the resorts were compulsorily closed by the authorities.

Another aspect of the social amenities at this time reveals itself in a dancing saloon between Dutoitspan and Kimberley, a favourite haunt of coloured and black women and of their non-white gallants, who became dangerously jealous of their white rivals when such appeared. Frequent fights were the result. 'It was', wrote an habitué, naming the most famous of prostitutes' rendezvous in Victorian London, 'the Argyle Rooms of the Fields.' Round the stage door and entrances to the theatres hung companies of harpies of all colours, especially on the pay nights of the actors, who would be, though but temporarily, rich men. Chroniclers almost inevitably tend to concentrate upon and exaggerate the glamour of vice to enliven their pages; virtue, being unsensational, is generally ignored. Frank Rhodes writing to his mother unconsciously revealed Kimberley's reputation for immorality, even in emphasizing the respectability and honesty of

134

many women who came to live there: 'It is quite a mistake to suppose that there are no nice girls out here.'

'Diamond diggers', wrote a correspondent to the local Press at Kimberley, 'are now sufficiently numerous and civilized to require, appreciate, and have provided for them, plenty of amusements, aye, and are able to pay handsomely for them too.'

6

Crime

MOST of the available evidence provided by the diggers emphasizes the general high standard of law and order maintained by the population of the Diamond Fields, and particularly by the first comers. Many witnesses stress the absence of brutal crime among them and contrast their orderliness with the disorder of the mining camps of America and of Australia.[1] 'There were very few outbreaks of ruffianism in the camps,' writes one of the most authoritative historians of the South African Diamond Fields, 'where the great body of miners was disposed to be orderly, and occasional sprees were the chief disturbance. The swaggering bullies and cheating gamblers and lurking garrotters who infested the seething camps of Nevada and Colorado, rarely drifted as far as these isolated Diamond Fields, and the few who came were held in check.'

It is still a matter of pride at the Cape that the attempt of an English convict-ship to land its cargo of criminals there in 1849, was frustrated by the opposition of the inhabitants, who offered so inhospitable a reception that the ship went on to Australia. The memory of this incident led one observer on the Diamond Fields to point more particularly the contrast: 'The basis of Cape Society differed materially from that of Australia. South Africa had never been a convict settlement, nor had there ever been a convict settlement in its proximity. There was no material for the making of bushrangers or highway robbers. There was plenty of card-playing, but the stakes were mild, and there was none of that gambling that leads to duels and assassinations as in the gold fields of other countries. Pickpockets and burglars were at that time as scarce in the Colony as money, and that was scarce enough in all conscience. . . . There is no such thing as unmitigated good in the world; amongst all the blessings which came to the

---

[1] Beet, in this respect, differs from the mass of evidence: 'Like the American and Australian goldmining camps of earlier times, Du Toit's Pan had its full quota of dangerous and unscrupulous blackguards, outlaws from all parts, who were prepared to "raise the wind" by any form of violence or guile.'
The Grand Old Days of the Diamond Fields, p. 60.

country through the diamond discovery, it brought a few pickpockets and burglars. The prevailing crime of South Africa up to 1870 was sheep-stealing, but there were no sheep on the Diamond Fields to steal, and digging for diamonds, although not generally very profitable at first, was even then more profitable, and held out better prospects than stealing sheep.'

One sign of the general obedience to law and order was that South African diggers, unlike their American and Australian counterparts, seldom carried arms.[1] 'The diggers are, as a rule, a good tempered race and respecters of law and order. Revolvers are *not* carried, at any rate never openly. I remember a time, though, when one or two daring highway robberies in the neighbourhood of Du Toit's Pan caused me – as well as many others – to take out my six-shooter at night, but I am sure I should have got along just as well without it.'

Firearms, in fact, were not approved by the diggers who regarded them not only as unnecessary, but as a positive nuisance. At the popular auctions of miscellaneous goods, when everything useful, mining tools, drapery, sporting guns and such, fetched high prices, revolvers were almost the only unsaleable article; 'and indeed they are of very little use here, for we are a quiet and peaceable community, with the exception of a few wild spirits who will go in for a "big drink" on Saturday night, and occasionally wake up to find themselves lying on straw in "Chokey" on Sunday morning, in the pleasant companionship of sundry strong-smelling aborigines.'

Another deterrent was the strict government tax of £1 a barrel, which led to weapons being left unclaimed at the Customs House, until ultimately, old and rusty, they came to auction and often enough became the highly valued possession of some native. They were, in fact, much coveted by the natives, who often came to work on the Fields chiefly to obtain a gun of some kind – the working of which they seldom understood.

Indeed the smallness as well as the inefficiency of the police force at the Fields bears witness to the comparative absence of violent crime, while the *bona fide* diggers, tired after long and exhausting hours of work, were in general little disposed for nightly rowdyism. What crimes occurred were mostly committed by hangers-on of the camps, not by the diggers. 'As a rule the diggers were honest, law-abiding and industrious, and too much occupied with their digging operations to give heed to, or consider any deviation from rectitude. . . . Whilst attending to their work in the claims, they left their tents fastened merely by a bit of string, yet when they

---

[1] The only contradictory evidence is Beet's: 'each invariably carried a revolver or bowie knife in his belt.' The mass of evidence is contrary.

returned they found everything just as left; the only depredator would, perhaps, have been a stray dog that endeavoured to ferret out the larder.'

A less idyllic picture, however, is painted by others. Robbery with violence certainly did occur, increasingly as the numbers and variety of the population increased. Indeed the diary of one digger merely for a single week of September 1871 somewhat discredits the happier reminiscences. In that one week a digger was attacked by robbers during a dust storm. His cries for help were heard by the police, but the strong wind and dust prevented their finding him until after the escape of the robbers. A man was, however, soon arrested on suspicion. Then news of several other highway robberies and garrottings at the De Beers Mine arrived. 'So, for the moment, revolvers are at a premium, and much worn at night.'

Six days later *The Diamond News* advertised a reward of £25 for information about three men, 'believed all white', who knocked down a man and robbed him of his money and diamonds at the junction of the Dorstfontein and Bultfontein roads. The next day a gentleman returning on horseback from Dutoitspan to his tent at New Rush 'was knocked off his horse and brutally kicked by three men, probably the same gang as those of the preceding day. As he was losing consciousness some people came in sight and the ruffians decamped without robbing him.' His injuries, however, were said to be not serious.

A particularly mean theft occurred this same week when a Boer took from a little boy a diamond he had found in stuff thrown out from a sieve, and falsely claimed it as his own. The Diggers' Committee, however, forced the man to return the stone to the boy. The following week, a native was seen to pick up a diamond of 10½ carats in stuff thrown out from a sieve and was brought before the magistrate. In this case, however, the stone was returned to its original owner.

At this time, too, a young man dragged an elderly one into the veldt, shot him just below the eye, destroying it, and left the man dying. Coolly and with apparent unconcern, the aggressor, brought before the magistrate and charged with attempted murder, pretended it was an accident. Although insanity in his family was pleaded and it was rumoured that the victim had robbed the murderer of some diamonds, the motive for the crime was thought to be robbery, and feeling among the diggers was strong against him. His fate is not known.

Occasional brawls and disputes ending in a bout of fisticuffs were inevitable: 'a good pair of fists still counted for something'. A quarrel and bitter fight between an English digger of indifferent character and a Boer occasioned a large audience, while 'the police kept the ring'! The Boer emerged victorious, but 'both were a good deal knocked about'. Drink, of course, largely contributed to violence and crime, and we read of an Australian digger who, when drunk, brutally attacked his frail little wife, 'knocking her down and kicking her furiously, inflicting very severe injuries'. He was marched off to the police station between two constables with drawn swords, while the indignant diggers hoped he would be sentenced to at least 'four dozen lashes and six months'.

Increasing crime, among other reasons, led to the formation of the early Diggers' Committees, and the drastic and immediate punishments prescribed. Rightly based upon the protection of the community and the maintenance of justice, instead of the modern often too sentimental and sometimes even unjust 'rehabilitation of the criminal', they were not only the chief reason for the scarcity of crime, but proved more effective than the slow, laborious and often devious methods of Governmental legalism introduced later. Thieves, whether by direct theft or through Illicit Diamond Buying, got short shrift from the Diggers' Committees, for all forms of theft were particularly dangerous to the diggers as a whole. In the first place, there was the ever present danger of personal loss in such a community, when their so vulnerable tents and huts had to be left unoccupied for many hours each day; in the second place, in general even more important was the danger to the whole diamond market and so to the whole community by the covert sale of stolen diamonds at absurdly low prices.

One mode of punishment imitative of contemporary advertisement in England, was adopted by the Committee for the crime of theft. The supposed thief was sandwiched between two large boards slung round his neck, displaying in large letters the word THIEF. The man thus placarded was placed in the middle of a small procession and so marched through the camp, while a man walked in front ringing a large hand-bell to draw the attention of all to the thief's ignominy. If proved guilty, he would be roughly expelled from the camp – the usual treatment of such offenders. But in the particular case described, some doubted his guilt and opposed further punishment before a more detailed examination of the matter was made. The boards were therefore temporarily removed, and he was taken back to the tent for further investigation. During this new search the missing article was found, the owner having forgotten that he had in fact hidden it for safer keeping. The owner was therefore made to pay a small sum for compensation to the wrongfully accused, and the quondam 'THIEF' was discharged without a stain on his character. This, however, appears to have been a quite exceptional incident. The Committee generally used great caution to prevent mistakes.

Perhaps the most notorious case of injustice was the conviction of Henry Tucker, well known to the community and respected for his honesty. An experienced politician, Tucker was also President of the Committee of Public Safety formed amidst the rising spirit of revolt against the Government during the period of the Annexation. He was also elected later to the Legislative Council. During his career he had probably made by his honesty many enemies, both political and purely personal, particularly by the part he played in framing laws against Illicit Diamond Buying. Forgetting on one occasion that his licence to buy diamonds had lapsed and not been renewed, he innocently and openly bought some diamonds from a friend, who in equal innocence registered the sale and so unwittingly gave his enemies their opportunity of revenge. Thus Tucker was sentenced to nine months in prison under a law which he himself had helped to frame.

During this later period, as the new influxes of fortune-hunters followed one another with the spreading fame of Kimberley, crime increased, and this was assisted by the long indeterminate status of the territory while Britain, the Free State, and the South African Republic disputed possession. The factional fights and general rebellion which ensued are described in a later chapter; but all confirm that 'lawlessness ran riot, frequent disturbances took place.' The cause, however, was almost entirely political grievance and revolt, not ordinary crime.

Ultimately, with the coming of mechanization and 'big business', Kimberley became a quiet town; British law was respected and crime declined to normal proportions.

It was fortunate that in the earliest days life on the Diamond Fields was so comparatively peaceful and free from professional criminals, for both police and, at times, even law courts and prisons were more strongly suggestive of comic opera than of actual life. The Frontier Armed and Mounted Police (F.A.M.P.) of the South African Republic (or Transvaal Republic) were established in a pleasant little camp on the top of a kopje just outside the town. They looked, and indeed were, a smart body of men in their service uniforms of dark brown corduroy, peaked leather helmets, well mounted and with horse revolvers. There were, nevertheless, 'a good many scamps and ne'er-do-wells among them; others had come to the fields without sufficient capital, and were "broke".' Many of them did in fact prefer police life with little to do, to hard digging at the mine. Although some minor irregularities such as occasional drunkenness were winked at by the authorities, they were strictly disciplined and any serious misdemeanour was severely punished. Thus one digger saw 'two policemen, convicted of a trifling theft, tied up to a wagon wheel to receive each four dozen lashes with the "cat" laid on vigorously by a black executioner – a most degrading and painful punishment, and, I should think, a salutary caution.'

The Free State Police offered the most complete contrast to the Frontier Force, being 'the most deplorable lot of seedy-looking ragamuffins that can well be conceived.' The only inducements to join the force were the miserable pay, and for the inspector alone a strip of gold lace round his cap. In these circumstances no decent working man or labourer would dream of enlisting, and inevitably its members consisted of the very lowest class on the Fields. 'Drunken, dissipated, seedy-looking reprobates, in garments of every shade, cut and pattern, but in dirt and dilapidation generally resembling those of the typical British scarecrow – such were The Free State Police.'

They were about twenty in number, and their appearance when they paraded outside the magistrate's court excited a mixture of pity and amusement. Their only arms were a few swords and rifles in the police office. Generally, however, they carried no weapons, nor any other sign of their function. Only when on some specially dangerous errand did they take their swords, and their most imposing occasions were those when with drawn swords flashing in the sun they escorted some prisoner to the police station. At other times they were perpetually loafing round the chief canteens, very ready to accept a drink at anybody's expense; thoroughly inefficient in the discharge of their duties, lazy and unintelligent, they were little more than utterly worthless as guardians of the public peace and order. It is not surprising that these were the police who kept the ring at the fight previously described, instead of preventing it. In addition, their duties on that occasion were said to be: 'to see fair play and enjoy the spectacle'!

How primitive magistrates' courts were even after Annexation, Chapter 9 will incidentally reveal. Nor were all the magistrates, in the early period at least, everything that could be desired. One magistrate, named Truter, a Swede, was conspicuously efficient: 'a conscientious man and a courteous gentleman', as all agreed. We shall meet him again, later, at the time of the Annexation. But all were not Truters. One was generally disliked for his too free use of the lash, and the unrestrained temperaments of another magistrate and his wife inspired the following revealing passage by a trustworthy and educated witness: 'There were lively times in Klipdrift just then. The Magistrate's wife on the Klipdrift side was going the rounds of the camp with a loaded revolver in her pocket to shoot anyone whom she considered offensive, and his worship her husband, who sat in robes on the Bench, went for knocking men down with his fist as a preliminary to having them locked up.'

Perhaps there was some excuse for such conduct. The duties of magistrates were exacting and wearisome: fining Boers for their favourite practice of firing their guns at night, sentencing natives to short terms of imprisonment or to the 'cat', for drunkenness or theft; and there were also many civil cases: disputes, breaches of contracts, assaults, damages, and so forth. Nor was the court interpreter's task easy, for quite apart from Europeans speaking foreign languages, there were many different tribes of natives on the Fields, each with its own tongue.

Although some observers claim that few appealed to the law in civil disputes, one even asserting that the delay in establishing courts was due to their not being needed, and indeed that the miners as a whole were opposed to law-suits, others very definitely express an opposite opinion. 'Diggers', wrote a barrister, 'are decidedly a litigious lot, and half a dozen sound and sober lawyers would thrive amazingly.' Certainly some were very ready to go to law, even including two 'partners' who legally contested their first 'find', two tiny diamonds of $\frac{1}{3}$ carat each, hardly worth 10s. the pair.

How completely ignorant of law litigants might be, is revealed in the case of two Boer partners who appealed against an interdict on working their claim which another Boer had obtained from an official. When the man who had obtained the interdict was questioned as to what right he had to do so, and whether the claim was his property, he replied 'No'. What then was his legal authority, he was asked. The claim, he explained, belonged to a friend, and he thought the two working partners were not doing their best. Asked for his power to interfere, he said that he had none. Asked if his friend had made any declaration constituting him his trustee – he did not know of any! The interdict was dismissed with costs. Yet those wrongfully interdicted never dreamed of claiming damages for loss of time, or even made any complaint.

Police stations and prisons on the Fields were at this time as primitive as the majority of their occupants – natives. The station at Dutoitspan was 'a little building of "wattle and daub"; the prison, "tronk" or "chokey", was a wretched, barn-like little place, the floor littered with dirty straw, on which were generally reposing one or two inebriated or felonious niggers, and now and then a dissipated white man.' Next to the police court was the official whipping-post, brought into use when prisoners were sentenced to a flogging, a punishment hardly ever inflicted upon white malefactors.

Indeed when Truter became magistrate and presided over the new, large wooden court-house at Dutoitspan, floggings were few and much milder than at Klipdrift, where even diggers who had taken a drink or two too many were put in the official 'stocks' standing beside the door of the court. 'I don't remember anybody ever being put into Klipdrift prison, in fact it would not have been of much avail to do so, for the walls were so loosely put together that a prisoner might have pushed his way out without much difficulty.' Trollope, seven years later, found the Kimberley prison by no means beyond criticism. 'I could have wished that the prison had been better – that is more prisonly – with separate rooms for instance for those awaiting trial and those committed. But all this will be done within those twenty next coming years. And I know well how difficult it is to get money to set such things afloat in a young community.'

The fate of individuals brought within the law's embrace was often very uncertain. 'The principles of the law varied so much that it was sometimes difficult for a man to know how to act with a certainty that he was doing what was lawful and right. And the worst part of it was that we had no Court of Appeal, so that suitors and criminals were comparatively at the mercy of the Magistrate.' One temporary magistrate at Dutoitspan was particularly disliked for a too free use of the lash. 'This Dutoitspan', wrote one, protesting, 'is a very quiet and orderly camp, although we have at present only six of the Free State Police to keep order in an assemblage of about twenty thousand people.' Such comments explain the preference many felt for the original Diggers' Committee.

Of all the offences with which the Committee had to deal the most important, most prevalent and most generally detested was illicit diamond buying, known as I.D.B. I.D.B., indeed, would almost appear to have been a vocational disease of the Diamond Fields, especially of the Kimberley Mine which doubtless presented by its size and depth better opportunities for such thefts than the rest of the Fields. 'Here adventurers of the worst types of all races abounded, having come to the fields for the express purpose of illicit diamond buying – a remunerative calling then rampant. It was estimated [later] the diamond-mining companies were robbed of at least £3,000,000 worth of diamonds every year by their employees who sold them to illicit diamond-buyers. This trade flourished in spite of severe penalties.' 'The worst evils were beyond all question, diamond-stealing and illicit diamond-buying; beyond this there was practically nothing to tempt the professional thief or receiver of stolen goods.'

That I.D.B. was the commonest of crimes on the Diamond Fields is not surprising. There were particular circumstances which greatly encouraged it. In the first place it was an ever present temptation; in addition, stealing was as easy as detection was difficult. To trace and identify the diamonds stolen, to obtain the necessary evidence also, even when there was no actual doubt about them, was far from easy. And above all other temptations was the large fortune that the thief or thieves might gain, leaving, when really lucky, no necessity of taking the same risk afterwards. Thus I.D.B. flourished, and today, in the modern, mechanized diamond mines, continues, no longer as a merely personal and individual adventure, but as a well-organized criminal conspiracy on a vast scale.

Most of the actual stealing then occurred on the mines themselves during one or other of the various stages of production. Many were stolen directly from the claims by the workers with pick and shovel. These were generally raw natives who, finding a diamond while digging, and while the owner or overseer of the claim was above at the sorting table, quickly appropriated and secreted it before resuming their work. This was, of course, done in various ways according to circumstances. Some, on seeing the diamond lying in the turned-up ground, would quickly throw it along with a spadeful of earth behind him, and then at night return in the darkness and secure it. Others would very quickly pick up the exposed stone with their toes and then at the first possible moment transfer it to a better hiding-place in their own bodies: in their ears, in rotten teeth, in a self-inflicted gash in the leg, in the quick of a toe-nail, or by swallowing it or in other such places of concealment. Their skill in all these operations was remarkable, and if several natives were working on the claim at the time, the theft could be yet more easily achieved. Even when white overseers were present, prevention was almost impossible.

The stone might well be filched while being transported to the sorting table, or even while on the sorting table itself. But the best opportunities for theft were presented when the blue ground was reached and its stones, both more numerous and more valuable, discovered. For the blue ground, when broken up, had to be left for six months or a year outside the mine to disintegrate in the sunlight, and was then beaten to powder by gangs of natives armed with wooden mallets. Once this stage was reached, the number of thefts on the Diamond Fields greatly increased. 'The opportunities were unfortunately too apparent and easy for filching and disposing of diamonds. The sharpest oversight could scarcely prevent nimble-fingered workers from slyly secreting tiny crystals in picking over the concentrates on the sorting tables, or in handling the deposit in the rockers and puddling pans.'

Nor, even in the first stage of I.D.B., did the natives always act on their own initiative. For the camps were soon haunted by many who lacked the means to buy a claim, or the desire to dig, yet hoped for riches by quicker and often more certain methods. These soon began to entice natives to steal diamonds from their masters in every possible way. Dishonest kopje-wallopers, 'canteen-keepers, proprietors of eating-houses, and of butchers' shops, were the principal instigators and receivers in days when the only law was the "unwritten law".'

One particularly ingenious type of rogue who exploited the natives' stealing of diamonds was the fortune-teller or wizard previously described,[1] who imposed upon the more ignorant and credulous diggers, including the Boers, by claiming to reveal the presence or absence of diamonds on their claims.

The next stage in I.D.B. was the secret transference of the stolen diamond to some intermediary, white or black, generally some well-dressed Cape 'Boy' or, as often, a Polish Jew, who received it from the practically naked native for a mere song, and easily disposed of it at a somewhat greater profit to one of the unscrupulous licensed diamond buyers, who would be by far the greatest gainer from the crime. Although he knew quite well that the stones he bought were stolen, theft was difficult to prove and 'ignorance' profitable.

Among these illicit buyers were 'respectable' persons: church-goers, club-men, loud denunciators of I.D.B. and its associated evils. Indeed the story goes that one Kimberley clergyman, possibly hyperconscientious, but certainly surprised at the generosity of his congregation when the collecting-boxes were emptied, expressed from his pulpit a pious hope that he was not being made an unwitting receiver of stolen goods.

Inevitably the hotels and bars of Kimberley became clearing houses for I.D.B. Though perhaps somewhat over-dramatized, the following description of a typical scene in such bars – in this case 'the company you could meet in The Red Light, at all hours, but especially about midday' – convincingly suggests the actual local colour: 'Crowded with humans, from all climes and cities and aristocratic quarters too. There stands a parrot peer, garrulous, trembling hand, glassy eyes, smoking a pipe, waiting for tardy remittances from "home"; not disdaining to accept honours of the bar from the red-scarved poppy-headed Hebrew; flashily dressed, with enormous watch-chain and important diamond ring, he speaks coster-like, with offensive familiarity to the fallen aristocrat, wondering all the time to himself how he ever arrived at such an altitude. But he is a gentleman of means, a coward, who never risks his own skin,

[1] v. *supra*, p. 148.

but supplies runners (natives), with the money to buy for him from the raw niggers working in the mines. . . . When not engaged in these exciting practices, he lived at ————— in the Transvaal; immune from English law, he pursued his traffic, a thief who disdained to thieve himself. . . .

'There is a royal rogue from Russia with deep scars received in Siberia, marked upon his cheeks, a frowsy-looking Pole in jack-boots, and who has evidently had a good time, for he flashes a huge bundle of notes, and openly exchanges some of them over the bar for £100 in gold. The use for which he intends the coin is obvious, and the transaction attracts not even a passing remark. Sadly leaning against the counter, regarding hungrily the cash, is a thin, genteel, well-bred looking man, with fair, drooping moustache and tired, disappointed and dissipated face. He knows few people. Long ago he lived in England: had heaps of friends and money, had been to College, lodged at Claridge's; but falling the prey to ladies, had been convicted of some offence and in due course shipped to Africa to try his luck. Lots of such men – good chums – but Fortune's outcasts.

'Around the bar were detectives mingling and drinking with the fish they hoped to catch; broken-down, grandiose captains; jewelled gamblers stinking of scent; liquor-loving lawyers; Irish "patriots" of combative and fiery inclinations; a few flabby actors, unwashed and unabashed with last night's triumphs plastered on their faces; newspaper reporters, down at heel; unemployed nondescripts; they were all forbidding and repellent. Stubborn Swedes; sallow Sicilians; swarthy Spaniards; Square Heads from Silesia; such were the exotic members of La Légion Noire – the modern, the mediaeval, the antique, laughing gaily, drinking merrily, smiling serenely, but all the time with the shadow of the breakwater[1] haunting them and phantoms of prison warders grinning over their shoulders.'

Great quantities of stolen diamonds were also smuggled out of the camps for sale in the coast towns or in foreign markets. Indeed the number so disposed of has been estimated (probably somewhat over-estimated) at 50 per cent of those found each year. Nor were all the diamonds sold in the various weekly auctions at Cape Town 'honestly come-by'.

To discover means of smuggling the stones out of the camps and secreting them throughout the short or long journeys involved, human ingenuity was again severely taxed. A favourite and particularly revolting method of getting them outside the camp was to feed the diamond to a dog in meat, then lead it out of the camp and kill it. Similar methods were also used to conceal the stones during longer journeys: by feeding them to horses and

---

[1] Convicts were sent to build the breakwater at Cape Town.

dogs, even to the lowest types of men and women, who also, like the natives on the mines, concealed them about their bodies at critical moments. Some of these loose women travelled regularly between the camps in South Africa and Europe. They would come out to the Diamond Fields, spend a few weeks there, then return to England or the Continent with their secret cargoes. Few but whites engaged in these smuggling expeditions, whether long or short. To reach the Cape and overseas, was difficult; but a quick dash across the border into the Transvaal or Orange Free State was comparatively easy, not only because of their close proximity to the Diamond Fields, but also because the Governments and Police of the two countries were indifferent, while even Natal showed little enthusiasm for preventing the illicit traffic across its borders.

I.D.B. soon became one of the most important crimes with which the Diggers' Committee had to deal. That the punishments they imposed were drastic is not strange, for to the honest diggers I.D.B. was almost the worst of all crimes, threatening as it did the ever insecure foundations of their work. For besides the danger of immediate personal loss for the individual whose diamonds were stolen, there was the much greater effect of I.D.B. upon the fortunes of the diggers as a whole. The general uncertainty as to whether diamonds were being secretly stolen from the claims led inevitably to increased uncertainty as to whether any particular claim was not in fact richer than appeared, and this in turn adversely affected the prices of the claims when sold, particularly as some, which appeared to be very poor and could only be sold, if sold at all, at a very low price, might really be producing fine stones secretly stolen. Nor was this all. The low prices that the thieves must accept for the stolen stones also affected the diamond sales by lowering prices, and, if not prevented, might destroy the whole diamond field. In these circumstances the diggers' fight against I.D.B. was a fight for survival.

In the absence of legal remedies the diggers took the law into their own hands. Punishment of the native thief was physical and severe. Lynching never appealed to South Africans as it did to Americans, and although one responsible writer of the time says 'Judge Lynch was sometimes active' in Kimberley, no evidence of lynching appears. The usual punishment for the native was whipping, the culprit being tied to a log of wood and flogged with a sjambok, while the other natives, as a deterrent, were forced to watch the operation. One writer remarks that these floggings were 'not very severe'; but in 1878 one native was given fifty lashes and nine months' gaol, nor was the loss and consequent exasperation of the diggers likely to inspire a merciful disposition towards the offenders. Indeed one of the penalties suggested, but never apparently accepted by the miners, was branding on the face with a hot iron. Although many natives stole diamonds, others were entirely honest, and we hear in one case of a native, who, working alone on a claim, found a diamond of no less than 154 carats, which he at once took to his master.

In those days, before organized robbery controlled I.D.B., the thefts were still, like everything else on the Fields, individualistic. At such a time, to small traders and kopje-wallopers not doing very well on the Fields, the temptation to take a chance with I.D.B. must have been strong. Since no native might dig on his own account but must bring all stones found to his master, any diamond offered by a native to anyone but his master was probably stolen. In such circumstances the native depended upon the 'generosity' of the buyer, who might offer him little or nothing. Indeed to give much was to court detection, as a native with money would attract the attention of the police.

Thus, at the moment when a fine stolen stone was suddenly and secretly offered and a willingness to accept a merely nominal price shown, the temptation to buy it and immediately gain a fortune if not detected, must, especially to some canteen-keeper or kopje-walloper in adverse circumstances, have been very strong. But strong also was the buyer's punishment if detected. In such a case the whole crowd of miners marched in a body to the tent, shop or canteen of the accused, smashed it up and set it on fire with all its contents, emptied and smashed the bottles and barrels of wines and spirits when found, and roughly forced the man to stand by and watch all his belongings disappear in the flames. Then he was kicked out of the camp. At the river diggings he was also dragged through the river. 'Day after day, and night after night,' said *The Diggers' Gazette* on 19 July 1872, 'one or another of the camps is regaled with the edifying spectacle of natives flogged, tents in flames, white men surrounded by angry crowds hardly to be restrained from exemplifying their vengeance with a short shrift and a stout cord.'

But even such harsh measures failed to suppress the illicit diamond buyers. 'How easily,' the tempted man would think, as the native tendered the stone which might hold many thousands of pounds for the buyer: 'How easily, but for my ill luck, this native might have been *my* servant, and the stone *my* own legitimate property!' So the temptation to right this wrong of Providence became irresistible. Evidently the spirit of Abstract Virtue was not predominant over the Diamond Fields: 'The proper motto of the Fields is – "Make Money" – honestly if you can – but anyhow, make money. I was sometimes swindled when I first came on the Fields, so I will do my best to "skin" others. So the scoundrel white, by threatening to give the native to the police, often gets a big diamond for the merest trifle – a bottle of grog, or even nothing at all.' And as another observer remarks, 'The evil could not have continued but for the unscrupulous fellows hanging about mines for this purpose, to buy them, as otherwise the natives could not have disposed of them.'

In time a special corps of diamond police was formed, consisting of a Chief, some twenty-five natives, nine white detectives, and a number of others who were engaged in scouring the region and in service abroad. In 1880 a special court was established to try I.D.B. cases, and a Diamond Trade Act ordered that every parcel of diamonds taken from the Fields must be formally described and registered, and every transfer recorded from the date of discovery until its final shipment from the Cape.

Trapping was, of course, one of the most important duties of the police. Information was obtained from many different sources, suspected persons were watched, and traps were set for them. The white buyer's house, generally, of course, a tent or corrugated-iron shanty, was quietly surrounded by the police, usually at night, and a trained native decoy, carrying one or two concealed diamonds, was despatched to the 'house' to pretend to sell the 'stuff' to the suspect. Before leaving the police, the decoy was carefully searched to see that he carried no money of his own – so proving that whatever money he brought back must have been paid by the suspect for the offered diamonds. Upon the decoy's gentle knock on the house door, the suspect's native servant (a collaborator with his master in I.D.B., and expected by him to introduce only 'safe' customers) would open it.

Having convinced the servant that he was a genuine thief, the decoy would be brought into the buyer's room, easy and tempting terms would quickly be reached, and the decoy paid in gold and silver coin. Once safely outside the house the decoy would whistle a signal to the concealed and waiting police who would then rush in and arrest the man, often before he had had time to get rid of the diamond or diamonds. For a conviction the police must prove: (1) that their trap found a stone or stones on the accused; (2) that they found on their decoy the money he had received for them. Sometimes, indeed, the police by bribery or intimidation persuaded genuine diamond thieves to become decoys.

Strange or amusing stories of traps and of hairbreadth escapes, of course, are legion. There were, for instance: the wife who, when the police rushed in to seize her husband, hid the incriminating diamond in the stuffing of a goose she was cooking; the men who, as their only way of escape, swallowed the stone; the hotel proprietress who, having saved her husband by seizing the diamond and throwing it away at random as the police dashed in, found it eighteen months later, when the police searches had ceased, wedged between the corrugated-iron roof and the wooden ceiling. Another writer tells how, having been informed by his friend the Chief of Police that a raid was to take place at Dutoitspan which might be interesting to see, he waited and watched a Cape cart with four horses standing opposite an hotel in the central square, until a young man emerged from the hotel carrying a large overcoat slung over one arm, and slowly walked to the waiting cart. But before he reached it a police whistle sounded and the police dashed in, seized, handcuffed and searched the man. In a pocket of the overcoat they found £200,000 worth of diamonds, which got for him twenty-five years of hard labour. If he had reached the cart and got away over the border into the Free State only three miles away, he would have been made rich for life.

Sir Lionel Phillips on one occasion accompanied a leading detective named Fox and his men on an I.D.B. expedition, which took place one night during one of the terrific thunderstorms of the region. Completely drenched they crouched in a hole in the ground full of water, watching, before rushing the house and arresting the buyer, red-handed. Just as they were leaving after thoroughly searching the premises, one of the detectives suddenly swung round, drawing his revolver, believing he had been shot at; but it turned out to be only a loud thunderclap.

These illicit diamond buyers were usually well known. Their buildings abounded in exits, and their native servants' quarters were generally larger than usual as they employed more 'boys'. The 'boys' they employed were generally the sophisticated, insolent kind, often with a smattering of education from a Mission school, which made them, Sir Lionel Phillips thought, 'worse than without'. When a Government regulation gave the right to search for stolen diamonds, search-houses were installed at the exits from the mines. The white men employed (this was in the later period) objected, and a strike followed. Threatening crowds of strikers formed, joined, of course, by the illicit fraternity, and the Kimberley mine was put in a state of defence. An attempt to rush the defences was met by shots from the defenders of the mine, some strikers were killed and others wounded, and despite the fierce threats of the strike-leaders, the strike quickly died away.

Not less exciting were the experiences of I.D.B. agents who worked farther afield. One famous case was that of a thief named Harding. Stripped of its inessentials, the tale runs that Harding, when passing the little corrugated-iron post office at Kimberley, noticed a registered letter-bag lying close to the unguarded, open window and yielded to the sudden

Dry sorting of ground brought up from the claims, 1872, before the advent of the washing pan

Sorting machine erected by Weils and Barker, 1880

The first 'horse whim' (windlass) erected at Kimberley, May 1874

Kimberley Market Square 1880-5

impulse to take it. On opening it in his tent, he found diamonds worth £60,000 inside and determined to escape with them to Europe. He reached Cape Town unsuspected, but 'going on the spree' there, just before his ship sailed and being lavish with his money (and doubtless the worse for drink), he attracted the attention of the police who boarded his ship at the last moment before sailing and examined his luggage, but without finding stolen diamonds. As they were about to leave, however, one of the detectives picked up Harding's double-barrelled gun, and finding it unusually heavy, pulled some packing out of the barrels and turned it to point to the ground. When a string of diamonds immediately fell out, Harding was arrested and finally sentenced to seven years hard labour – doubtless at the Cape Town breakwater.

Nor was a gun by any means the most unlikely of the various hiding places invented by the long-distance thieves: bullets, books cut into square recesses in their middle pages, dresses with secret pockets, shoes with hollow heels, and, as with the thieves on the Diamond Fields, the human body. One case is recorded of the escape of some to Europe with the stones hidden in a hollow malacca cane that had been in the hands of a detective – evidently a less astute one than the man who had handled the double-barrelled gun at Cape Town.

The question as to who should guard the guardians sometimes arose, for not every policeman could resist bribery or the temptation to engage in I.D.B., temptations to which he was peculiarly exposed, and for which conviction in such cases was particularly difficult. For example, in later days when De Beers had become the great power in the land, a clever deception of this kind was successfully attempted by a policeman whose duty was to watch convicts working in the mine, to take any diamonds they found on the floors, and to enter to their credit the usual percentage rewards for stones that the convicts found. When the policeman died, a large quantity of diamonds was found among his effects. They were identified as De Beers diamonds, and De Beers bought them back for £1,000. It was finally discovered that all were stolen. By consistently entering in his records throughout the years the weight of the diamonds received at less than it actually was, he had been able to steal the excess weight for himself.

Another case in which one of the official guardians was closely concerned revealed a different method. The man, who had been given a valuable stone to use as a bait in detection, complained that thieves had drugged his drink and stolen it. Long afterwards the diamond was found in the possession of a woman, a relative of the suspect for whom the trap had been set.

Incorruptible guardians of the laws against I.D.B. were the well-trained police dogs introduced later to prevent the transference of stolen diamonds by native thieves in the compounds to accomplices outside. Messages would be exchanged between the thieves, the stones hidden at some marked spot and dagga placed there in exchange. At first, when this traffic was discovered, the company itself played the part of the dishonest agent by carrying on the correspondence through pretended thieves and so regaining the stolen diamonds for the cost of the dagga. Soon, however, the idea of training dogs to prevent this traffic across the boundaries occurred to them and was found most effective.

The most famous, or rather infamous, of all the diamond thieves was Adam Worth, a man of international disrepute, 'wanted' by the police of Europe, America and even of Asia Minor for daring robberies throughout the world. While visiting the South African Diamond Fields, Worth learned of a parcel of diamonds worth £40,000 that was being despatched to Cape Town for shipment to England. To prevent its departure by the steamer as arranged, Worth's gang ensured the necessary delay by breaking up the railway track, and before the diamonds reached Cape Town the ship had gone. Awaiting in the post office the next steamer to England, as Worth had planned, the parcel was stolen by his men in a successful burglary which for many months left no clue.

In the meantime Worth lived in luxury in a West End hotel in London and opened a diamond dealer's office in Holborn Viaduct, where he sold the diamonds for £40,000. Thus supplied, he took a flat over Fortnum and Mason's in Piccadilly, set up as a wealthy man of leisure with his carriage and yacht, and later stole Gainsborough's famous 'Duchess of Devonshire', the return of which to its owners Worth negotiated as 'honest broker' for £2,000. Worth outwitted the law to the end and died in bed, 'a lusty old sporting gent'.

One or two glimpses of the guests in Free State hotels near the border suggest that escaped diamond thieves regularly found sanctuary there. One person observed two such in the hotel at the same time as himself, in addition to a detective set to watch one of them. The first, happily presiding over the dinner table in a most beautiful smoking-cap and dressing-gown, had been charged with I.D.B., had been allowed out on bail and had escaped over the border. The other, 'a grave and morose American, Major B——', had shared a claim at Kimberley with two partners, had appointed himself the receiver of all their finds, and, when they became suspicious and demanded their property, had refused to give it them. On their appealing to a magistrate, Major B— had fled to the Free State where he was momentarily safe. But closely watching him and his black portmanteau, presumably holding the diamonds, was a young man, booted and spurred and ready to take to the veldt at a moment's notice, who had followed on the major's trail, armed with a warrant. The portmanteau, however, must have been innocent, for the worthy major, leaving it behind as a decoy, escaped in the night and was soon followed by the agent of justice in hot pursuit. The end of the story is unknown.

Strangest of all, perhaps, and not unremarked was the safety in which diamonds were transported by cart, without any protection, from the Fields to Cape Town. 'One can scarcely understand such recklessness on the part of any Government, as would and does allow twenty, or fifty, or a hundred thousand pounds' worth of gems to be carried fortnightly in an open cart, driven by a wild Hottentot, over mountain and river, seven hundred miles, without a policeman or soldier to protect it. More than this, the mail-carts are supposed and encouraged to take passengers, thus helping out a meagre subsidy. It is as sure as any event can be, that, sooner or later, two or three quiet-looking gentlemen will engage the vacant seats, and – teach our Government an elementary lesson of prudence. No better testimony to the diggers' character could be produced than the long immunity of the post-carts.'

But even when a supposed robbery of the mail cart occurred about this time, and an offer of £500 reward was placarded on almost every tree between Klipdrift and Hopetown, the lost bag with its £20,000 of diamonds was found by chance on the veldt by a farmer who casually picked it up and brought it to Hopetown: incidentally, another unconscious testimony to the honesty of the Diamond Fields. The following police notice clearly shows how unclaimed, recovered, stolen diamonds were treated by the police.

NOTICE

The undermentioned rough and uncut diamonds having from time to time been recovered by this Department, notice is hereby given to all whom it may concern, that unless proof of the bona fide right to the possession of such diamonds be given, or a proper permit for the same be produced within ten days from the date hereof, such diamonds will be sold and the proceeds of such sale carried to the account of the Government.

John Fry.
Chief of Detective Department of Griqualand West.

May 24, 1883.

Underneath this notice was a list showing the number of carats, from whom recovered, how acquired. The number of carats ranged from ½ carat to 6,375 carats in the possession of one man, and the total number was 8,443 carats recovered from fifty persons. Two days later a similar notice stated that 1,573½ carats had been found in the possession of a well-known illicit diamond buyer. The total value of the two lots was nearly £40,000.

Even in Kimberley gaol I.D.B. was very active, white prisoners receiving money from visiting friends to buy stolen diamonds secreted by native convicts. Some white illicit diamond buyers did not scruple to employ native or coloured mistresses to undertake the more dangerous tasks of their criminal activities. Despite the loyalty and affection these women often showed, at best they got no reward beyond their bread and butter and soon afterwards dismissal to the streets. The story of the well-educated society man familiar with the leading European capitals, who in Kimberley had a coloured mistress, the mother of his child, and who deserted them to live luxuriously in Europe after his mistress had not only nursed him through a dangerous illness and supported him by her diamond thefts, but also made him rich for life, is but one instance out of many of brutal baseness in I.D.B.

So dishonest an activity as I.D.B. inevitably carried other vices in its train. Some of those drawn into the traffic were originally decent persons who had come to the Fields without aptitude for such a life, without business training or any other means of earning their living honestly in Kimberley. After wandering about 'like lost sheep', they fell in with idlers and gamblers, finally becoming tools of illicit diamond buyers. The continual mental strain, the ever-present possibility of spending the rest of their lives at work on Cape Town's breakwater, soon led them to drink and dissipation, and then disaster was seldom averted, for no drunkard could outwit the police for long. Some of the I.D.B. devotees, however, are said to have been entirely honest in all other matters, to have shown generosity to the poor and fallen, and indeed to have been 'incapable of a base action'! Doubtless a choice minority in that community!

That the innocent should at times have suffered for the guilty was almost inevitable in such an environment. Charges brought to the police against individuals were as likely to be the result of spite as of a disinterested pursuit of virtue, while a pretty wife, particularly if her affections wandered at times, could be to the husband a very real source of danger. Information came to the police from all sources: enemies, friends, women rivals, prostitutes, even from minor I.D.B.s themselves, caught by the police and released only on condition that they helped to secure the arrest of more important criminals. Some of the police too were dishonest, could be bribed, or even practised I.D.B. themselves. The detectives hid everywhere: on roofs, in cupboards, under beds, wherever opportunity offered a post of vantage. They made friends with suspects, and an evening's drinking between a detective and his 'friend' might well end with the latter being handcuffed and conducted to the local gaol.

The possibilities of sexual exploitation of such a situation are too obvious to need detailed comment. 'Friendly' relations between detectives and women both white and black, whether as relaxation or in the stern pursuit of duty, were inevitable. Sometimes, far from assisting the cause of justice, they frustrated it. An illicit diamond buyer who, on entering the bedroom of one of his white women-clients to complete a deal, found a detective had preceded him, and turning hastily and tremblingly away to make his escape, was reassured by the detective who, regarding the ceiling stonily to observe nothing below, remarked sweetly, 'Oh, never mind me!' The benefits obtained by some of these ladies were sufficiently substantial to set them up in Europe as well-to-do persons.

At times both I.D.B. and attempts to prevent it misfired, with unfortunate effects. For example, a master, suspecting the honesty of his black servants, employed a very honest Hottentot to act for him as a decoy and tempt the servants with diamonds he provided for the occasion. The servants, however, mistaking the unfortunate decoy for a genuine diamond thief, denounced him publicly, and before the master could come to save him, the Hottentot was severely flogged and barely escaped lynching. Another occasion when justice was too hasty, occurred when a native servant, secretly practising I.D.B. without his master's knowledge, was discovered, and the indignant crowd, mistakenly believing 'like master like man' in reverse, almost burned down the innocent man's store.

Nor could masters always be sure that their attempts to test the honesty of their servants might not in other ways recoil upon themselves. To put rock crystal secretly in the stuff to be sorted, and, if it disappeared, to assume the servants had mistaken it for a diamond and had stolen it, was all very well. But as likely as not, a police search would prove fruitless and immediately afterwards all the servants would disappear. However, the fact that many diggers left their servants unwatched, suggests their general honesty.[1]

[1] Many comments, however, state the very opposite. See Chapter 8.

In 1891, when Lord Randolph Churchill visited the Diamond Fields, he was particularly impressed by the peculiar legislation for the suppression of I.D.B. 'The special character of this industry has produced some rather curious legislation. In order to protect the diamond industry – an industry in which the product is at once so valuable and so portable – the Cape Parliament has passed a series of enactments which have created a statutory crime known as "Illicit Diamond Buying", and this crime is punished with remarkable severity. The ordinary presumption of the law in favour of the innocence of the accused is abolished, and a man is liable to a maximum penalty of fifteen years' penal servitude for merely neglecting to report to the proper quarter, and at once, a diamond which he may have chanced to have found. In the case of the native employees extraordinary precautions are taken. During the term of their service, for three months or more, they are treated as prisoners. Every day they are stripped and searched on leaving the mines, and for a week before the conclusion of their contract they are isolated and subjected to a *régime* which makes a theft of diamonds a physical impossibility.'

By that time, of course, the system of compounds introduced in this later industrialized period was in force. By this means, stealing was more difficult; no longer could the natives roam the mines at night, and peace and order were much assisted. In addition, good food and lodging was provided in the compounds for the natives, drunkenness was checked, restrictions essential to common security were enforced, and steady industry promoted.

Nevertheless, despite compounds, stealing continued on such a scale, that as a final means of preventing valuable stones from passing outside the compounds, where discovery would be more difficult, De Beers, acting on a suggestion of Cecil Rhodes, arranged to buy back stolen diamonds from the natives, believing that it was better to buy them back cheaply than not only to lose them, but also to have to face the competition of the cheap stolen-diamond market in other hands. Trained native detectives were employed to this end in the mines and compounds, not only to buy back stolen diamonds, but also to prevent thieving by giving the native diggers 10 per cent of the value of all the diamonds they found, if they brought them at once to the overseer.

In the case of the stolen diamonds, however, the method was this. To the thief who evaded all their various precautions up to the last one in the compound, they offered purchase of the stone, immunity from prosecution or punishment, a handsome reward and release from his labour contract on the condition that before attempting to pass his diamond across the compound defences, he should voluntarily report his theft to a responsible official and surrender the stone in return for the purchase-money, the reward and freedom to go. It was rightly judged that such thieves would generally prefer to accept the offer, knowing how much they would otherwise be at the mercy of illicit buyers and must face all the risks and penalties of detection. Nor were they ignorant of the fact that the bigger and more valuable the diamond, the greater was the risk of discovery, and the greater was the difficulty of disposing of it.

By this system, too, the induced honesty of the natives who voluntarily surrendered their stolen stones came in conflict with the interests of the I.D.B. detectives who also obtained rewards for detecting the undeclared diamonds. An astute thief, knowing himself to be thus suspected, might evade the police in the mine until he could pass his theft to an outside accomplice, or, frustrated, declare it in the right quarter as a voluntary action. One thief who acted thus is said to have stolen the famous Excelsior diamond and to have evaded the police by suddenly disappearing in the fastnesses of the mine, only to reappear that night at the office, receive his reward of £500, a horse, saddle and bridle and a pass home, after which he rode away. At that time it was the biggest diamond in the world of the first quality, and the reward the police would have received would have been great also. So the diamond was bought back, just before midnight on 30 June 1893. Had it been sold a few minutes later, it would have become the property of different owners who at midnight by previous agreement became proprietors of the mine.

Trollope's opinion of the dealers in stolen diamonds in Kimberley, and of the whole ethos of I.D.B. is interesting both for the details he mentions and not less for the revelation it provides of his own attitude to it as an 'outsider':—

'The diamond dealers whom I saw were the honest men who keep their heads well above water, and live in the odour of diamond sanctity, dealing only with licensed diggers and loving the law. But there are diamond dealers who buy from the Kaffirs – or from intermediate rogues who instigate the Kaffirs to steal. These are regarded as the curse of the place, and, as may be understood, their existence is most injurious to the interests of all who traffic honestly in this article. The law is very severe on them, imprisoning them, and subjecting them to lashes if in any case it can be proved that a delinquent has instigated a Kaffir to steal. One such dealer I saw in the Kimberley gaol, a good-looking young man who had to pass I think two years in durance among black thieves and white thieves because he had bought dishonestly. I pitied him because he was clean. But I ought to have pitied him the less because having been brought up to be clean, he, nevertheless, had become a rogue.'

Trollope's visit to the diamond dealers at least made him realize the temptations to I.D.B. himself. 'The various diamond shops to which I was taken were near the mine, or in the streets leading down from the mine to the square. These were little counting houses in which the dealers would sit, generally two together, loosely handling property worth many thousands of pounds. I was taken to them to see diamonds and saw diamonds without stint. It seemed that one partner would buy while another would sort and pack. Parcel after parcel was opened for me . . . I could not but think how easy it would be to put just one big one into my pocket. The dealers, probably, were careful that I did nothing of the kind.'

Trollope's belief that the mails carrying diamonds to Cape Town were never robbed was mistaken, but it is surprising, particularly in the circumstances he describes, that robberies were so few. 'The stones were packed in paper parcels, each parcel containing perhaps from fifty to two hundred according to their size. Then four or five of these parcels would be fitted into a paper box – which would again be enclosed in a paper envelope. Without other safeguard than this the parcels are registered and sent by post, to London, Paris or Amsterdam as the case may be. By far the greater number go to London. The mails containing these diamonds then travel for six days and six nights on mail carts to Cape Town – for four-fifths of the way without any guard, and very frequently with no one on the mail cart except the black boy who drives it. The cart travels day and night along desolate roads and is often many miles distant from the nearest habitation. Why the mails are not robbed I cannot tell. The diamond dealers say that the robber could not get away with his plunder, and would find no market for it were he to do so. They, however, secure themselves by some system of insurance . . . I should have thought that property of such immense value would have paid for an armed escort. The gold in Australia, which is much less portable, is always accompanied by an escort.

'I was soon sick of looking at diamonds though the idea of holding ten or twenty thousand pounds lightly between my fingers did not quite lose its charm. . . . And these dealers when the stones are brought to them for purchase, have no certain standard of value by which to regulate their transactions with their customers. The man behind the counter will take the stones, one by one, examine them, weigh them, and then make his offer for the parcel. . . . A dealer offers £500 when the buyer has perhaps expected £2,000! And yet the dealer is probably nearest to the mark. The diamonds at any rate are bought and sold, and are sent away by post at the rate of about £2,000,000 in the year. In 1876 the registered export of diamonds from Kimberley amounted in value to £1,414,590 and reached 773 pounds avoirdupois in weight. But it is computed that not above three quarters of what are sent from the place are recorded in the accounts that are kept. There is no law to make such record necessary. Anyone who has become legally possessed of a diamond may legally take it or send it away as he pleases.'

While Trollope was examining the diamonds, a kopje-walloper of Kimberley was not less intently scrutinizing the famous author, and has left us this interesting and obviously accurate description of what he saw: 'The fame of the diamond fields having spread round the world, distinguished men favoured Kimberley with their presence, amongst them Anthony Trollope. He visited sundry offices there, where he was shown large parcels of diamonds, at which he gaped in astonishment and then through his spectacles glinted suspiciously round at the partners present as though he was hoping they had come to these riches honestly. Once was exhibited for his edification a huge collection of yellow stones, all larger than plovers' eggs. He almost gasped with astonishment and ejaculated "Bless my soul! Bless my soul! I could not have believed it."'

The observer, though an admirer of Trollope the novelist, found his personality less attractive: 'particularly brusque and gruff, and if he could write like an angel, he didn't talk like one. He appeared to have a somewhat coarse manner, and there was a vehement roughness in his strongly expressed and contradictory opinions, which he uttered in blustering fashion, enough to crush at once, and for ever, any opposition to his views. He certainly didn't court flattery, and became restless when it was ladled out to him; but I'd have pitied the men who had the temerity to criticize him.' But, far from criticism, Trollope received from the inhabitants of Kimberley, as our observer also noted, 'much congratulation on the success of his books, especially by those gentlemen who had never heard of them'. Trollope, staying with VIPs and important officials, was probably in some degree suffering from the temporary egomania which sometimes afflicts visitors to South Africa, intensified in his case by his tendency to regard diamonds and diamond-digging as temptations of the Devil.

But despite all precautions, laws, punishments and blandishments, not to mention moral disapproval, I.D.B. continued and continues to flourish. When in those early days one of the comparatively rare convictions in court occurred and the thief was given a heavy sentence, the enthusiasm of the watching public was extreme. When one dishonest dealer was sentenced to three years' imprisonment, loud applause filled the court and rejoicings outside were very audible within. Yet even many who came to support laws for the suppression of I.D.B. had profited by it before they were wealthy enough to be converted to better ways. As the genial Kimberley crowds asserted, chanting an old music-hall song as they promenaded the streets, 'They all do it!'

7
Climate, Health, Religion

WITH almost complete unanimity the diggers praised the climate of the Diamond Fields as healthy and bracing: 'very healthy', even 'gloriously healthy'. 'Those days were entrancing; the gloriously healthy climate filled our young, well-trained bodies with a *joie de vivre* indescribable. We worked by the sun, fourteen hours in that blazing orb at midsummer, decreasing to ten hours on the shortest day in winter. . . . We heartily enjoyed every moment of those active days, in which brain and body worked at concert pitch. One felt a sense of daily accomplishment, exhilarating to any right-minded being.'

Some, however, are less enthusiastic: 'not absolutely unhealthy, but in many respects extremely trying to newly arrived Europeans'. In fact, many of the diggers' experiences throw doubt upon the more rapturous commendations, at least to the extent of distinguishing between the 'healthy' and the comfortable or pleasant. 'A mere existence,' wrote a newcomer from the river, 'requiring fortitude and money to sustain and luck to endure.'

The health of the diggers was on the whole good. Both this good health and the sudden and extreme changes of temperature which many found so trying were fundamentally due to the position of the Diamond Fields, situated as they were on an elevated plateau, 4,000 feet above sea-level. On the other hand, the periods of widespread illness, which occurred particularly in the summer, appear to have been due to the terribly insanitary state of the camp in those early days, rather than to the climate. Some common ailments, such as sore eyes and hands (an 'occupational disease' of digging), were intensified by climatic conditions of heat, dust and sand, when hot winds brought clouds of red dust from the veldt and mixed it with that perpetually rising from the mines.[1]

What Nature inflicted upon the diggers was less disease than temporary

[1] Cf. Beet, p. 19: 'Our first peep at the famous Du Toit's Pan was certainly unsatisfactory; little was to be seen but dense masses of fine dust ascending heavenward.'

inconvenience, though at times this became actual physical suffering, through excessive heat or cold, and thunder and rain-storms. It was not pleasant when the wind filled the air with dust and sand and blew down the diggers' tents, or when the rain drove them from their claims. Nevertheless, the dry air was good for consumptives, and the clear winter days were invigorating, despite their extremes of heat and cold. Whatever the sickness on the Diamond Fields in general, it was due to the negligence of man, rather than to the malevolence of Nature.

Yet even in 1877, when the early insanitary conditions of Kimberley had been abolished, Trollope complained bitterly of climatic influences upon himself.

'During my sojourn at Kimberley though I was the recipient of the kindest hospitality, and met two or three whom I shall ever remember among the pleasant acquaintances of my life – yet the place itself was distasteful to me in the extreme. When I was there the heat was very great, the thermometer registering 106 in the sun, and 97 in the shade. I was not absolutely ill, but I was so nearly ill that I was in fear the whole time. Perhaps having been in such personal discomfort, I am not a fair judge of the place. But an atmosphere composed of dust and flies cannot be pleasant – of dust so thick that the sufferer fears to remove it lest the raising of it may aggravate the evil, and of flies so numerous that one hardly dares to slaughter them by the ordinary means lest their dead bodies be noisome. When a gust of wind would bring the dust in a cloud hiding everything, a cloud so thick that it would seem that the solid surface of the earth had risen diluted into the air, and when flies had rendered occupation altogether impossible, I would be told, when complaining, that I ought to be there, in December say, or February – at some other time of the year than that then present – if I really wanted to see what flies and dust could do. I sometimes thought that the people of Kimberley were proud of their flies and their dust.'

Whatever the later inhabitants of Kimberley thought of their flies and dust, the early diggers were by no means proud of them. Flies and dust were two of the greatest curses of the diamond camps, making the summer heat infinitely more distressing. These flies in fact were horrible. They came in myriads, big and little and of various kinds, 'settling on humans with a grip like a sting'. They swarmed into the tents, prevented the miners' afternoon siesta, spoilt every article of food or drink not closely covered, and indeed even when covered, for generally, when the meat was put into a tin for protection, one or two flies got in unseen at the same time, and when the tin was opened on the following day, the meat was found to be flyblown.

Digger after digger witnesses to the fear and hatred the flies inspired. 'The flies', writes one, 'are of two kinds: a little black fellow, like the common house fly of Europe, and a rather large, bright green fellow; the latter the more endurable insect of the two, because he very seldom settles on the person or attacks the face, in which the little black beast is most pertinacious.' 'Horrible insects' he calls them, and after describing the rotten carcases of animals lying about the camps, on which the flies settled in clouds, he adds: 'The horror felt at the contact of a fly can be easily imagined.'

'They are far more aggressive than the European insect, they come at you with a loud threatening buzz, and their contact is exceedingly irritating, producing almost the sensation of an actual sting. Moreover, they are particularly fond of plunging into the corners of your eyes, and sticking there if you will let them, or into your ears, nose, etc.' 'I must speak of the flies, for at this moment they began to put us in terror of our lives. The canvas walls of the canteen were black beneath their hosts. Dishes and drink choked with them. They actually bit our flesh and drained our mortal juices. . . . The horror of illness was more than doubled by this plague. We, hale men, grew sick with the terror and nausea of them. What must poor sick fellows have suffered!'

Thus in the dust and heat of summer, while the canteens drove a roaring trade, the diggers, often assisted by their wives and children, worked at the sorting tables under improvised awnings of rugs and blankets, with a 'scraper' in one hand and in the other the tail of a horse, or cow or wildebeest with which they tried to keep the flies at bay.

Nor were flies by any means the only insect plague: 'Our tent swarms with the most ferocious flies; fleas annoy us now and then; and today we are invaded by black ants, and they don't seem to mind hot water.' 'Fleas were a plague,' writes another: 'It was the morning after the night before that one's body bore evidence of the innumerable bites of these pests.'

Most of the diggers at one time or another suffered from one or more of the vocational diseases which affected eyes and limbs, the former being ophthalmic, the latter pustulous. The sores, which broke out especially on the hands and arms, discharged pus, sometimes formed even when there was no scratch to start them, and took several weeks to heal. The diggers' complaints of these ailments are many and emphatic. 'Working in the mines in this particular earth's spot of sin and sorrow and sore eyes was hardship indeed. A slight break in the skin would speedily develop under the festering attentions of myriads of poisonous flies into a villainous wound, and to the hundreds who suffered from ophthalmia caused by fearful and nearly ever-present dust storms, conditions must have been torture indeed.'

The sorting process was a chief cause of eye disease. Sitting all day beneath the hottest of suns with eyes fixed on grey-white gravel, in the current mostly of some four or five riddles sending out ceaseless clouds of lime, the sorters were particularly exposed to this complaint. Many wore goggles of wire or gauze, but seldom before the mischief was done. Some imputed the prevalent ophthalmia principally to the flies. Whatever the cause, the effect upon the appearance of many diggers was only too obvious: men 'from the sorting table, with faces white and blood-shot eyes. Nearly all the "working" men are badly scarred on hands and arms. The slightest scratch will fester when the poisonous, limey sand gets into it.'

Nor were the really serious diseases, such as dysentery and enteric fever, primarily due to the climate. For these, apart from the great heat in summer, the appallingly insanitary condition of the camps in this early time was responsible. Again and again diggers complain of the defective sanitation and of the bad water, which was also held responsible for much of the prevalent sickness. 'Abominable defective sanitary arrangements'; 'abominable deficiency of all sanitary arrangements'; 'the public latrines were huge open trenches, lying in many cases in the midst of the tents'; such are a few of the many condemnatory comments which strew the pages of the diggers' memoirs. We need not, therefore, question the probable accuracy of the following: 'It is time something was done, for in certain parts of the camps the stench is dreadful – almost sufficient to knock me down. Surely if this continues we will be visited by some pestilent disease.'

Not less insanitary and pestiferous were the rotting carcases lying about the camp. 'Sheep and goats are slaughtered alongside the tents, the offal is allowed either to fester in the sun, or dragged about the camps by packs of half-starved cur dogs' – that is, such offal as the natives had not already seized and eaten. Outside the camps were 'hundreds of carcases of cattle which have died of different diseases, in different stages of putrefaction'. Inevitably diarrhoea, dysentery, and enteric or 'diamond-field fever' were prevalent in the hot months.

The summer of 1871 was a time of widespread illness. 'Many down with enteric, doctors were plentiful enough, but there was no hospital, and nurses were unknown.' Rumours, many exaggerated, of extensive disease and many deaths were flying about the camps. Nor must we forget the general insanitary way of life of the natives and its dangers for themselves and for the rest. 'We had a sensation at Bultfontein today, of the most unpleasant kind; a Kaffir boy fell dead across the kitchen threshold: he had been ill of a slow fever about two weeks past, but no one had thought the matter serious. Shortly afterwards, my attention thus abruptly called to the sanitary condition of the camp, I find the air to be full of gruesome rumours. The belle of Dutoitspan lies dying of virulent typhus; a woman was brought in from the veldt this morning, dead long since, with a bundle untouched beside her; a well-known digger has died today, another lady is given up. New Rush appears to be one great hospital. . . . We had great difficulty in getting our poor Kaffir buried.' However, these fears of some dreadful epidemic proved unfounded. Nevertheless, these diseases claimed many victims. 'Many healthy young men of good physique, who come to the diamond fields full of hope and confidence of "making good", succumbed to the dread disease [enteric fever], among them some young officers of Imperial regiments . . . who had been granted leave to try their luck. . . .'

One result of this unhappy summer of 1871 was the vigorous prosecution of plans for the foundation of hospitals on the Fields. In September: 'The rate of mortality in the camps is rather on the increase. The necessity for speedily providing good hospital accommodation and sanitary arrangements is becoming a topic of general discussion, and I believe proper measures will at once be taken for the carrying out of both these objects.'

Nor was the foundation of hospitals the only planned innovation; closely associated were plans for the building of churches on the Fields. One result of the general social spirit of the river camps had been their respect for religion and the various churches. Churches of several denominations had been extemporized or built very quickly by the river diggers, and the Berlin Missionary Society had established its station near Pniel long before the discovery of diamonds.

The dry diggings were no more to be outshone by the river diggers in religious zeal than they had been in diamantine. Even as early as mid-September 1871: 'The Bishop of Bloemfontein is here, earnestly advocating the erection of a suitable Church, and funds are being rapidly subscribed; a Hospital too, which will be sorely needed, is getting liberal support.' A week later: 'Dutoitspan and the neighbouring camps are busy with church and hospital schemes, and subscriptions and money are forthcoming in abundance for all these good purposes.'

The strict observance of Sunday as a 'holy day', to be devoted to public and private worship and abstention from all mundane tasks, then enforced in England by both law and custom, was almost automatically continued on the Diamond Fields, at least to the extent of abandoning for the day the frantic pursuit of diamonds. Many indeed attended at least one religious service on Sundays, and the Boers were notable for their love of psalm-singing and church meetings. Non-church-goers went their own ways, repairing tents and equipment, or going into the country – always with an eye for stray diamonds. Even little children playing about the camps often picked them up, and there was hardly a child above five years of age who could not distinguish a crystal or artfully broken bit of glass from the real thing.

Nevertheless, whatever the minor deviations, the general unanimity with which Sunday observance was accepted by the mass of diggers was remarkable. 'Without conference, consultation, fixed law, or framed regulation every man knocked off work on Saturday night and made his appearance on Sunday morning, no matter how high the Saturday night jinks had reached, washed and brushed and with as much of a Sunday-going-to-meeting look about him as circumstances admitted. This Sunday observance was voluntary, not brought about by clerical influence, and it must be remembered that of the thousands of diggers not a few were men who had been roughing it all their lives, who seldom talked of religion, never affected piety, and the majority of them had made no pretence of being church or chapel goers when living in cities, towns or villages.

'It is true that they visited bars and liquored up on a Sunday all the same, but there was neither card nor billiard playing. They left off work and put on a Sunday appearance which was the extent of their Sunday observance, but still observance of the day, which was very remarkable seeing that every one of them was engaged in a race for wealth, and it involved a loss of one seventh of the time they had at their disposal for the getting that which they had come hundreds of miles to get. Sundays hung very heavily on the hands of these diggers, and the observance could not have lasted long in this fashion.' But as in England, many relieved the dullness of such Sundays by visiting friends. The 'luck' of the preceding week was, of course, discussed.

Temporary clergy at the river were soon succeeded by resident chaplains. The first marriage ceremony among the river diggers which the first Church of England chaplain was called upon to perform, was that of a young coloured couple, and the diggers decided to celebrate it in fine style. The 'church' was also the 'Rectory': the chaplain's residence, a one-roomed wattle-and-daub hut, originally intended for the local prison. The bridal couple were far from ignoring the demands of fashion. The sixteen-

Morning market, Kimberley, 1880-5, with the ubiquitous 'Cape Carts'

De Beers Boys 1890

Klipdrift High Court and public offices 1872-5

President Stafford Parker of the Diggers' Republic

year-old bride was dressed in blue silk with lace tippet and a bridal veil. The bridegroom wore a fashionable morning coat, lavender-coloured trousers, a white waistcoat, a sky-blue tie, patent-leather boots and a black silk hat. Both wore white kid gloves.

The diggers decorated the walls of the 'Rectory' which could accommodate only the chaplain, the bridal pair and their best man, with evergreen from the willows overhanging the river. While the ceremony was taking place, the diggers crowded quietly round the building, and at the end, when the two became man and wife, they cheered so heartily that the diggers across the river joined in. Then the diggers entertained the couple at a local canteen and sent them off on their honeymoon with vociferous good wishes. 'And,' wrote the 'best man', 'it must be said to the credit of the diggers who took part in this festal celebration, that they were as respectful to the bride as if she had been a sprig of nobility, and not an unseemly word was spoken in her presence. . . .'[1]

In Kimberley, even in the first year of its existence, a Wesleyan church was built, and soon afterwards an Anglican. Trollope, who observed with approval that churches were 'provided plentifully' by the town, also praised the sermon he heard as 'much in advance of those which I call the sermon at sermon par.' But he was worried by the preacher's wearing an enigmatical green ribbon.

Almost immediately after these first moves other churches appeared, and were well attended. As early as February 1872: 'We have four churches in Dutoitspan at this time, English, Calvinistic, Roman Catholic and Independent – very.' The 'Calvinistic' was doubtless the new Dutch church recently built. The number of Roman Catholics was considered 'surprisingly large' for 'a land so thoroughly Dutch'. The social aspects of church life, when they took the form of a 'musical entertainment' for the English Church Fund and a 'grand bazaar' in aid of the Dutch Reformed Church, were especially appreciated by the diggers, who showed in all such ecclesiastical festivities an admirable theological tolerance.

In the meantime the building of hospitals did not lag behind that of the churches. By the end of the year, such was the speed attained, there was a hospital at Kimberley, another at Klipdrift, a 'Catholic Hospital' at Bultfontein, and a 'Diggers' Central Hospital' at Dutoitspan. 'The hospitals', declares one diarist, 'are much needed at times by poorer diggers when suddenly ill, out of work and without friends or relatives.'

The condition of such, left sick and solitary in their tents, reveals itself intimately in this same writer's diary, when he lay ill with dysentery during

---

[1] For a much less respectful treatment of a wedding party, v. *infra*, p. 216.

the unhappy spring and summer of 1871: 'From the 5th of October to the 5th of November I find a total blank in my diary, for during that time I was prostrated by low fever, being delirious several nights and parts of days; dysentery and very severe diarrhoea came on before the fever left me. I got hardly any rest or proper food, and lay in profound misery on my straw mattress, sweltering in heat, tormented by legions of green and black flies, which I now and then had energy enough to flick away from my face with a wildebeest's tail as they came swiftly on me with a hideously loud buzzing, making most pertinacious attacks on the corners of my eyes, my nose, and mouth. It was so hot that I could not bear any covering over my face. Sometimes, too, I was without water. With very few exceptions, which I shall ever gratefully remember, almost everyone was too much engrossed in the incessant, eager, hurrying work of the Rush to think for a moment of a poor fever-stricken wretch. Had it not been for the great kindness of two good Samaritans, fellow passengers from England, I should have fared badly indeed.

'After making several attempts to fight against the effects of the combined fever and diarrhoea, and crawling feebly about on a stick, hardly recognized by many of my associates – such a lank, hollow-eyed skeleton was I – I at length determined to remove to the riverside at Pniel till I recovered a little of the strength I felt I could never regain in the pestilential air of the New Rush with its filth and bad water.' And a little later, safe in Pniel, he added: 'I heard of many more cases of sickness – one death – in a very short time, from the same disease which had attacked me, and felt happy to be away from the camp.' 'The summer of 1872 will, I trust, be less fatal than that of 1871,' he wrote a little later, and in a briefly noted survey of the health conditions at the Fields, 'principal ailments this summer are – low fever, acute diarrhoea and dysentery, colic, inflammation of the lungs, and a very mild form of scurvy – some deaths from intemperance of which there is a good deal – heat, dryness causing thirst, temptations offered by innumerable canteen keepers and total abstinence of all restraint. A young man who drinks is totally lost on the fields. Many who might have returned home in health and wealth now lie in a nameless grave on the veldt, beneath the black flag, killed by drink, which is totally incompatible with this climate.'

On the very day that the sufferer left for England, 5 December 1871, a Cape Town newspaper announced: 'Sickness at the Fields is terribly on the increase.' The following February another digger summed up the situation in a passage which incidentally reveals the humanitarianism of many diggers in a far better light than his predecessor suggests. 'There is more sickness on the Fields now than at the time of my arrival. Beyond doubt these fiery but open plains are amongst the unhealthiest parts of the world. There is everything to contend against: reckless disregard of sanitary rules on the diggers' part, and a somewhat lax supervision from the police, bad food, insufficiency of vegetables, bad drink and too much of it; a debilitated constitution on the part of many people; empirical doctoring, and not enough of that; drugs of a bad class, and woeful deficiency of them; lack of all strengthening and tempting diet. The kindness of men to one another is no novelty in suchlike situations. I know of parties which have kept an invalid for months – more than a year in a certain case, feeding and doctoring him with every care the fields could furnish, never leaving him alone. The mortality, considering all things, is astonishingly small. Nine died last week, grown men, by accident or disease in all this camp of no one knows how many thousand inhabitants, tent dwellers, in an atmosphere polluted by open wells of filth, and carcases decaying. Children suffer more, but there do not appear to be so many of them as formerly.'

Five years later Trollope found a very different provision of medical services in Kimberley, one of the few elements there which, including particularly the nurses, won his unqualified approval. 'There are hospitals which have caused infinite labour and are now successful – especially one which is nearly self-supporting and is managed exquisitely by one of those ladies who go out into the world to do good wherever good may be done. I felt as I spoke to her that I was speaking to one of the sweet ones of the earth. To bind up a man's wounds, or to search for diamonds in the dirt! There is a wide difference there certainly.' But Trollope apparently overlooked the fact that without the diamonds there would have been no hospital.

Even at its best, life in early Kimberley was no bed of roses. Dust storms and flies, tropical lightning and rain which flattened tents and sometimes even the weaker wooden hovels, lack of individual privacy, inevitable in such circumstances, frequent scarcity of food and water, dangers of 'camp fever' and similar diseases, led many to abandon their hopes of wealth and quit the Fields. Yet despite such drawbacks, the mass of evidence insists upon the extraordinary general healthiness of the camps even in the height of summer, and the tougher type of digger, cheered by the prospect of a rich claim and 'good luck', would forget all local evils and continue a task which at any moment might, as by a magician's wand, convert toil and often poverty into wealth and luxury 'beyond the dreams of avarice'.

The winter months, May, June and July, were on the whole the pleasantest of the year. The nights were cold; so cold that the veldt round the camps was often white and glistening with thick hoar-frost, and even the water in buckets outside the tents and the cold tea inside froze, while horse-riders wrapped sacking round their stirrup-irons to save their feet from frost-bite. But with sunrise the air began to warm and soon the early morning ushered in a pleasantly hot day, not too hot for sustained physical activity. This was the best time of the year for work with enjoyment; the diggers, however unmusical, would at times break into song in sheer light-heartedness. During the occasional rain-storms and cloudy, overcast days of winter, rare and of short duration but very cold, the claims were deserted, and hotels and canteens crowded with convivial diggers. Most days, however, were cloudless, and the sun powerful, causing light head-gear such as broad-brimmed straw hats with light muslin puggarees, and pith helmets to be worn.

How great and rapid the changes of temperature were, the following complaint shows: 'There is one thing the new comers grumble at, and that is the weather. They say they came out to South Africa expecting to be "frizzled"; but they did not bargain for being frozen. Now we have had some very keen frosts lately, even to finding water frozen inside our tents of a morning; and fancy getting up and lighting a fire at daybreak then, with the bullock dung all over hoar frost and refusing to be lighted, while the unhappy digger stamps about with icy feet and blue fingers. But in a couple of hours what a change! Such is the clearness of the sky and the power of the sun, that by nine o'clock all is warm and glowing; and I can sit on my little heap and sort with a light canvas jacket on, and no collar or necktie. Collars are a good deal worn on Sundays.'

Winter was also the shooting season, for there was a very fair choice of game near the camps, and from De Beers and the Colesberg Kopje very pleasant and successful shooting excursions were made. 'Some of the aristocratic diggers of those camps see no harm in turning out with horses and dogs on Sundays, and organising a *chasse* on a large scale, the result of which is that many a buck, hare, bustard and partridge may next day be seen hanging among the legs of mutton and pieces of beef on the big mimosas outside their tents, which form their winter larders. The wooded banks of the Vaal provided an abundance of guinea-fowl, wild ducks, sometimes even wild geese, and plenty of smaller game, while good fishing could be had at both the Vaal and Modder rivers.

In the spring, which included the months of August, September and October, the weather was generally bearable enough, the days hot but not oppressive. The nights and early mornings were still cold, sometimes still with a light frost.

Throughout the summer months a strong wind was nearly always blowing, while often a hot north-west wind from the Kalahari desert enveloped the camps in a cloud of horrible, clinging, red dust. If no wind blew, the heat became sultry and stifling, making exercise almost impossible, and even breathing difficult.

The ever-present dust rising in clouds from the mines, as day after day with little intermission the digging, hauling and sifting continued, was one of the greatest curses of the Diamond Fields, as many a disgusted digger complained. It was, as one wrote: 'to be classed with plague, pestilence and famine, and, if there is anything worse, with that also'. When the wind from the Kalahari desert brought the red dust to the Fields, it and the white dust from the mines formed vicious clouds, amidst which the diggers had to go about their work 'with eyes smarting and lungs oppressed by it'. The two kinds of dust were equally objectionable. 'The supply of both', writes one observer, 'seems unlimited; they are both equally fine and penetrating, so much so as to stop a hunting watch; very few watches can be kept in order on the Fields, the works get clogged up in no time. As it is nearly always windy, our camps are generally enveloped in clouds of this irritating element.'

When the occasional whirlwinds arrived, a tall, revolving column of this dust swept through the camps, while everything light and loose, hats, papers, even sheepskins, were tossed high in the air. 'Wonderful,' Sir Lionel Phillips described these dust storms, and he continued with what is perhaps the best description of one: 'In a perfectly still air one could see a distant wall rise far away on the plain. In a few minutes it would be on us with a roar, darkening everything, filling one's eyes, nose, and ears, stinging one's face, forcing one to turn one's back upon it. Usually in ten or fifteen minutes the hurricane swept by, but it left behind gritty mouths, gritty food, and a thin layer of fine dust on everything. The streets were swept bare – a veritable scavenger. Often sheets of galvanized iron were torn from roofs or verandahs and hurled about like leaves of paper, to the peril of the passer-by. Wonderful whirlwinds frequently rose at that season. Without any apparent reason, a small pillar of dust, revolving at high speed, would come into being, growing in dimensions as it gained momentum, and carrying upwards in its gyrations anything in the shape of old tins or other similar unattached articles in its path. The column would rise high above the earth and travel on its giddy course without any apparent cause, for it was surrounded by still air, finally dying down from sheer exhaustion.' What this particular whirlwind could do was shown by its lifting one of the diamond buyers' little offices, a wooden frame and canvas affair, some fifteen feet by ten feet in area, and ten feet high, ten feet in the air, as it passed, while some hundreds of pounds' worth of diamonds that were being sorted there were scattered far and wide and mostly lost.

Another, and far worse dust storm, at Dutoitspan, has been described in such detail as to make it, even for the distant modern reader, a living experience: 'In the evening a dust storm raged over Dutoitspan. It is the commonest incident possible in this merry New Year time, but no habit can reconcile one to its recurrence. The day had been blazing hot, as usual. . . . There is a sort of aggressive heat on these fields. The sun does not shine in a friendly manner. It rages and blazes, and seems to delight in torturing poor people. We have no clouds on such a day as this. The sky is palely blue, with a lurid light on the horizon. Without warning or change of wind . . . one quarter of the heaven suddenly hides itself in a dun red mist. The distant line of mountains is swallowed up; the horizon vanishes. Then shouts and yells ascend from every group of Kaffirs on the slope. They scream to one another in high metallic notes. They shout and laugh in chorus awhile, answering from mound to mound and claim to claim, from one end of the kopje to the other. Dutoitspan, three hundred yards away, takes up the cry, and gathering figures crowd its lofty hillocks.

'Another moment, and they are scattered, black men and white, all making for their fragile tenements, shrieking and swearing, and shrilly hallooing. The great dun cloud sweeps on, heralded by sharp, fierce lifts of wind. An instant more and it is on us, a furious tornado of grey dust. Tents fill, and wrench, and struggle at their cords, striving to break away. Men cling, shouting to their strained tent-poles. They throw themselves on the ground, and grapple with the canvas, often to no avail. The bellying stuff breaks from them, and is whirled away, or snaps its pole and falls a struggling heap, or flies to ribbons in their hands. No man can help another. The area of one's vision is but a yard or two across, and beyond it are forms blurred and broken, like a picture smudged. The eyes are filled, and nose, and mouth, with poisonous dust that stings the flesh, so fiercely is it driven. The man overtaken before he has cleared the claims, scarce dares advance; for on every side are yawning holes, invisible until he stands on the very brink, where a sharper gust might cast him in. His coat is nigh turned inside out upon his shoulders if he face the storm, and if he show his back the wild wind drives him like a balloon. For ten minutes, or twenty, such are the pictures shrouded in that whirling veil of dust. When the tempest passes, the sun shines mercilessly out again. Men begin, swearing, to repair their damage. Kaffirs reseek the claims, laughing cheerily. Such a sudden fury has raged across the scene while I write. It is past now. The door that banged and rattled on its lock five minutes since, as if to rive the lintel down, stands wide open without a tremor. The driving sand, that beat like rain upon the glass, has all passed by. Nothing is left to tell the tale save the thick layer of dust upon my papers, and the dusky, lurid fog driving fast towards the distant hills.'

But far worse than these dry dust storms were the terrible, frequent and devastating thunderstorms which came with the spring and summer season. From November to the end of January and often much earlier, such storms were an almost daily occurrence, generally bursting over the camps about sundown. 'Often these storms were terrific, opening with the rising of a yellow streak above the horizon, and the rapid spreading over the blue sky dome of rolling masses of heavy, lurid clouds. Then from the coppery bosom of this pall there came such blazing streams of lightning in sheets and contorted shafts, such rending explosions of thunder peals, that the awful flare and crash would shake the nerves of hardened men. With this appalling discharge there poured from the clouds torrents of rain, or a volley of huge hailstones rattling on the canvas roofs and driving man and beast to the nearest shelter.'

'Many strong men grow nervous when they see the lurid coppery clouds gathering up to windward. Lightning so vivid and thunder so painfully loud I have hardly ever experienced elsewhere, but I am happy to say that fatal accidents are comparatively rare.' Nevertheless, accidents through lightning did happen, and not so 'rarely' as one might suppose. The diggers' records are studded with instances. Thus of three quick strokes of lightning (without rain), the first killed a mule at the brink of the Kimberley mine, the second killed two Europeans stretching a wire rope, and the third not only killed a native sifting gravel, but also melted the sieve: 'a shocking spectacle'. By the river the storms were even more violent; choosing one or two fatalities for reference among many, we read of five natives sleeping in a tent, three of whom were killed and the remaining two seriously injured; at Pniel five out of eight natives asleep in a bell tent, and lying head to head, were killed, while the remaining three were crippled for life.

Many of the diggers attempted a dubious security against such dangers by fixing lightning-rods or 'glass bottles on the iron spikes of their tent poles'. Sometimes these thunderstorms were accompanied by showers of huge hailstones, sometimes by terrific deluges of rain, which made all work on the claims impossible. In addition: 'These constant thunderstorms have a very weakening effect on the nervous system, except in men of very strong constitutions.' Nevertheless, he concedes one benefit: storms cool the air.

That they could occur not merely in the spring but even before the close of winter, the following extract from a digger's diary vividly shows, revealing also, far better than any general description can do, the vicissitudes of a digger's life: '*July 2nd, 1871*. Monday, very cold and windy – stuff damp from Sunday's rain and very difficult to sort. Tuesday, after heavy rains during night, stuff too wet to sift. Terrific thunderstorm and very heavy rain in evening. Wednesday, cloudy but no rain. Thursday, incessant pouring rain made work impossible and flooded most of the tents. Friday, awoke from my second night of sleeping in a puddle, to find that one side of the tent had blown in, and our rugs, blankets, provisions, etc., were all soaking with water and mud; and as we had not a bit of dry wood or even a dry match, we fled from the miserable scene in disgust, and betook ourselves to Benning and Martin's hotel, which we found crowded with "washed-out diggers". We breakfasted and dined there, and slept upon the table. Everybody being damp and cold and having no work to do, there was, of course, a good deal of hard drinking, and in the evening there was any amount of singing, music, and general fun and jollity. I am happy to say that, although I saw many who had taken too much Cape Smoke, there was no fighting, only a little rough horse-play now and then, and one or two attempts at rows. On Saturday it was fine again, but hardly any of the claims could be worked, except by washing, and most of our diggers are not provided with cradles for the wet work, dry-sifting being the regular thing at Dutoitspan.'

Seven weeks later, spring brings a combined dust- and thunder-storm: '*August 20th, 1871*. We had some very trying weather at the beginning of this month; it commenced with a furious gale of wind late one night. One corner of our tent was torn from its fastening; in rushed the wind with a cloud of dust, away flew the lid of our coffee tin, and dust and coffee, hideously commingled, were thickly spread over and amongst our blankets. We both had to get up many times that night, and rush out to fix extra fastenings. About 3 a.m. there was a thunderstorm, followed by a copious downfall of rain. Part of the tent collapsed, and I woke in the early dawn to find myself lying in three puddles, rain pouring in upon me, a chill blast driving over my face, and my blankets soaked through with rain and smeared with mud, the results of the aforesaid mixture of dust and ground coffee. I sat up shivering in the driest part of the tent that I could find, and my partner awoke and groaned dismally. Then we thought of Mark Tapley, and endeavoured to be jolly, but it was rather a failure.

'Still the wind howled and the rain poured down in torrents. We opened portmanteaus, got out dry clothes – for we were wet to the skin – and fled from the scene of desolation. We found refuge in a corrugated iron hotel, where we did ample justice to a very substantial breakfast. We found it [the tent] half down. Our newspapers and other light articles were flying all over the camp, and the whole interior of our tent, with a miscellaneous and muddy chaos of most heterogeneous articles, was exposed to the public gaze. Putting the tent up again in that gale being out of the question, we covered the things over with the loose canvas as well as we could, and took a precipitate departure from our desolate Lares and Penates, resolved to dwell in something more solid until fine weather returned. Many other tents were down, including the big church tent, and the hotels were all full of "washed out" diggers.

'Though it was Saturday, there were hardly any sales in the afternoon, the weather not permitting much open-air work. In the evening, however, there was an entertainment given by some talented amateurs on behalf of the funds of the English Church. The iron room in which it took place was crammed to suffocation with diggers in working dress, who besides hearing some capital songs both comic and sentimental, recitations, readings, an excellent impromptu stump speech, and a lecture on astronomy by our worthy pastor (I don't think we cared much for the last named), had the privilege of gazing modestly and reverentially of course, at the unusual apparition of two charming young ladies in evening dress, and several more in ordinary costume.

'Sunday again was a pouring wet day, but a temporary lull of wind and rain in the afternoon enabled us to get our tent up, though sleeping in it was out of the question. On Monday it began to clear up. During the week the weather was cold, fine, but windy, with three very sharp frosts and a hailstorm.'

Only four days later, another similar experience occurred: 'I did not think that so soon after despatching my last letter I should have to chronicle a recurrence of that awful weather which entails so much misery on poor diggers. On the evening of the 24th, after a storm of wind and dust all day which had rendered work impossible, and covered everything in our tent with a thick layer of red dust, the gale increased so much that we feared the tent would come down. Fastening after fastening gave way; we were soon almost smothered in dust; then the wind veered round, and rain poured down in torrents. In the morning, after an almost sleepless night, we found ourselves wet through, everything soaked and muddy, and the tent half down. Needless to say that we again had recourse to the friendly shelter of the hotels. But there was no fire in any of them. It was bitterly cold, and, having wet clothes on, we were in a state of "cold shivers" all day. Substantial meals slightly alleviated our misery, and in the evening, dropping into a store, we found two or three friends assembled round a piano, and heard some capital music and singing. I slept that night on a table in the principal hotel, with only one blanket over me, and was *not* comfortable. The weather improved a little the next day, and yesterday being quite fine, we came back to pitch the tent in a fresh place, and so securely that there would be no danger of it coming down in future.' And incidentally, as a fitting climax to this situation, they found that during their absence the tent had been robbed.

But these storms ended as suddenly as they began, and only four days later: 'The weather is lovely today, warm as an English July. The wives and daughters of lucky Boers are parading the camp in gorgeous apparel; tired diggers have been hard at work washing shirts all the morning, and now everybody feels fairly entitled to Sunday's rest and cleanliness.'

Throughout that week the day temperatures were in the eighties and nineties Fahrenheit, while the night temperatures fell from 40° into the twenties. The maximum day temperature was 93° while the minimum temperature of 28° was registered that same night.

Ten days after the last storm a whirlwind with its accompanying dust cloud swept through the camp as September began, but an hour or so later the digger's diary recorded: 'Weather still lovely and summer-like, only rather too hot for hard work and time approaching when many will have to leave the hot, glaring and dusty dry-sifting camps for the various river-side diggings.' A week later another storm momentarily eclipsed the brightness of the spring: 'A very pretty storm it was. The usual business; hurricanes, then dust storms, so that you could not see a yard before you for dust, then awfully vivid lightning and deep thunder, then torrents of rain, then more wind, and so on. This time our tent stood it bravely, though the rain came through in places, and we got but little sleep, the tent and everything in it shaking continuously. But yesterday morning it was quite fine again.' With the return of the good weather the diarist's spirits rose. His entry for the day, 10 September, ends on a note of positive gaiety: 'Spring time is coming; flowers are blooming on the veldt and birds are building their nests. A pair of saucy little fellows, like sparrows, have chosen the tent of a friend of mine as a residence.'

A week later the record runs: 'This has been a week of intense heat. Black men have discarded all clothing; white men would very much like to do the same. Awnings or large umbrellas have been erected over sorting tables, and "new chums" have been asking the portentous question, "If this is only the beginning of spring, what will the middle of summer be like?" ' But September was not to go out so peacefully. On the 29th he wrote: 'During the week we have had three thunderstorms, in one of which the lightning was painfully vivid, while the instantaneous and deafening explosions of the thunder were louder and more startling than I have ever heard before. The hot weather is fairly setting in now, and with it frequent storms and heavy rains, also plagues innumerable in the shape of flies, fleas, ants, etc.'

How devastating these storms were to social occasions can well be imagined. In 1871, the first wedding at the New Rush was not only spoiled by one, but barely avoided tragedy. For in the evening a dance was being given in an enormous circus tent which was blown down on the dancers when a sudden thunderstorm with heavy wind and torrential rain swept down upon it. The dancers lay flat on the ground beneath the canvas roof until it could be lifted, and when they emerged, 'their clothes, especially the ladies', were a sorry sight'. But the danger they had escaped was far greater than damage from falling tent-poles and tackle and heavy canvas, for only the fact that the rain had so soaked the canvas, prevented its catching fire as it fell on the many paraffin-lamps lighting the dance.

Another social occasion, this time a Sunday dinner at Mrs Brown's hotel and restaurant in October 1871, came to grief in a similar way. And once again a storm illuminates not only the diggers' troubles, but also new details of their way of life: 'We entered the big marquee which was Mrs. Brown's dining-saloon. It was a big tent supported by three strong poles, the table, flanked by rude benches, and, of course, quite innocent of a table-cloth, was capable of seating at least fifty persons. A long row of tin plates with stout knives and forks adorned it on each side, while here and there a cruet stand, a salt cellar, or a bottle of pickles, added ornament to the scene, and a promise of luxury to the dinner. It was early yet, only about half-past five, and Mrs Brown's dinner hour was six; still there were several diggers and merchants there, spruce in Sunday rig, the latter especially, all holding an animated conversation on the two pet subjects – diamonds and gold – with a slight reference now and then to fever and dysentery, quinine and chlorodyne, the sanitary condition of the camp, and the approaching annexation of the Fields.'

After an adjournment for drinks at the bar in an adjoining tent, the writer and his friends returned to the dining saloon: 'But it had all the time been quickly growing darker, the thunder louder, and the lightning more vivid, and now the usual premonitory gale was upon us. In an instant we, the table, and everything inside the tent, were covered with a thick coating of red dust, not ornamental to us, but still less improving to the salt and pepper. Then came a tremendous blast, several of the tent ropes gave way, and one of the big poles leaned over alarmingly. It was evident that if something were not done we should soon have the whole tent down upon us, and might very probably be suffocated; so, as nothing could be done outside in the midst of that fierce wind and impenetrable cloud of dust, several of the hungry diggers inside volunteered to stand by the poles. They leaped upon the strong tables, and three or four held stoutly to each wavering pole. Thus they had to remain, brave and patient caryatids, while the storm burst upon us in all its fury. The dust filled the inside of the tent so that one could not see across it. One little party of men were constantly employed in keeping the candles alight; all looked anxiously towards the windward side of the marquee, whose canvas flapped and whose poles creaked so ominously.

'After the dust came a furious downpour of rain, much of which leaked through the seams and trickled down the sides of the tent, here and there pattering down and making mud of the red dust that covered the table. But especially did it pour upon and trickle down the necks of the brave men who were holding up the tent poles, for in that part the wet canvas was flapping about them, and the rain leaked through, of course, far more than where it was still stretched taut. This rain lasted about half-an-hour. During the whole of the dust and rain storm the crashes of thunder had been deafening, the lightning simply terrific in its vivid blaze. Many of the expectant diners were avowedly nervous. And where was the dinner all this time? Cooking in a very frail little kitchen outside the tent, which was probably blown down, and surely the most enthusiastic cook could not stand by the fire in such a storm as that?

'Soon there came a lull, the wind fell eventually, the rain almost ceased. In an instant all was activity. Mr Brown and his assistants rushed out; hauled in guy-ropes, knocked in pegs, and soon had poles and canvas all firm and taut again; while inside the tent, a couple of men with buckets and huge cloths or swabs hastily washed down the long deal table and cleared it of dust, and performed the same kind of office to the benches on which we were shortly to sit. Plates, knives, forks, all had to be washed, salt-cellars to be replenished, but about half-an-hour after the original dinner-time an excellent meal was served, the only really noticeable result of the storm being that the meat was a little over-done. So diggers and buyers, strong men and invalids, all forgot their late troubles, and chatted gaily as they did justice to the good dinner, at which figured plenty of roast joints, a curry, some pies and a plum pudding. We inwardly congratulated ourselves, however, that the dinner had not been served before that horrid dust storm came on, in which case everything would have been spoilt.'

November, December and January, the summer months, brought great heat. At Pniel in early November the thermometer often stood at 100° Fahrenheit in the shade. The glare of the sun, reflected from the white limestone, light-coloured soil and the white canvas tents, would 'try head and eyes most severely'. With the advent of summer the storms even intensified: 'Half the population of the Fields had to hold on by poles and ropes like grim death during the time the storm lasted. In some cases holding on was no use. Bell tents went after bell tents by the score, especially at the New Rush and De Beers.' On that occasion also the Central Hospital tent was almost destroyed.

'It will easily be understood that, during the summer, very few Europeans feel inclined to engage in the more active operations of picking, shovelling, hauling, breaking or sifting. It is quite sufficient for them to sit under an awning and sort, leaving the Kaffirs to perform all the other stages of the work. During the worst of the summer, December and January, even existence in the camps becomes intolerable, and many diggers, especially those who reside in Cape Colony, leave the diggings and visit their homes for a month or two. They may lose money but gain health.' But most remained all the summer at the diggings, although 'many a strong man has found a grave on the barren veldt beneath the solitary black flag that marks our cemetery, or at least has had his constitution radically injured thereby'.

With autumn, which covered the months of February, March and April, however, 'the weather begins to be tolerable again and all hands are back at the fields, resuming work with activity.'

8

The Natives

WHEN Trollope visited Kimberley in 1877, although he was prejudiced against the town and the diamond diggings, which seemed to him the veritable 'Cave of Mammon', nevertheless, he most surprisingly found there almost the last thing to be expected; for to Trollope Kimberley almost seemed what Rome seemed to Virgil – a civilizing and pacifying influence! But for Trollope this influence was an influence over the native workers there. 'Because of this,' he wrote, 'I regard Kimberley as one of the most interesting places on the face of the earth. I know no other spot on which the work of civilizing a savage is being carried on with so signal a success.'

Nor did Trollope restrict his appreciation to this civilizing process in Kimberley. He also appreciated as similarly unique the fact that instead of exterminating the natives, South Africa had allowed them not only to survive, but remarkably to increase. 'The savages, whom we have encountered in our great task of populating the world, have for the most part eluded our grasp by perishing while we have been considering how we might best deal with them. Here, in South Africa, a healthy nation remains and assures us by its prolific tendency that when protected from self-destruction by our fostering care, it will spread and increase beneath our hands.'

Reliable estimates of the number of natives on the Diamond Fields or of the proportion of white to black during the earliest period do not exist, but some of the attempted assessments are not without a certain general significance. One digger on the spot in 1871, previously quoted, estimated the total number of whites in the three camps at 10,000 to 12,000, and the blacks at two or three times that number. Another estimate of the numbers a few years later by a writer of today is 60,000 in all, consisting of some 20,000 whites and 40,000 blacks. Thus, allowance being made for the slightly later period of the second estimate, the two agree fairly well.

Trollope, indeed, contemplated the social and industrial scene at Kimberley and its neighbourhood in a practical but sardonic frame of mind. Religion in the hands of the missionaries, he thought, had failed to civilize

the natives; working for the whites even in the humblest and most material-
istic way would, by gradually inducing the habits of white civilization, be
more effective. 'The work of civilizing,' he wrote, 'as it has been carried
out by simple philanthropy or by religion, is terribly slow. One is tempted
sometimes to say that nothing is done by religion and very little by philanthropy. But love of money works very fast. . . . Here [the natives] are
brought together, not by the spasmodic energy of the missionaries or by
the unalluring attraction of schools, but by the certainty of earning wages.
The seeker after diamonds is determined to have them because the making
of his fortune depends upon them; and the Kaffir himself is determined
to come to Kimberley because he has learned the loveliness of ten shillings
a week paid regularly into his hand every Saturday night.

'Who can doubt but that work is the great civilizer of the world – work
and the growing desire for those good things which work only will bring?
If there be one who does, he should come here to see how those dusky
troops of labourers, who ten years since were living in the wildest state of
unalloyed savagery, whose only occupation was the slaughter of each other
in tribal wars, each of whom was the slave of his Chief, who were subject
to the dominion of most brutalizing and cruel superstitions, have already
put themselves on the path towards civilization. They are thieves no doubt
– that is they steal diamonds though not often other things. They are not
Christians. They do not yet care much about breeches. They do not go to
school. But they are orderly. They come to work at six in the morning and
go away at six in the evening. They have an hour in the middle of the day,
and know that they have to work during the other hours. They take their
meals regularly and, what is the best of all, they are learning to spend their
money instead of carrying it back to their Chiefs.

'Civilization cannot come at once. The coming, I fear, under any circumstances must be slow. But this is the quickest way towards it that has
yet been found. The simple teaching of religion has never brought large
numbers of natives to live in European habits; but I have no doubt that
European habits will bring about religion. . . . But the missionary has
endeavoured to gratify his own soul by making here and there a model
Christian before the pupil has been able to understand any of the purposes
of Christianity. I have not myself seen the model Christian perfected; but
when I have looked down into the Kimberley Mine and seen three or
four thousand of them at work – although each of them would willingly
have stolen a diamond if the occasion came – I have felt that I was looking
at three or four thousand growing Christians.'

Trollope's enthusiasm for the Diamond Fields as a primary agent of civilization and religion in Africa was evidently largely affected by comparative standards, by other aspects of life known to him in and around Kimberley, and which others, too, matter-of-fact persons remote from the imaginative sympathy and vision of the artist, had also seen and described as among the strangest experiences of their lives. Strangest of all was the endless procession of natives streaming into the town, 30,000 of them each year, many weary, dusty, ragged or almost naked, with bleeding feet and dragging limbs, hungry, almost fainting survivors of a long, arduous trek from the heart of Africa, their fallen comrades left lying dead along the way. Others, who had come by shorter and easier routes entered jubilantly, yelling, chanting, shouting in a hundred different tongues, wildly dancing, many with head feathers waving and arm and leg bangles flashing in the dazzling sunshine, in the excitement of reaching their *el dorado*. For these were raw natives, as yet untouched by civilization, yet drawn by the prospect of such good wages as they had never before known.

The welcome the new arrivals received from their brother natives already installed at Kimberley, was hardly in accordance with Rousseau's pathetic belief in 'the noble savage'. For these 'old stagers', watching the procession of new-comers emerge from the bush, received it with howls, jeers, derisively eloquent gestures, showers of rotten fruit and even of stones. Soon, however, the new-comers were accepted as friends and allies by the old.

The native workers, indeed, showed amazing endurance in reaching the Diamond Fields; some after journeys of 1,000 miles, in which they overcame all the formidable obstacles presented by the vast country and its climate: mountains, ravines, rivers, mud, sand, desert, heat, cold, frost, tropical storms, wild animals and wild men, hunger, thirst, sickness and weariness, sometimes arriving covered with sores, scratches, bleeding feet, ill and exhausted. 'In an unspeakably miserable condition; literally they were nothing but skin and bone.' But their powers of recuperation were such as the primitive only know, and after a week or two on mealie-meal porridge they began to recover, while a month later they would appear sleek and in excellent form. As for those who died, a native's life was held cheap in those days on the Diamond Fields – and so too was a white man's.

The immense demand for labour and the comparatively high wages paid attracted the natives from far and near in their thousands. Kaffirs, Korannas, Hottentots, Griquas, Fingoes, races of all colours, 'from pale, sickly yellow to polished ebony, swarm at the Fields.' The Kaffirs were regarded as the most trustworthy of the labourers, and among them the Zulus had the best reputation, and next came the Basutos. Unfortunately, however, there was a permanent feud between the two races and they would not work together. Most of the workers, however, came from Bechuanaland and the Transvaal.

'Of all tribes and all colours, not a little do they contribute to the picturesqueness of the scene, though truth compels me to say they are sometimes more picturesque than decent. Some of the women have good features and many of the younger ones have splendid forms. They are a noisy lot, singing and shouting over their work, and specially glad when a diamond found and proclaimed gives the signal for a loud "Hurrah!" from all the neighbouring claims, or when the mule cart for Pniel dashes by with its six fine mules at full gallop – or at any other excuse for a shout or a yell.'

When at times the labour supply became scarce, a few speculators would go out into the country, and when one of them met a starving crowd of natives on their way towards Kimberley (perhaps two hundred of them), he would conduct them into the town, and place them with masters short of servants, for a commission of £1 a head. Generally, however, any good master could get the 'boys' he needed, even his own labourers gladly bringing their own relatives to him when required.

If for any reason, however, a glut of labour occurred, the situation of many natives became bad indeed, as they lay starving to death in the outskirts of Kimberley. 'A nigger's life in Kimberley', wrote an *advocatus diaboli*, 'was regarded as possessing about the same value as that of a tiresome fly's existence, and I have seen them die the cruellest of deaths without as a rule, a hand to help them.' Yet that some of the diggers were concerned and offered charity, though sometimes, apparently, with little effect, appears incidentally: 'Many charitable persons would give them money to alleviate their wants, but in few cases would the coin be spent in buying food, but carefully deposited in a little leather bag suspended round their necks as a first instalment towards buying a gun – the ambition of every native. One morning I saw a skeleton-like nigger discovered outside a compound in a dying state. He had had no food for four days, he told the kindly man who found him and gave him some wine to revive him – he could not eat. The nigger said he had been offered five shillings a week to work, but that was not sufficient to save on, and he had travelled far beyond the setting sun – and only for a gun. When it was pointed out his obstinacy not to labour for less than the customary wage might cause his death, his reply was pathetic and characteristic: "If he died he would not want a gun, and if he lived he would have one".'

This yearning for a gun, the natives' chief aim in coming to the Fields, also accelerated their departure. Within a year or less, the necessary £5 or £10 were saved, and the gun bought. The happy possessor then left for his ancestral kraal, sometimes also taking for his family, blankets, boots and clothing. 'He is then a mighty hunter, is sure of getting a good wife [that is, one who will work for him], and is ready to take an important part in any war that may arise between his and the neighbouring tribes – a very frequent occurrence.' This continual coming and going, however, prevented the camps being swamped with native labour.

The general quality of the 'guns' sold to them may be judged by the diggers' genially cynical name for them, 'gas-pipes'. Cheap guns from Birmingham and old muzzle-loaders of the past were joyfully bought by the natives, and as there was no law to prevent the sale of arms to natives, the whites did a big trade in them. Many of them burst and injured their owners so often, that the natives became wary, and on Sundays would go out into the neighbouring veldt and fasten their newly-purchased 'gas-pipes' to the numerous thorn-trees growing there, and after tying a long string to their triggers, would fire them off at a safe distance to test their reliability.

When political tensions over the possession of the Diamond Fields developed later, and many natives attacked the Boers, the possession of a gun became an even more important matter than before, and white traders hastened to make hay while the sun shone for them. Thus one observer describes the crowd of natives buying rifles at Klipdrift during an emergency: 'Those who bought were Korannas and Kaffirs. The street appeared to be possessed by a negro army. Round the shops were a crowd of hundreds pressing in. From its open door a stream of armed men struggled out ceaselessly. Each carried a rifle, some with the bayonet screwed on. The purchasers hung round the outskirts of the crowd, comparing the merit of their respective arms, until a body of eighteen or twenty was collected. They then marched away in line. So fast the bargains were concluded, these groups seemed to file past in a grotesque parade. Many of them had no covering whatever, except a tail of jackal hanging in front. Those were the Zulus. But every man carried an excellent rifle, Tower marked, one of the muzzle-loading Enfields discarded from the English army. These were sold at £3 each, £3 5s. with bayonet. It was stated that five hundred stands had been disposed of that morning.'

The miners preferred raw natives to those partly educated in Mission schools. 'The raw, untutored, unclad Kaffirs, fresh from their "kraals" up the mountains,' one claim-owner advised, 'are by far the best and most trustworthy workmen. The contact of civilization seems to be almost in-

variably pernicious and demoralizing to the peculiar organization of our
Kaffir friends. Above all things, mistrust a Kaffir who speaks English and
wears trousers!' These raw natives, especially, were quite unskilled at first,
not even knowing anything about their simple tools or even how to handle
them when placed in their hands. The only implement with which any of
them had been previously acquainted was the hoe. 'What pathetic speci-
mens of savage manhood', wrote Sir Lionel Phillips, 'used to seek work
in those days! They came sometimes hundreds of miles on foot to the
scene of industry, and on arrival were usually living skeletons. They had
never seen a pick or a shovel, and had to be fed up before their initiation
in the use of those instruments could begin.' Nor did the servant's duties
begin and end in the mine. Both before and after the hours of diamond
digging there were domestic duties at his master's tent: lighting the fire
for cooking, boiling water, fetching water from the wells, and if the native
were not too dirty, the washing of plates and dishes.

The inevitably squalid appearance of the claims was greatly intensified
by the widely varied but unaesthetic drapery with which the natives covered, or rather partly covered, their splendid bodies. For their native gala
dress was seldom if ever seen on the Diamond Fields. The Zulu splendours,
for example, of ox-tail girdles, gold and ivory armlets, anklets, bracelets
and earrings, were, like the great ostrich plumes, considered too valuable
and too inconvenient to be worn amidst the dust and dirt of the Great
Hole. 'A greasy, gaudy handkerchief twisted around a black head, and partly
coloured bunches of rags, or moochies made of tails or skins of wild animals, were a camp parade dress too precious to use in quarries.' Some at the
most would wear only a scanty loincloth or a leopard skin or old and dirty
kaross or as often huge bunches of tall feathers.

There was, however, another reason for this general abandonment of
native dress. Respect and reverence for the white 'bosses' extended to their
garments, and the gift of some old clothing would be received with unbounded delight: 'One of my "boys",' writes a digger, 'once found one
leg of a pair of trousers, and straightaway put it on; but finding it inconvenient, frequently slipping down and hindering him in his work, to which
I naturally objected, he finally converted it into a sort of turban, and wore
it triumphantly on his head.'

One observer describes the raw native arriving at the camp in 'only a
loin-cloth, with perhaps gaudy plumes of feathers on his head, a necklace
of tiger claws, shells or beads, and probably no language but his own, or
a few words of Boer Dutch.' Such, the writer advised, should be taken to
the magistrate's court and registered, so making a contract to which he

must put his mark. This not only impressed the native but also enabled the master in the event of his laziness or disobedience to bring him to the police station 'for probably a dozen lashes of the "cat". This is better than taking the law into one's own hands.'

The natives' preference for European dress was not nicely particular or discriminating. An old flannel shirt or old jacket made the most acceptable present, especially an old military red coat which made the recipient 'supremely proud and happy'. When a gale blew an old hat into his tent, says one digger, and he gave it to his 'boy' along with a gaudy feather, the native 'grinned exceedingly and said: "Boy is *gentleman* this morning" ' and set out on his Sunday walk, 'with solemn dignity', wearing only the hat and a shirt. The same observer noted the striking variety of dress among the different tribes and classes of the natives. 'Many wore merely a parti-coloured bunch of rags before and behind, barely sufficient for purposes of decency. One will strut about with nothing on but a hat and a loin-cloth; another with an old shako and red coat, formerly a private soldier's.' Others would wear hat, jacket and shirt but no trousers. Many still retained coloured handkerchiefs twisted round their heads, and feathers. 'These semi-barbarians, half-naked negroes, are said to be the most honest and best workers. Educated, and consequently fully clad natives are looked upon with distrust. The bare-legged fellows go about singing weird native songs, of strange tone and wonderful discord.'

'In those days,' wrote one digger, 'discarded uniforms were plentiful, and sold to anyone – so one often saw the blacks with their primitive dress, on which was superimposed a coat of some glorious regiment; perhaps also a paper collar round his bare neck, held together by a piece of thread.' 'I have seen,' said another, 'a nigger walking about most complacently, dressed in a hat, an old paper collar, and a courier bag, not a rag else, barring the *mutya* [loin-cloth].' An offshoot, as it were, of their passion for European dress was their affection for umbrellas. This affection appears to have been entirely aesthetic, not utilitarian, for they would sit happily under their umbrellas in the moonlight at night, and the umbrella was also a popular present for their favourite wife (and doubtless also for themselves), when they returned to their native village.

The women came too: 'Women innumerable, black, brown and yellow, are to be seen in our camps. . . . They dress decently, with a natural pre-ference for gaudy colours. They find ample and remunerative employment as washerwomen, household servants, etc. But it must be added that a great many of them are too lazy to work, and prefer to get money more quickly and easily, as is soon apparent by their bolder and richer apparel, their constant promenading about the camp, and their impudent looks. Both men and women in many cases, smear their faces with red ochre which has a comically hideous effect.' And 'the dark ladies wore beads, quite decent and very picturesque.'

Thus the natives brought into the somewhat dreary and squalid scene of the Diamond Fields a striking if tawdry contrast. 'The niggers were, I must own, a very strong element of the picturesque in the appearance of the camp at night. Hundreds of dusky figures, in every variety of fantastic headgear, squatting round the bright camp fires, or perchance dancing their war dance, or singing barbaric songs. They are very happy as a rule: they may well be so when they are getting such wages. Many of them will carefully save their money.'

They also brought their naturally sociable and happy temperaments, whatever the hardships to be endured. But the camp offered in many ways benefits beyond anything of the kind obtainable in their own village existence. Otherwise they would not have come voluntarily and indeed eagerly, as they did.

They enjoyed the liveliness, noise and general animation of the camps. With their instinctive childish gaiety they enlivened their labours with cries, shouts, yells and laughter as they heaved and strained at boulders, worked cradles or sieves, quarried, sorted, and spotted diamonds while their masters surveyed them, sheltered from heat and rain. When a specially large diamond was discovered, their excitement expressed itself in louder whoopees of delight. Any little incident or accident was enough to provoke their ever ready laughter: a broken rope, a dropped bucket, a slipping ladder or climber, or even the skittishness and whinneyings of the mules.

'There is great fun whenever a bullock waggon passes along the narrow little road left among the claims. All the niggers who are digging near, shout and yell at the oxen in the most contradictory and confusing manner, some shouting "Yek!", "Trek!", the stimulus to increasing speed; others, "Ah now!" and the apparently cosmopolitan "Wo!" – the signals to stop. The effect of these, all yelled at once by some dozens of strong-lunged Kaffirs, is to put the oxen into a fearful state of bewilderment, and their drivers into a considerable rage. The other day four bullocks, confused and terrified, started off up hill at full gallop, and a lot of boxes somewhat loosely packed in expectation of uniform slow progress, were precipitated into the road. How all the niggers, aye, and diggers too, laughed, and how the old Dutchman swore at them.'

These and similar descriptions provide a necessary corrective to dismally one-sided accounts of the natives such as this: 'Naked they toiled throughout the day in a scorching atmosphere, either obscured with odious, blinding dust and disgusting dirt, or pitiless rain accompanied by death-dealing lightning and terrible claps of thunder.' True enough so far as it goes, but one must not forget that in their own kraals the natives would have been equally exposed to dirt, dust, and the various unpleasant climatic conditions. Nor would they, wisely in their climate, have abandoned the 'nakedness' so often envied by sweating diggers. What, however, they would not have found in their own villages was the money to buy a gun!

The following glimpse pleasantly illuminates the natives' relations with their employers. 'From the direction of the mines, on their way home, came troops of dusty, naked natives, singing Kaffir songs of glee, and following their white masters who walked ahead of them, as would a leader of a regiment. They were a splendid stamp of men, these early claim-holders. Big, brawny, fine made fellows, and in many instances highly educated; they did honour to England, Ireland, Scotland and Wales. I knew where most came from at once by their accent, when they had cause to speak reprovingly to their stalwart "boys". There was no nonsense about this breed of miners. They were Anglo-Saxon to the core and looked it. Each band of Kaffirs, docile as children as they followed their boss, numbered thirty to forty, and when, after a fortunate day, their great gaunt master stopped them in front of a canteen for a "soupee", then their joy knew no bounds. "Zing! Zing" they sang as standing in a row they chattered to each other, their huge mouths open and their eyes gleaming in anticipation of a glass of Cape "smoke". Carefully the white man, probably a former naval or military officer, sees that each of his servants gets his quota, at times handing the beakers round himself. There is a wild display of enthusiasm after drink, by the Kaffirs, who do a war dance and with their eternal "Zing! Zing!" follow the silent and self-immersed figure of their master home.'

Such a glimpse, surely, gives us a better comprehension of Trollope's belief in Kimberley's civilizing influence upon the natives. He himself gives another equally illuminating glimpse of them; this time, as they leave work: 'Perhaps the most interesting sight at the mine is the escaping of the men from their labour at six o'clock. Then, at the sound of some welcomed gong, they begin to swarm up the sides, close at each other's heels, apparently altogether indifferent as to whether there be a path or no. They come as flies up a wall, only capering as flies never caper – and shouting as they come. In endless strings, as ants follow each other, they move, passing along ways which seem to offer no hold to a human foot. Then it is that one can best observe their costume, in which a jacket is never absent, but of which a pair of trousers rarely forms a portion. A soldier's red jacket or a soldier's blue jacket has more charms than any other vestment. They seem always to be good-humoured, always well-behaved – but then they are always thieves. And yet how grand a thing it is that so large a number of these men should have been brought in so short a space of time to the habit of receiving wages and to the capacity of bargaining as to the wages for which they will work. I shall not, however, think it so grand a thing if any one addresses them as the free and independent electors of Kimberley before they have got trousers to cover their nakedness.'

White diggers could not resist taking advantage at times of the natives' naïveté, to make genial fun of them, often using their ignorance of English to give them fantastic, sometimes even horrifying names, when they registered their servants. Indeed so hectic did the nomenclature become that the Government had to step in and stop the practice. Among the printable jokes so played is that of the poor native named, without his suspicion of its significance, 'Ballyfool', a name so harmonious with his own soft-sounding language as to delight him. Arrested for some slight misdemeanour and placed in the dock, on being asked by the magistrate for his name, he replied 'Ballyfool' with a pride, directness and emphasis so strong that the irate magistrate, mistaking the name for a reference to himself, sent the bewildered man to prison at once for contempt of court.

Another joke of the whites at the expense of the natives (or rather at the expense of the missionaries, whose attempts to convert and civilize the natives were regarded by the diggers as eminently unsuccessful), was the story of the claim-owner who during a great scarcity of labour was delighted to obtain forty natives from a Mission station. All but one, a raw native, had been educated at the Mission, and the way they began work on his claim exceeded his fondest hopes. Indeed as they worked, he found them singing the 'Hallelujah Chorus'. Feeling these needed no watching, he went away to tell his friends of the treasures he had found. When, on returning in the afternoon he found them enthusiastically singing 'God Save the Queen', his delight was unbounded. But later his feelings changed when the one 'raw' native told him that the leader of the chorus, their precentor, had concealed something in his belt. A search and questioning produced the depressing facts that he had stolen a 5-carat stone while leading them in the 'Hallelujah Chorus', and a 10-carat while loyally leading them in 'God Save the Queen'.

In general the standard of honesty among the native servants seems to have been but little lower than that of their white masters, despite obvious and manifold temptations. Diamond stealing was prevalent, but a smuggled diamond often appeared to both white and black as no worse than a smuggled watch or bracelet seems to a white tourist returning home from a foreign land. Apart from diamonds, the 'honest' natives seldom did more than help themselves to their master's grog and tobacco, and would have considered any complaint on that score as hyperconscientious. In any case the grog-stealer needed no Sherlock Holmes to run him to earth, as he would immediately be found there, peacefully sleeping on the floor of his master's tent or on the ground just outside it. In fact, the victim's chief complaint was not about the stolen grog and tobacco, but about the lost day's work, as the delinquent remained *hors de combat* for the rest of the day.

Nor, despite the fact that the great majority of the first natives on the Fields were drawn straight from savage life, was crime among them higher than in later years when more 'civilized' and 'educated' natives appeared. 'Notwithstanding the preponderance of natives drawn from savage life, not a single white woman was molested in the early years of diamond digging.' In those days of the simple rather than 'noble' savage he took no personal interest in diamonds, not knowing that the possession of them could be useful to him. The white man's passion for these 'light stones' as the natives called them merely confirmed the servant's belief in his white master's childishness or insanity. Not until they learned their value from the white, civilized Christians did diamonds become a temptation. Equally unsophisticated, too, was their first attitude to money. Never having seen a coin before, they logically enough concluded that value was proportionate to size, that the larger the coin, the greater its value. Thus they would reject a sixpence or a half-sovereign for a penny or a half-crown, and run away chuckling at their own cleverness, before the expected pursuit by the outwitted white man could overtake them. In this way, until the natives learned better, they were themselves often deceived by dishonest whites.

Indeed it was later, when the naked savage at the mines had acquired more civilized standards, including a taste for some articles of European dress, and learned that not only his wages but also stolen money and diamonds would bring him the things he wanted at the Kaffir canteen, that native dishonesty increased. One Kaffir eating house became a recognized meeting place for the sale by natives of their stolen diamonds. All, however, were not dishonest, and we hear of such incidents as that of a native who in pulling up the roots of an old tree for firewood, found an 80-carat diamond buried there and brought it to his master.

Some in Kimberley believed that the native chiefs ordered and trained their subjects to steal diamonds when they reached the mines, and to bring them back for the benefit of the chiefs themselves. Trollope accepted this belief, as the following interesting account he gives of the part played by the natives in I.D.B. clearly shows: 'The Kaffirs are great thieves – to such an extent of super-excellence that white superintendence is spoken of as being the only safeguard. The honesty of the white man may perhaps be indifferent, but such as it is it has to be used at every point to prevent, as far as it may be prevented, the systematized stealing in which the Kaffirs take an individual and national pride. The Kaffirs are not only most willing but most astute thieves, feeling a glory in their theft and thinking that every stone stolen from a white man is a duty done to their Chief and their tribe. I think it may be taken as certain that no Kaffir would feel the slightest pang of conscience at stealing a diamond, or that any disgrace would be held to attach to him among other Kaffirs for such a performance. They come to the Fields instructed by their Chiefs to steal diamonds and they obey the orders like loyal subjects. Many of the Kaffir Chiefs are said to have large quantities of diamonds which have been brought to them by their men returning from the diggings – but most of those which are stolen no doubt find their way into the hands of illicit dealers. I have been told that the thefts perpetrated by the Kaffirs amount to 25 per cent of the total amount found – but this I do not believe.

'The opportunities for stealing are of hourly occurrence and are of such a nature as to make prevention impossible. These men are sharp-sighted as birds and know and see a diamond much quicker than a white man. They will pick up stones with their toes and secrete them even under the eyes of those who are watching them. I was told that a man will so hide a diamond in his mouth that no examination will force him to disclose it. They are punished when discovered with lashes and imprisonment – in accordance with the law on the matter. No employer is now allowed to flog his man at his own pleasure. And the white men who buy diamonds from Kaffirs are also punished when convicted, by fine and imprisonment for the simple offence of buying from a Kaffir; but with flogging also if convicted of having instigated a Kaffir to steal. Nevertheless a lucrative business of this nature is carried on, and the Kaffirs know well where to dispose of their plunder though of course but for a small proportion of its value.'

Certainly the standard of honesty must have been greatly encouraged by the speedy and drastic punishments inflicted upon them in the lawless, earliest days. One example is that of a Hottentot who, after stealing a stone and running away, was chased over the veldt by no less than 150 horsemen until captured. Sentenced to fifty lashes, he was tied to the wheel of a wagon, while an ex-naval man inflicted the punishment with a cat-o'-nine-tails. But instead of crying for mercy, the Hottentot called out derisively to his captors at every stroke.

With the establishment of law and order punishments were not only less drastic but less speedy, and for the innocent victim of theft or other lawlessness, more inconvenient, as generally several attendances at court were required, full evidence beyond question must be produced, and as the following example shows, unusual linguistic difficulties often complicated matters. 'I found', writes a digger, 'that our tent had been robbed in our absence, of four or five suits of clothes, two rugs, a blanket, a roll of tobacco, a gallon of brandy, and sundry other articles. We questioned our Kaffir but he professed utter ignorance. In the afternoon, however, while our "boy" was absent, fetching water from the dam, a neighbouring digger called me over to the fire-place of some other Kaffirs, where he had seen the corner of a blanket sticking out of the ground, and had found several articles of clothing, besides a roll of tobacco and a bottle of brandy, all lightly buried in the loose sand. On searching the neighbourhood we discovered nearly the whole of our missing property similarly concealed. One of the Kaffirs said that our "boy" brought the things there. I immediately got two policemen, and had our "boy" arrested as he was returning from the dam. His back will probably be made acquainted with the "cat". He accused four other Kaffirs, whom I believe to be implicated with him.'

At the police court the native pleaded 'not guilty'. 'I identified all the stolen things,' the record continues, 'but could not prove his possession of them there, so the case was remanded. But I was fortunately able to return in half an hour with three witnesses: an Englishman who found the buried things, a Zulu Kaffir and a Hottentot who saw our "boy" bring the things there, and to whom he gave brandy. Native dialects here become perplexing, as my two black witnesses could speak neither English nor Dutch. At last it was managed as follows: the interpreter of the court, who understood Zulu, translated the Zulu's evidence, the Zulu translated the Hottentot's evidence to the interpreter in Zulu, and the interpreter retranslated it to the court in English. Our scamp was convicted and sentenced to twenty lashes with the "cat", and a month's labour. As soon as the court closed I saw him tied up to the whipping-post and flogged. The lashes were inflicted very lightly, and he didn't seem to feel them much.'

A magistrate's morning in court and the punishments he inflicted can be imagined from the following odd items: two Hottentots who had stolen sheepskins and, incidentally, had offered them for sale to the very man from whom they had been stolen, were ordered fifteen lashes with the 'cat'; another was fined 5s. for being drunk and beating his wife; two Kaffirs were fined 2s. 6d. for being out after hours; a charge of assault brought by a Kaffir against a Hottentot was dismissed; a white man found at night in another man's tent, who pleaded drunkenness and mistake, was fined £1 or twelve hours' imprisonment. Next, a number of Dutchmen were charged with firing their guns and rifles in the camp after sundown – so celebrating the discovery of a large diamond in their usual way; there had been bullets in some of the rifles, and the police had taken eleven guns and summoned the owners to court, where they were severely reprimanded and fined 2s. 6d. each. Such were the cases that came regularly and interminably before the magistrates in those days.

Drink, of course, was a common cause of crime, among natives as among whites. When the Diggers' Committee issued a proclamation forbidding canteen keepers from selling drink to natives without authority from their masters, under a penalty of ten pounds, one digger commented: 'It was much needed. The scenes at New Rush especially, began to be disgraceful.' In those days, before compounds were created, many natives, after drinking the potent Cape brandy from lower-class canteens, would swarm about the diggings at night, a menace to the safety of the community, and indeed to themselves as they stumbled about among the wells, and the deep holes of the mines. The effect of alcohol on the natives was always very strong and exciting, and led to many faction fights, during which the police had often to be assisted by white civilians. Diggers walking through the so-called 'town' at night were always careful to go in parties of at least three or four, and armed with sticks or other weapons in case of attack. 'These', writes one digger, 'were indeed rough and exciting times.'

The introduction of a ten o'clock curfew for natives was generally approved by the diggers, and led to a great improvement in nocturnal conditions on the Fields. 'The evenings in camp are pleasant enough. I hardly ever feel inclined to stir out, but lie on many buckskins and rugs, and spend the time between dinner and 10 p.m. in reading. But others are not so quiet; there are plenty of amateur bands frequently promenading or playing in neighbouring tents, so I get plenty of music. At ten a bugle sounds, which is the signal for all natives to retire to their respective locations. Any unfortunate darky found in the "streets" after that hour, is taken to "chokey", the slang name for our little prison, and receives fifteen lashes.'

At Kimberley, as on the gold fields, tribal fights occurred almost every week-end, as well as individual bouts of fisticuffs during purely personal quarrels. These latter were even encouraged by many of the miners, who liked to look on, often as a lunch hour distraction, gambling with one another as they backed their particular choice. No digger, however, wished his own 'boys' to participate in these fights, and many strictly forbade them even to attend them, as all feared the loss of days of work through their 'boys' being injured in the fray.

But the tribal fights, especially between those chronic enemies, Zulus and Basutos, were much more serious affairs, taking place indeed upon appointed days. The vivid detail of the following description gives it unusual interest. 'It was evident enough that there was something unusual among the niggers. . . . I had seen numbers of tall strong Zulus, and the scarcely less well-formed Basutos, hurrying all in one direction, and I even thought I saw here and there an *assegai* carried. Most of them had thick, hard sticks, or powerful bludgeons; many were armed with pick-handles, while those who had been unable to find anything suitable in the timber line, had collected large bagfulls of big rough stones. Not pleasant missiles at a short range these latter! Most of the Kaffirs who did not belong to the hostile tribes, like our "boys" for instance, were also moving out of the Camp in the same direction; while a gay crowd of diggers, many of them in their "Sunday best", i.e. a new felt hat with a clean ostrich feather in it, a clean flannel shirt, a paper collar, bright cord trousers, and shining boots, were following the swarm of natives, many simply to "see the fun" as they phrased it, but many to identify their "boys" for purposes of punishment. It must have been a grand sight when the two bodies of dusky savages, for they were little better, stood facing one another under that hot African sun, bathed in that wondrous glow of light which we, with our cold, damp, dark western skies never even dream of, but which here flooded with its radiance the open veldt wherever they stood.

'But here are our niggers, many hundreds of them, drawn up in "battle array" – the Basutos and their allies apparently out-numbering the Zulus. They have chosen temporary chiefs to lead them to the conflict, the barbed *assegais* are ready to be poised and hurled, pick-handles and bludgeons are grasped, stones are about to be thrown, the concentrated animosity of ages seems to gleam forth from the keen eyes and fiercely grinning teeth of these dusky warriors – not "boys" or servants now, but each transformed into a fierce, brave warrior for the nonce.

'Diggers are standing on the surrounding ridges, looking, some with eagerness, some with anxiety, for the approaching commencement of the fray.

'But what is this little band of horsemen galloping so swiftly towards the combatants? Hurrah! Truter, the Landdrost, followed by his Inspector of Police and one or two mounted diggers. Grave Truter – come to preserve the public peace at all risks. Clad in a neat dark uniform, with a gold laced cap, hotly spurring on a handsome horse, he rides impetuously, drawn sword in hand, into the very midst of the belligerents.

'A few fierce indignant shouts and many low mutterings are heard, even some *assegais* are poised, and stones seem about to be hurled at the person of the interfering magistrate; but he, nothing daunted, lays lustily about him with the flat of his sabre on the woolly and bare shoulders of the ringleaders, Zulus and Basutos alike. The Inspector and C—, the Natalian, are there, with gleaming revolvers. Many of the spectators from the adjacent hillsides are hurrying up, animated by Truter's bravery, to place themselves on the side of law and order. So at last, reluctantly enough, and with many a muttered curse and threats that they *will* fight next Sunday, and no one shall prevent them, Zulus and Basutos retire slowly to their respective kraals, to gorge themselves with mealies or meat, and to indulge in wild war dances and yelling barbaric songs round the glowing camp fires in the evening.

'C— rides swiftly back to his tents: his "boys" have all been there, contrary to his express command; so, as the disobedient niggers come slinking back to the kraal, C— vigorously administers to each a sound personal chastisement of a dozen lashes. His example is followed by many other diggers – most masters lecture their boys on the folly of the affair; moreover, the determined appearance and conduct of the Landdrost has made a powerful impression.'

When the day's work was ended, the naturally sociable spirit of the natives was given full play as they sat with their friends round the blazing camp-fires they made, for the nights were cold, smoking, talking, singing, and dancing among themselves. 'They make a fearful hubbub till eight or nine o'clock, when they curl themselves up in their blankets or skins, and sleep soundly till daybreak, when the rays of the rising sun, or the foot of the rising "baas" warns them to get up and make the fire.' The natives suffered from the cold at night, and some of the more generous and kindly diggers would give their servants a rough tent to sleep in. Without this, the more active natives would make comfortable little huts for themselves from branches or bushes brought in by them from the country during their week-end holidays.

They were great smokers of the cheap Boer tobacco, and the gift of an old, short clay pipe delighted them. Without such an implement, many resorted to the method of smoking they practised in their own villages. It was, however, more ingenious than satisfactory, for it consisted in moistening a small piece of ground sufficiently to allow a thin stick to be thrust in, making a narrow passage some nine inches long; the making of a small hollow at one end, into which the lighted tobacco was thrust, and the placing of their lips to the other end, in order to use it as a pipe. The native plutocrats smoked cigars; preferring, with a particular nicety, so at least we are told, to put the lighted end in their mouths!

Whatever the civilizing influence of the Diamond Fields upon the natives, many uncivilized, even barbaric customs remained. 'The public slaughtering place is not very far from this tent,' wrote one digger, 'and whenever my "boys" hear of any oxen or sheep going to be slaughtered, they will ask leave, rush off to the scene, and shortly return with huge festoons of the filthiest offal, and so besmeared with blood and dirt that we cannot on these festive occasions allow them to clean our plates and dishes. And the quantity of offal they will gorge at a sitting is perfectly astounding, though it does not incapacitate them from taking their usual huge plateful of mealie-meal porridge to fill up gaps with.'

Their staple diet was mealies or maize, with once or twice a week a little meat refuse, and on Sundays a glass of 'Cape smoke', all provided by their masters. They seldom washed either their clothes or themselves, and one master complains that if you give them an old flannel shirt they will not take it off until it falls to pieces. 'Baas, give little bit soap,' said one fastidious fellow, 'head plenty full of —— insects unmentionable to ears polite.' Cape brandy they much preferred to water.

Some natives were well behaved, hard-working, economical, and returned to their kraals with money and the goods they had bought. 'Some, it is true, are not so careful, they yield to the "white" vices of drinking, gambling, etc., are often to be found in "chokey", often changing masters, and never saving money.' The Bushmen, Hottentots and Griquas particularly disliked working at the mines, while even the better natives had to be watched, not only lest they stole diamonds, but also because they were always apt to loaf, stand still and stare about until they felt the stones thrown at their bare legs to bring them back to earth.

One of their most trying characteristics from the diggers' point of view was their naturally wandering disposition: their refusal to remain, once they had accumulated enough to buy the much coveted gun. They knew nothing of the 'civilized' man's passion for wealth in itself, the passion which kept many a digger who could have retired on a competence to his native land, or if South African, his native region, digging (often vicariously) amid dust and heat and the dreary environment and primitive way of life of the early camps, in the gambler's faith that the next moment his wealth would be doubled or more.

Civilized or uncivilized the natives were not without guile, nor were their 'bosses' always unkind. Frank Rhodes, the brother of the famous Cecil, reveals his own consciousness of this, as well as his generosity (at his brother's expense!) and suggests the attitude of many decent diggers to real, or apparently real, hardship among their servants, when, left during his brother's absence in charge of his claim, he informs his family: 'I am alone in my glory, and in charge of claims and Kaffirs for the time being. I think the Kaffirs rather like it, as they impose on my ignorance, and ask for all sorts of things which I immediately give them; one has just been in here and explained by pointing to his naked legs, that it was too cold. I immediately gave him a pair of Cecil's trousers, which Cecil will be awfully pleased at, I should think.' Indeed the natives showed a peasant's cunning at times, and the logic by which they would lay claim to undeserved wages or presents was more ingenious than effective; as when Sir Lionel Phillips, having on one occasion given his best workers among his natives each a half-crown extra, found his office immediately besieged by all the rest demanding the same extra pay. On explaining that those boys had been rewarded for specially good work, the rest replied: 'If those boys did more than we, they did a little work for us!'

Whatever the casual kindnesses shown to the natives, however sympathetic some of the diggers might be towards their condition, the differences between them and their 'bosses' were too many and too great for understanding. Even one of the most sympathetic observers, one who had described with sorrow and indignation the sufferings of the natives, admitted that he 'never liked them, few colonists do'. Another witness, objective and unprejudiced, was little more enthusiastic. The natives, he said, 'on the whole cannot be said to show to much advantage as patterns of native growth, or raw material; since the heavy hand of the Free State has been taken off, and the mild paternal sway of the Colony substituted, some of these people are disposed to be grossly insolent and presume upon the forbearance of the authorities and that of the white population generally; the money they have come into possession of lately, accounting in some measure for this disposition. Before diamonds were discovered the highest wages paid by a Boer were about 5s. a month, and for this sum, natives had to work hard under jealous taskmasters – the Boers stand no shirking or nonsense – but the demand for labour consequent upon diamond enterprise, changed all this, and the wages now paid in the fields, are from 6s. a week to 30s. a month, with food, and even at this rate it was not easy to keep natives at work, for the moment they had scraped a few pounds together they were off to their kraals to display their wealth and live in the idleness their souls delighted in. The Zulu Kaffirs brought from Natal are a very different class. They are really splendid fellows and make trustworthy, staunch servants; they wear no clothes worth speaking about, and in all things afford a marked contrast to the others. Any little kindness was quite wasted upon the inferior blacks, and from first to last I found them troublesome, exacting, ungrateful and difficult to deal with in every way. As for some of the Griquas, Hottentots – so called – and Bushmen, they are in many instances but very slightly removed from their original Darwinian condition.'

Certainly the Zulus, although soon to be brave enemies in a war against the Whites, were then (as they still are) the most liked and respected of all the native tribes. 'Two friends of mine', writes one, 'brought up from the interior of Natal six of the best Zulus I ever saw. They were fine, tall, strong-built young fellows, of rather prepossessing countenances and splendid figures, all clad in bright red coats, so that as they marched through the camp to or from the claim, singing their loud and not inharmonious songs, their appearance was most imposing. Moreover they were thoroughly good "boys", hard working, polite, good humoured, and lively. They used to go through grand performances at their "kraal", war songs and dances pantomimes of hunting and other scenes, with great spirit and talent, causing large audiences to assemble to witness their barbaric sports.' In addition the Zulus were said to be thoroughly trustworthy, not only could they be left to go on steadily working alone on their master's claim, but even to bring to him any diamonds they found.

But with the growth in size and civilization of Kimberley and the Fields as a whole, the natives, too, changed and the more sensitive diggers regretted the passing of the picturesque, colourful element. No longer, complained one writer, did the returning native take away with him to his kraal the wonderful umbrella and tin box which used to be the most coveted of presents on such occasions, but 'smart pieces of stuff, marvellous blankets and probably cheap jewellery. The old picturesque costumes are disappearing and being replaced in a big town, for both men and women, by the latest fashions and flashiest of dress. Intercourse with whites of the lower classes has not improved their opinion of us, and they are far less respectful than of yore. There is, however, a natural dignity about a Kaffir, and he is quick to recognize a gentleman.'

Change in some degree began in fact quite early on the Diamond Fields. Compounds for the natives were so quickly instituted, that when James Bryce visited Kimberley in 1874, he thought the compounds 'the most striking sight there and unique in the world'. He described each as 'a huge enclosure, unroofed, but covered with wire netting to prevent anything being thrown out of them over the walls, and with a subterranean entrance to the adjoining mine. . . . Round the interior of the wall there are built sheds or huts in which the natives live and sleep when not working.'

At the time of Bryce's visit there were 2,600 natives in the compounds, of many tribes, some of which he named: Zulus, Ferigos, Pondos, Tembus, Basutos, Bechuanas, Gungunhamas, Matabele, Makaelaka and natives from the Portuguese territories, as well as many from both sides of the Zambesi: 'a living ethnological collection such as can be examined nowhere else in South Africa.' By this time, too, a hospital and school had been built in the compounds, the latter assisting the natives to employ some of their leisure in learning to read and write. All the supplies required by the natives were sold at a store inside the compound, kept by the company; no spirits or visitors, black or white, were allowed inside the compound, and every entrance was strictly guarded for various obvious reasons.

There was, not unnaturally, opposition to the introduction of the compounds among the commercial fraternity on the Diamond Fields, who rightly saw their own sales and profits considerably threatened. But crime, too, had greatly diminished. The charge of 'slavery' was brought against the new system, both honestly by enthusiasts for 'human rights' irrespective of particular conditions, and dishonestly by those whose commercial profits were threatened. The supporters of the system which, of course, was also instituted mainly for commercial reasons, not primarily for its moral advantages, replied to their critics by asserting that the essence of slavery was that the slave was bought for life and not paid, whereas the natives in the compounds freely contracted for a few months' or years' service, were well paid and housed and fed, were also protected from the temptations of drink and other vices and from the deceptions of unscrupulous whites, besides being paid at the end of their service a substantial bonus for honesty.

Thus, as gradually the new industrial age dawned on the Diamond Fields, widely different conditions from those of the recent past affected both white and black there. The natives were now brought to the mechanized mines and industrial centres by a well-organized recruiting system. Rest houses and good food were provided for them on their journey, and they reached the Fields in good health and well nourished, no longer weary, emaciated and ragged as before. Most of them were in fact already acquainted with some kind of regular work; almost all knew how to handle simple implements, many had had practical experience of pumps, engines, ploughs and similar machines, and their general education was at least in these ways much improved.

The days of the old soldier's discarded coat and the dirty paper collar were gone, and so too was much that went with them. 'I remember', wrote Sir Lionel Phillips, 'seeing a neighbour one morning whipping every one of his "boys" as they started work, and, in reply to my question as to his reason, he said: "If they don't want it now, they will!" In his case the punishment was not severe, just a reminder, but the mere action gives an idea of those times.' When Sir Lionel wrote, even the 'idea' had almost passed out of memory, and as another digger mournfully remarked: 'No one dreams of corporal punishment now!'

For (as always in periods of marked change) there were *laudatores temporis acti* who watched the transformation of the Fields with saddened eyes. Many, particularly old diggers dispossessed of their claims by the advancing diamond companies, loudly lamented the passing of the earlier times and considered the natives by no means personally improved by the improved conditions. In the past, many, probably with reason, had believed the 'raw' natives made the best 'boys', and the mission-educated ones the worst. Most doubtless agreed with the digger who had warned them to mistrust 'the nigger who speaks English and wears trousers'. To these it seemed, and doubtless correctly, that with better education and better pay and conditions, the old reverence for the white man (*omne ignotum pro magnifico*) had greatly declined even if it had not entirely disappeared. The old prostration before their masters was changing often to self-assurance, even impertinence, impudence, disrespect. Doubtless the complaint was justified, and the change was also largely due to the unconscious influence of the flood of inferior types from white nations who had in later years poured into the Fields; for as Sir Lionel Phillips had said: 'The Kaffir is quick to recognize a gentleman.'

And he, too, noted the change in the natives' manners. He described them as in the earlier days 'real savages in all respects, with a tremendous reverence for the white man, who, in their eyes, could do everything but tie up the sun ... otherwise, the poor benighted creatures had an inordinate respect for us and were quite abject in attitude, an inherited legacy, perhaps, from the slave days.' Many of the earlier diggers' opinions were expressed by one who said: 'Too much kindness or familiarity makes them think themselves too valuable to lose. They will ask for higher pay, lose all respect for the "Baas", be insolent and disobedient, and finally run away; probably with some of his diamonds or other property. A nigger is all very well as long as he is kept in his proper place, that is, "kept down"; to treat him in the "man and brother" style of Exeter Hall philanthropists, is only to spoil him and injure yourself. New-comers to the colonies find this difficult to realize, thinking that kind treatment *must* succeed, but they soon get woefully undeceived. Of course I don't mean you should ill-use Kaffirs, but keep them in their places; punish them when naughty, and never be familiar or laugh with them.'

Even Sir Lionel Phillips noted some aspects of this decline with reasonable regret, as he recalled the vanished influence of the white man upon the savages of those days, particularly one occasion when he and a friend, 'poker in one hand and revolver in the other', stopped a tribal battle by rushing in and 'using his poker pretty freely', while stones and bottles were flying, and every native had some kind of stick. 'But such was our prestige in those days, that the moment we were recognized, our Kaffir names were shouted out, and the tumult died away in a very few minutes. Tackling such situations was always a nasty perilous job, and I do not believe two white men today could undertake it. The police would have to be sent for. To a native then, every white man was an *inkoos* – a chief.'

9

Annexation and Revolt

UNTIL the discovery of diamonds, the Vaal River region had long enjoyed the peace of a land in which no government is interested. Apparently mere desert, like that of which the neighbouring states had already far more than they wanted, the Diamond Fields lay in a no-man's-land without settled legal boundaries of state control. In 1854 Britain, believing that in the face of Boer and Native opposition the game of retaining the Orange River Sovereignty (in which the then undiscovered Diamond Fields lay) was not worth the candle, handed the territory back to the Boers upon their agreeing that certain parts, not precisely specified, should be given to the native tribes there as reservations. From that time the land relapsed into its ancient peace.

But when fifteen years later the first diamonds were discovered and hordes of diggers began to descend upon the region, the adjoining countries (the two Boer republics of the Free State and the Transvaal) and also Great Britain as protector of Cape Colony all began to cast longing eyes at it, while each became really or mystically aware of definite claims to its ownership, hitherto overlooked. Nor were these all, for several native chiefs including the missionary-educated, Boer-Griqua half-breed, Nicholas Waterboer, presumably incited by speculative agents, also laid claim to parts of the territory, including the Klipdrift, Pniel and Dutoitspan Fields. Besides these, the Berlin Missionary Society at Pniel and Hebron claimed to have previously bought that diamondiferous district from the native Koranna reserve there, and when the diggers appeared, the clergyman in charge quickly issued licences to them and took the fees of those who were willing to pay them. The remainder simply ignored fees and licences and prospected happily in freedom.

Hitherto, both the Orange Free State authorities and those of the South African Republic (Transvaal Republic), although rejecting native claims to the particular diamond regions, had not attempted to exercise authority or to interfere in any way with the diggers who, except for their own self-constituted Diggers' Committees' regulations, followed their own sweet wills. But when the diggers learned that the President of the Transvaal Republic, Martinus Wessels Pretorius, had granted to a privileged firm of three persons monopoly rights to search for twenty years from 22 June 1870 for diamonds at the Fields, subject to a royalty to the Republic of 6 per cent on all diamonds found, the diggers at Klipdrift rose in rebellion and formed their own Independent Klipdrift Republic, with Stafford Parker, one of their number and a leading spirit, as President.

Parker was a sailor turned trader who had come early to the district and indeed is said to have been present when diamonds were first discovered. His acquaintance with both Boers and natives is said to have served him well in successful speculations, ending in his turning diamond digger himself. Soon Parker acquired great influence over the camp at Klipdrift; 'all the camp yielded authority to him and passed the title of President which he affected.'

Parker's method of government was apparently drastic but effective. His chief executioner was an ex-butcher who carried out Parker's sentences upon offenders against the peace of the camp. The lightest punishment was ducking in the Vaal; next came 'the cat'; worse was 'dragging through the river', the offender being bound head and heels and dragged through the water over the rough river bed by men on each bank. Last came 'the Spread-Eagle': the culprit being staked down by his hands and feet, extended flat on the ground in the full glare of the sun, and at the mercy of the flies. 'But,' writes one who knew him, 'in justice to Mr Parker and his counsellors whom it is now the fashion to ridicule, I declare that one whisper of cruelty, other than these eccentric punishments, never reached my ears. They did many foolish acts and perhaps committed some wrongs. It may not be well to ask closely which way their revenue all went. But their procedure answered the demands upon it. No criminal lost his life, and no honest man felt terror. There were, during my stay, thousands of educated and respectable men who sighed for the good old times when "The Diggers' Mutual Protection Society" held its meetings in Klipdrift, and Mr President Parker kept such propriety in the camp as has not since been known.'

When the 'English gentlemen' to whom Pretorius had granted the monopoly reached Klipdrift, Parker's treatment of them was similarly drastic and effective. Already disconcerted to find the land they had last seen almost vacant now covered by the intervening influx of diggers, they were completely intimidated when President Parker 'took them aside, and in gruesome tones warned them: "Don't say a word. They don't know you're here. If they did, they'd hang you on a tree!"' The discomfited monopolists speedily departed to complain to President Pretorius of the reception given them. Pretorius therefore – a worthy man who often came to dig on his own claims at Klipdrift with, it is said, a licence from Parker! – finding such activities not suited to the dignity of the South African Republic, decided to exert his personal and official authority upon the unruly diggers of Klipdrift by making a State Visit to the camp, attended by a body-guard of police and officials. Thus, not only would the monopoly be confirmed, but also – the implicit intention behind the monopoly grant – the Transvaal Republic's claim to part of the diamond diggings.

President Parker (an imposing figure, we are told, in his grey top hat, frock coat and dark glasses) was also when required a tactful diplomatist. He now rose to the occasion by arranging a subscription ball in his own tent in honour of Pretorius, when he arrived at Klipdrift early in August 1870.

Whatever the ball lacked of state pomp and splendour was compensated for by such easy intimacy that, as one newspaper correspondent reported, liquor, pies and cakes stocked behind the bar were 'cribbed' by some adventurous spirits, who passed them round to others waiting in front. The washed gravel floor of the roofless tent was graced by some hundred and fifty dancers (including no less than sixteen ladies) 'in all conceivable costumes'. The chief illumination, the moon, supplemented by a few tallow candles, produced but a dim effect within the tent. The music was provided by an accordion, fiddle, flute and drum.

Whether chiefly intimidated by the ball or by the sight of more armed and angry men than he could muster in his own republic to fight them, Pretorius withdrew, leaving Parker victorious. To the complaints of the disappointed monopolists Pretorius is said to have replied peevishly: 'Look at the place, sir! And tell me what I can do. There aren't men enough in the Transvaal to turn these people out. Your rights, sir? Your concession, sir? It is all very well to talk in that way, but look for yourself – look for yourself!' So the President returned in state to his capital with its 300 inhabitants including natives, and laid the whole matter before his Council who, with no suggestions to make, simply 'dropped' the whole question, ignoring various demands for compensation, made from time to time by the discomfited 'monopolists'. Nevertheless, Pretorius sent a strong complaint to the British colonial authorities of the invasion, occupation and insurrection of the diamond squatters on the Vaal.

As news of increasing discoveries of diamonds spread, tension over the various rival claims proportionately increased. Waterboer, inspired by wily advisers, asked to become a British subject, while the British High Commissioner at the Cape, Lieutenant-General Hay, watched developments, alert to seize whatever opportunity offered of obtaining possession of the Diamond Fields. He now sent a representative, John Campbell, to Klipdrift with magisterial powers over the British subjects there, while President Brand appointed the Swede, Olaf Truter, (an ex-policeman from the Australian gold fields) to be magistrate and representative of the Orange Free State at Pniel, transferring him shortly afterwards to Dutoitspan when diamonds were found there. Hay meantime adopted a more threatening attitude, warning Brand against acting upon his claim, protesting at Truter's authority over British diggers, and warning Pretorius not to encroach upon tribes 'in alliance with Britain'.

Upon the appointment of Campbell, 'President Parker' readily accepted his authority and resigned, so bringing the 'Diggers' Republic' to an end, despite a commission from Waterboer, 'which added greatly to the gaiety of the assembled multitudes at the Diggings'. For some time, under the dubious control of a quarrelsome Executive Committee the little, short-lived 'republic' had been drifting towards anarchy. With the discovery of Dutoitspan, the evacuation of Klipdrift by the many diggers moving to the new dry diggings had left the place deserted. Thus when Campbell arrived, he found the Diggers' Republic declining and disintegrating.

Parker's republic has been ridiculed as a mere 'comic opera', but it was much more than that. Beneath the surface comedy and the very practical prevention of the monopoly was the intention to prevent assimilation of the diggings by the Transvaal Republic and to free them for subsequent absorption by Britain. 'If this hope was not openly avowed at first,' writes the chief historian of the Diamond Fields, 'it undoubtedly existed in the minds of many of the diggers, and no time was lost in communicating the situation to Her Majesty's High Commissioner at the Cape, Lieutenant-General Hay.' That the men of the Diggers' Republic really expected to preserve its independent existence for any length of time after it had served its immediate purpose, is most improbable, despite the fact that so far, few if any suspected how short would be the life of the river diggings.

But whatever loyal rejoicings greeted the advent of Mr Campbell, soon many diggers, irritated by new laws and restrictions, bitterly resented the change and regretted the days of Parker's administration, as soon became evident. Parker himself, when the Republic disappeared, departed for the Transvaal gold fields amidst the regrets and good wishes of those who still remained at Klipdrift. Nor did some, at least, suspect Parker's integrity. 'Mr Parker,' wrote one who knew him and was well qualified to judge, 'with all his opportunities, made no very great deal of money on the Diamond Fields. When he left them for the Transvaal gold fields he squared his accounts like a man, but he who brought little into these fields took little out of them. I do believe that when he went he did not leave an enemy behind him, and had the good wishes of all who knew him.'

On the gold fields Parker appears to have had no greater financial success than the diamonds brought him, and far less social importance; for when we next hear of him, Parker had declined into a 'Marketmaster'. 'When I met him the next time,' wrote the same friend, 'he was at Barberton – not President of the gold fields, but Marketmaster of the only town then existing in the gold fields. From President to Marketmaster could hardly be regarded as a *step* in the right direction, but rather a *stride* in the wrong one; but Parker, the Marketmaster of Barberton, was quite as jovial, happy and merry as the "President" at Klipdrift – and rather more so, I think. He was as ready to welcome old friends, hospitable to perfection, and altogether a swagger citizen of the Great Republic! Stafford Parker is naturally generous in private life, and is by no means wanting in natural ability within a certain range.' So Stafford Parker disappears from History, and, despite his Draconian punishments, with no little credit.

But long before the end of the Diggers' Republic and the departure of Parker, the territorial claims of the various disputants had become increasingly strident and increasingly complex, particularly after the dry diggings were discovered. Before, along the uninhabited banks of the Vaal, the only person in actual possession was the head clergyman of the Berlin Mission who claimed land along the river. A struggle had also developed between the owners of the land at the dry diggings and the diggers who invaded the diamond farms and refused either to give up the land they had taken, or pay more for it than the 10s. monthly licence allowed by the Diggers' Committee.

The Boer farmers, bewildered, disheartened and disgusted by the inrush of swarms of diggers beyond all restraint or control, finally sold their farms to the speculative English and Colonial companies which immediately sought to buy them at bargain prices. These companies next claimed the right, as owners of the land, to exclude the diggers and by means of native employees to dig for their own diamonds themselves. This the diggers and their committees naturally bitterly opposed, caring nothing about legal niceties. Such practices, they declared, were contrary to their Diggers' Committee's regulations – which, however, had no force of law. In effect they claimed that the owner of the land should have no right to possess it except so far as the diggers allowed him to do so.

It was now that the Orange Free State, which still held authority at this time over the territory, passed legislation confirming the diggers' regulations and even converting them into law, along with several additions of their own – all depriving the unfortunate landowners of their rights and privileges. Thus among other regulations the new laws declared:

1. All lands upon which diamonds and precious metals had been found were open to the public upon payment of the 10s. monthly licence fee.
2. The State to have the option to buy such land compulsorily at 2s. per acre.
3. The Diggers' Committee and its regulations to have the force of law.
4. The landowners to pay 10 per cent of their licence revenue to the Committee for expenses of police, health and Committee members' salaries.
5. The landowners to pay half their licence fees (5s. out of each 10s. licence), to the State.
6. The landowner may not work more than two claims for himself.

After such encouragement, the diggers became more violent in opposing any attempt by the owners to restrict their activities. One digger has left us this interesting glimpse of the happenings which followed the Free State decree, as soon as the news of it reached the dry diggings. 'At dawn Mr Webb [the owners' agent] and his household were awakened by a desperate clamour. The insatiable digger, with Dutoitspan scarce yet scratched by pick or shovel, has "rushed" Bultfontein also. Claims were marked up to Mr Webb's very doorway. They used the house-wall as a boundary. Big, rough fellows were tearing about with pegs in their hands, wrangling, fighting, rejoicing over the spoil. Others drove off with many a curse and blow, the Kaffirs who had been working for the proprietors' benefit. Henceforth they were to have no right to their own diamonds, excepting in two claims only.

'Mr Webb and two or three staunch friends struggled through the mob, amidst curses and threats. They attempted to plead for some small grace. They tried to point out that, after all, the land was theirs – paid for with their money, and at no mean price. But it was all useless. The diggers who hated and derided the Free State appealed to the law just passed by its Volksraad, though it had not yet been published. Active measures then were taken at the greatest personal risk. The upholders of justice drew out the pegs immediately surrounding the house. One huge fellow swore he would drive his pick through Mr Webb's foot if he dared obliterate his claim-mark. Three times the line was made, and three times was it gallantly smoothed out.

'The protected of the Free State howled and yelled at the little band. They threatened to hang Mr Webb and his friends on a Bultfontein tree. But a compromise was at length effected by some committee-men, who had no immediate interest in the matter. Sixty feet all round the house was reserved to the proprietors, and those who had marked out claims within that area growlingly withdrew. As to the remaining acres of Bultfontein farm, fifteen thousand or so, these were to be accounted gone, lost, from that hour, so far as diamonds are concerned. Not a scoundrel in the world but possessed for the future an equal field with the poor proprietors, and vastly more favour. He at least kept what he made, having as good a right to work as anyone; the proprietor must return 60 per cent of what sums were paid him. Earnestly did Mr Webb and his partners long for the British annexation.'

Shortly after the appointment of Campbell, Hay was superseded as High Commissioner by Sir Henry Barkly who was, if possible, even more anxious than Hay to acquire the Diamond Fields. After much more wrangling he persuaded Pretorius to submit the Transvaal Republic's claim to a court of arbitration, and agreed to a joint administration of the disputed lands pending the award. Barkly tried to persuade Brand to agree also, but Brand insisted on *foreign* arbitration, which Barkly would not accept. Divided control (rather than 'joint control') led to defiance of Truter's authority. Brand sent a commando to maintain order, and rumours were rife among the diggers before its arrival. 'A prominent topic at table,' wrote one, dining at Jardine's hotel at Pniel, 'was the impending "commando" of the Free State. People did not quite know whether to laugh or to be alarmed at the report that Mr Brand had ordered all his Boers to keep their war-horse and their rifle ready. In the meantime, they used the word in a joking fashion.' Barkly, in reply, sent a force of Cape Police and threatened to meet force with force. Pretorius, too, showed his teeth, sending a large commando to Klipdrift, where it stayed a month ' "in observation", much cheered and chaffed by the diggers,' until it withdrew.

Meanwhile, Barkly, supported by a new Colonial Secretary in England, the Earl of Kimberley, determined upon the annexation of the Diamond Fields, now proving more extensive and richer than was dreamed before. After more diplomatic manoeuvring Pretorius was induced to submit his claim to the Lieutenant-Governor of Natal, Robert William Keate, as the Court of Arbitration was too divided for a decision. Keate, apparently justly, deciding on evidence now claimed to have been inadequate, gave

the Diamond Fields to Britain, and Barkly on 27 October 1871 proclaimed
their annexation.

On 7 November the formal annexation took place. 'This ceremony',
declared a local journal, 'has been performed at the various camps with
much *éclat* and great rejoicing. There was not an obstacle raised, nor the
slightest opposition shown; but, on the contrary, the diggers as a body,
seemed delighted with the change. Du Toit's Pan, which we have been led
to believe all along had such strong Free State proclivities, was the most
enthusiastic in its reception of the Commissioners. There were Chinese
crackers, cheers, and a dinner and a ball.' There were also various enthusiastic public orations promising a wonderful future for the Diamond
Fields.

Nevertheless, a discordant note was not lacking, for on the same day
President Brand issued a counter proclamation, a protest against the
annexation and against the British forces which had occupied the Fields.
But at the same time he ordered the Boers to avoid all violence, as he was
confident that after proper representations to England the disputed territory would be restored to its previous owners.

Many diggers, too, now that the rule of the Boer Republics had been
eliminated as they wished, began to regard the new order with mixed feelings, fearing that the freedom they had enjoyed under their Committees
might be restricted. 'There was little or no enthusiasm, nor did any great
disturbance rise when an American digger hauled down the English flag
just after it had been hoisted on Dutoitspan. All contemplated with alarm
the probable results of British law upon their industry. They feared difficulties with the negro, needless interference with their rules. But at a
public dinner held that day at Dutoitspan, Mr Commissioner Thompson
[one of the newly appointed British Commissioners], gave great satisfaction by a short and simple speech. He said that although the Proclamation declared that the laws of Cape Colony would be administered here,
special note should be taken of the qualifying clause, "in so far as the same
be not inapplicable to the circumstances existing". This was an important
reservation. For instance, a strict and literal interpretation of the Masters
and Servants Act would bring about the sudden and immediate appearance
of a crowd of independent native diggers in their midst, which was neither
to be desired nor to be feared by anyone.' So one of the diggers saw it.

'Next day a criminal named Duffy, in custody of the Free State Police,
appealed to the passers-by, and claimed protection of the English authorities. He was released upon that ground by the new police. Thereupon,
Mr Truter, the Free State magistrate, solemnly arose from off his bench,

violently protested against this interference, and broke up his court. So ended Free State rule upon the diamond fields, with the protest of Mr President Brand.' Truter indeed deserved better treatment. He had carried out his duties with complete impartiality and dignity, and upon certain occasions which demanded it, with conspicuous courage which had gained for him the respect of the diggers in general. One described him as having 'a character which commends itself to the average digger, and in this respect he is well suited to his post. . . . Very satisfactorily he administered a rough and ready sort of justice. That he was enabled to do so is a legitimate boast of the diggers, for the police at his disposal were corrupt and incapable to a degree of which the magistrate himself bitterly complained. They were the best joke of the diggings.'

The landowners, having lost through the Free State legislation almost all their rights over their land and also 60 per cent of their fees from miners' licences, hoped for better things from the British administration when the territory was annexed. But in this they were speedily disappointed; more than disappointed, indeed, for their treatment by Britain was from the landowners' point of view far worse than that by the Free State. Before, they had been chastised with whips; now they were to be chastised with scorpions!

For not only did the new Commissioners declare the Diamond Fields 'open and public', they also transferred control of the licences and fees paid by the miners from the landowners to the Government Inspectors they now created, who were to issue and supervise licences and receive the fees – matters hitherto managed by the landowners or their agents. Upon this the owners' receipts immediately and mysteriously and sharply declined; for the Inspectors were inefficient, careless and lazy. Many diggers no longer troubled to pay fees at all. They evaded not only those of their digging licences, but also those for grazing their sheep and cattle on the land. Besides, they now began to sink their own wells for water on their claims, illegally, so that the landowners' fees for the use of the wells they had made – 1s. a month for two buckets of water a day to be filled and carried by the digger himself – also declined. The Inspectors, seldom troubling to patrol the Fields as the owners' agents had done, now only occasionally bothered to detect fraudulent diggers by examining their licences, and to punish them. Thus many continued to dig happily and illegally, without payment or much fear of being disturbed.

Nor was this all. Soon, despite assurances to the contrary, the landowners were forbidden to raise licence fees if they wished to do so. The Commissioners also decided to take 10 per cent of the owners' revenue from the Fields to pay their expenses, a deduction which, after keeping the owners waiting five months before any payment was forthcoming, was raised to 50 per cent. Indeed the administration intended to make the few diamond farms pay for the cost of administering the whole annexed region. 'By the dry digging precedent absolutely nothing is left to the landowner. He was just 40 per cent better off under the Free State.' To protests Lord Kimberley 'replied with emphasis, "The country should pay every farthing we could squeeze out of it." ' When it was pointed out that not the country but only one or two small farms were being made to take the burden, the reply was still the same. Thus, to take but one instance, the landowners who were not allowed to work their land themselves, received only £8 for licence fees from two brothers who almost immediately took from their New Rush claim diamonds worth £40,000!

That many of the diggers were largely indifferent to the annexation when it occurred, we have already seen. How widespread this attitude was, and how real, various accounts by observers show. 'The annexation has been formally made with evidences of satisfaction from the diggers, but without enthusiasm. The fact is, this matter has been thoroughly "discounted". Every one knew it must take place. Without such confidence, the digging population would long since have defied the Free State. They were quite content to endure for a little while a government which gave them their own most absolutely, and only robbed or harassed the landowners; but it was on the avowed condition that England would step in as soon as decently she could. Failing that, a republic self-constituted, with "President Parker" to rule in such fashion and for such time as suited the majority, was the programme. But I would not have it supposed, either, that the diggers are remarkable for loyalty. Emphatically they were not so when I arrived on the fields, and before I left there was something like positive treason in the air. No easy task is it to probe the feelings of a busy, eager, reckless population such as this. The results are apparent, indeed they show themselves with something more than candour; but the process of thought amongst an inadhesive crowd is long and difficult to trace.'

For this 'listlessness' about annexation there were several obvious reasons. So far as 'patriotism' affected the matter, it must be remembered that a large number of the diggers were not of British extraction; Germans, Boers and men and women from many different countries made up a large proportion of the population of the Fields. Besides, the Orange Free State had left the diggers almost complete freedom until the dispute with Britain, and recently had been very generous to the diggers at their own landowners' expense. The uncertainty hanging over the dispute with

Britain for possession of the Fields had not been without its influence on the diggers, tending to restlessness and anxiety. Fears upon annexation that the unknown devil might be worse than the known, that British officialism might interfere with the diggers' freedom far more than the mild Free State rule had done, above all that the natives might now be permitted to buy and work claims for themselves and by underselling their diamonds knock the bottom out of the diamond market: all these fears prevented undue enthusiasm among the diggers when annexation was at last proclaimed. Such were the conditions which 'made men listless in this matter of annexation at the first, and has finally bred in them a feeling of positive discontent.'

Fear, discontent and anxiety quickly bred disturbing rumours, often false or exaggerated among the diggers. When the owners of Dutoitspan and Bultfontein, unable to increase their digging licence fees, decided to begin to charge a ground rent of 10s. a month for each tent pitched on their farms, including grazing and water, the report went round that they were increasing the fees for the digging licences to £10 a month. Nor was such a belief strange, for the sums realized by diggers who cared to sell their claims were very large: especially if the claim were already proved to be a 'lucky' one. Well before the close of 1871, the unfortunate 'owners' of the ground, which they were not allowed to sell, saw small parts of claims being sold by the digger who paid them but 10s. monthly, for prices varying from £350 to £1,500, while, as one digger at the New Rush wrote: 'I suppose £10,000 would scarcely buy the best claims of this wondrous kopje.'

Fears of an imminent plague of typhus also arose when several persons were found dead on the Fields, fears which proved unjustified, but greatly increased tension. New causes for a revival of the old fears also arose; particularly the fear lest natives be allowed under English law to obtain claims. Worst of all, a proclamation suddenly changed the old regulations about the 'jumping' of claims. No longer might the 'jumper' obtain possession of a claim left untouched by its owner for eight consecutive days by merely lifting a spadeful of earth or making a scratch in the ground with a pick; henceforth he must properly excavate and sort the ground to be able to claim the 'jumped' ground as his own. But even this was only a six months' concession to the miners, for at the end of that time deserted claims were to be sold by auction by the official Inspectors: a change which deeply angered the diggers, who resented their 'democratic' rights being surrendered to the power of wealth.

Upon annexation, little time was lost in dissolving the Diggers' Committee and abrogating its regulations. On 29 November a proclamation was issued to this effect, while at the same time, to appease resentment, the population were invited to call a meeting at Dutoitspan to appoint another committee which should re-enact such of the old regulations as helped to preserve law and order, yet would not be contrary to English law. One account of the meeting, although somewhat lengthy, is too graphic, preserves too much of the local colour of the Fields to be omitted: 'When I got back to the Pan the adjourned meeting was just commenced. Captain R—, inspector of claims, had formally opened it, and invited those present to speak and vote. Thereafter he retired. The assembly met in the market square, where the tables on which our market-master is wont to stride gave its speakers a lofty station. There were, perhaps, a couple of hundred men to represent the thousands who sifted and sorted within our sight. It is idle to deny that they were not a prepossessing crew. The best men of the kopje shone by their absence. Those present appeared to be mostly agitators, who could not, of course, agree amongst themselves. But it was painful to remark how many bleared and disfigured eyes there were in the assembly. Diamond digging is a profitable occupation, but verily *on y joue sa peau.*[1]

'I perceived, also, that two classes, antagonistic to each other, were face to face. There was the digger, bleared and grimy, with loud voice, strong arm, and aggressive individuality. There was also the younger man, scarce less grimy, as strong of arm, and as loud-voiced on occasion, but bearing always that *cachet* in tone and manner which marks the gentleman or person of society. There is a *jeunesse dorée* of Dutoitspan, though it be not so numerous or so prominent as that of New Rush. These classes were evidently opposing one another, and the cheers of one were always chorused by the ironical laughter of the adversary.

'A certain Mr D— took the chair; that is, he mounted the table, and stood aloft under the shade of a great umbrella upraised by a black man. Who elected him to this honourable prominence I could not make out. Then somebody shouted out the name of a Mr K—, and another cried, "I second that!" Without further ceremony, Mr K— climbed the table, and began to make a speech. Whilst this proceeded, with considerable strength of lung, another name was shouted, another seconder backed it, and a third digger, "in his habit as he lived" – a very dirty habit – mounted to his comrades; a fourth was similarly appointed. But the *jeunesse dorée* began to get its back up. In the loud wrangle that ensued, I made my way to the table, and obtained the advantage of Mr K—'s eloquence. Its framework

---

[1] One risks one's life at it.

seemed to be a series of interjections, interrogations addressed to his "brother diggers"!

'Something in this style the oratory ran: "Did we invite this 'ere English annexation, brother diggers? No, we didn't: we didn't ask it, and we don't want it. We was content with the old committee and its rules, wasn't us, brothers? Those gentlemen understood the wants of diggers, and provided for 'em. These Commissioners don't know nothing about us. I ask you, brother diggers, was there ever a diamond digging like this afore? No! Well, then, what do these Commissioners know about it? What does the Cape Parliament, or what does the English Parliament know about it? Nothing! Very well, then, let us be ruled by them as does know; and if we are to vote, let us vote for the old Committee back again, and all the old rules. That's your ticket, brother diggers! The old Committee and the old rules!" – and some strong language followed. After twenty minutes of this, Mr K— jumped down amidst the throng, in a thunder of cheers from his friends, and ironical laughter from the other party.

'Then a Dutchman – a Boer that is – climbed up and attempted to address the meeting in Cape Dutch. It is so very seldom one sees a man of his race able to use any customs of this sort, that I was pleased to observe the ease and gravity of his bearing. What he said I did not understand, nor could have caught if I had comprehended, so great a row was going on. The swell party had proposed and seconded several of their number, who seemed to have quite as good a claim as the others. Things now had reached such a state of confusion, that Mr D— adjourned the meeting till 5 p.m.

'How many gatherings of the sort was I destined to see, all terminating in the same result – nothing! The reign of democracy had passed; the glamour of agitators had vanished before the dignity of English officials. Mr Parker, the most powerful of all the body, quite withdrew himself after the annexation; so did Mr F—, a man of great influence. To conclude this story; Mr K—'s advice was taken at the adjourned meeting, and the old Committee, just dissolved, was re-elected, under express instructions to repass all the abrogated rules. Of course the Commissioners declined to acknowledge this result.'

Such an ending to the diggers' demonstrations was little likely to assuage the general feeling of dissatisfaction in the camps. To the other causes of discontent was now added that of being some twenty-five miles distant from the centre and headquarters of the British Administration, with its High Court and three Commissioners, all stupidly situated at Klipdrift, which had only 'some hundreds of vagrant diggers, whilst the Pan [Dutoitspan] is looked on as a capital by fifty thousand substantial men'. 'One of the pleas on which the English Government took possession of the fields was that of preserving order and obviating perils which might ultimately have become most serious. How does it justify its action on this ground? By posing the seat of authority twenty-five miles away from the spot where danger might arise, across a broad and dangerous river, which sometimes becomes impassable for weeks. Here is shrewd action.'

Soon the truth of the complaint became obvious when, after a mass meeting of protest against the overruling of the new Diggers' Committee, the diggers seized upon several incidents to rise in a general revolt. 'Captain R— came up and dined with us. Mentioned in course of conversation, that the diggers of New Rush intended to try a canteen keeper for buying diamonds of a negro. So many alarming reports are always current, that we paid no attention to this warning.' Evidently the men of New Rush intended to ignore the new authorities, and to deal with delinquents as before, under the Committee rules of the past. At the same time the diggers at Dutoitspan were being angered by the landowners' prosecution of some who had been digging wells, instead of searching for diamonds, on their claims. In reply the diggers angrily claimed that they should be free to do what they pleased with the thirty feet of ground they paid for; ignoring the fact that the small fees they paid were for a licence to dig for diamonds, not for complete possession of the ground. The magistrate at Dutoitspan refused to settle the dispute which was then referred to the Commissioners at Klipdrift, where four months later a ruling in favour of the landowners was given, which further angered the diggers.

In the meantime, on 17 December came more disturbing news: 'About 2 p.m. rumours came down of disturbances at New Rush. I tried to get a cart, but earlier information had drawn everyone to the riot. I retired to Bultfontein, whither, about four o'clock, several friends came cantering over with the news. It seems that a certain A—, reputed to be a man of damaged repute, had for some time been suspected of buying diamonds from black servants. On Saturday, a specific charge was made against him, on the confession of a Hottentot. There really appears to be little doubt of his guilt. On Saturday, notices were sent round by some of the wealthiest and most respectable of the New Rush diggers, inviting a select few to meet at 11 a.m. this morning.

'About fifty attended; in fact, I believe there was only one absent of those invited. The Hottentot was produced by his master, and repeated his confession. After hearing it, but one verdict could be given. Some few suggested prosecution, but this course met with no approval. Marching from the council tent in a body, the self-appointed ministers of justice went towards A—'s canteen. Their purpose was widely known, and every digger in camp approved. By the time they reached their destination, there were not less than two thousand resolute men behind them. Nothing was said to A— beyond a few stern words. The leaders, I believe, had no intention of hurting him, but it appears that he was struck with an empty bottle, knocked down, and seriously hurt. His servants, too, suffered badly. Thereafter the place was sacked, the liquor started, every article of sale or furniture destroyed, and the canvas set blazing over the ruin.

'The leaders then would fain have had the crowd disperse; but this proved impossible. Carrying their reluctant instigators along, they went to canteen after canteen, holding before the door of each a trial, which would have seemed excellent burlesque, had it not been so cruelly serious. Five were condemned and burnt down, one after another. In the midst of the tumult, a Boer who had just been married drove down Main Street, where the rioters were thronging at that moment, with his bride and bridesmaids. The *cortège* was stopped, half a dozen big fellows clambered up and kissed the bride, and tickled the bridesmaids, to the roaring delight of those below.

'This sport exhausted, it came under earnest debate whether to burn the proprietors' tents – those luckless proprietors! – or to sack the stalls of the koopers. Little groups of the dangerous class gathered round each diamond-buyer's tent, loudly threatening, and waiting only for one spark of encouragement. Mr P—, the representative of the New Rush proprietors, was, I am told, in actual fear of his life; and a dozen wealthy diamond merchants have assured me that they expected a general sack from moment to moment.

'But while the crowd was hesitating, their leaders trying to disperse them, Mr Gilfillan, the resident magistrate of Dutoitspan, *pro tem.*, came up. He was loudly cheered by the rioters, who knew they had nothing to fear. It was a difficult, and, indeed a dangerous position for any one to occupy. Mr Gilfillan had no armed force to rely on; his police numbered about one to five rioters, nor were they either disciplined or contented. But it was carrying too far the conciliation policy to declare, as did our Dutoitspan magistrate, that the diggers had done nothing amiss; that he himself had been a digger, and knew and shared their feelings. "I am a digger myself," cried this gentleman, from the eminence of a cart, "and I understand you."

'But whilst excusing their illegal acts, Mr Gilfillan quietly suggested that enough had been done. He begged the mob to go home without further outrage. They cheered him, and passed up the street to burn an empty tent, with a few bottles in it, which some malevolent wretch denounced. When the act had been committed, it dawned upon the minds of some present that their proceedings were rather hasty. A shout arose for the accusing witness. He tried to conceal himself, but was discovered and pushed to the front. They say that the man's appearance instantly convinced all present that he had lied. It was earnestly debated whether or not to throw him amongst the glowing cinders, during which time he contrived to slip away, under protection of the chief rioters. A subscription, raised upon the spot, doubly or trebly reimbursed the tent-owner for his loss.

'Then, not warned by this awkward mistake, shouts arose for an advance on Dutoitspan, to carry out Lynch-law there. Mr Gilfillan, who had taken refuge in a canteen, now made himself useful. He induced the drivers of the carts to turn their horses round and refuse to go. Thereupon, as it was growing dark, the rioters dispersed to the pleasant diversion of chasing negroes round about, aimlessly punching their heads when caught. Not a policeman showed himself all through the time. He would have run no risk, for all knew him to be powerless, and well affected towards the malcontents. But the Free State party rejoices, saying that such disorders were unknown under Truter's rule.'

Meanwhile, at Dutoitspan fears of the impending march from the New Rush spread confusion, dismay, and yet stronger indignation that the headquarters of law and order should be miles away at Klipdrift. 'The Commissioners had not long been established in their comfortable quarters by the Vaal before receiving demonstration that the seat of Government is awkwardly chosen. The riots of New Rush took place, and most serious evils threatened. The burning of tents occurred at three o'clock; the march to Dutoitspan was arranged for five; special constables began to be sworn in at the latter place about four, and we were prepared for a desperate encounter. Where were the Commissioners? Safe at the metropolis, of course, "dreaming the happy hours away" [1] across the river. It is said that the news of what had happened reached them at midnight. Had the rioters followed their worst instincts, the same messenger might have brought news that all the dry camps were blazing.'

Nor did the exciting events of 17 December end with the day. 'This has been a day of alarm to many, and anxiety to all, at Dutoitspan.' So begins the diary for 18 December, and continues: 'A portion of the late rioters held a meeting in the forenoon, at which various storekeepers here were

---

[1] From the then popular 'drawing room' song:
Come where my love lies dreaming,
Dreaming the happy hours away—etc.

denounced as having sold diamonds to negroes. It was resolved to pay the accused a visit tonight; for the hours sacred to digging could not be encroached upon even for sacred vengeance. The threatened parties waited on Mr Gilfillan, and begged advice. I visited New Rush in the afternoon, but all seemed quiet. On my return there was a definite and well-formed rumour abroad. Mr K—, the "diggers' friend" and landowners' enemy, chairman of incendiary committees, and general agitator against common sense and justice, he who has led each crusade against proprietory rights, whom I myself have heard in the market square, perched on the market tables, deliver a vehement harangue against all authority but digger force – even he himself had been tried in his absence and convicted. Sentenced he was, without appeal, to have his house and store burned down.

'A formal notice to that effect was sent to him from New Rush. In pitiable terror he appealed for police aid. Mr Gilfillan promised assistance, and straightaway began to press in the passers-by as special constables. A Mr Fry— was amongst those first caught, and very droll was his indignation at the thought of defending, above all men on earth, Mr K—. But we were all interested in this case, for the post-office chances to be under the doomed roof just at present. Great excitement reigned when the news became disseminated. Diamond holders thoughtfully cogitated as to the best hiding-place for their store. The canteen keepers generally showed more stoicism, prepared for the worst. News from "The Mountain"[1], as one might call New Rush, an old revolutionary phrase, had a crowd of eager listeners throughout the day.

'I scarcely doubt that there was a scheme abroad for making mischief at Dutoitspan, but I feel quite sure the chief men of New Rush had no part in it. The project was hatched by the few persons of criminal antecedents who hung about the fields. We sat till a late hour, but no red glare lit up the sky. All was in readiness at Bultfontein House for an immediate sortie to the spot attacked, but no need arose. In fact, the seething camp beneath us never had been so still. Till midnight, there is in general a surge of life about it, a noise of laughter, shouting, and rude music, which re-echoes upwards to us, standing upon the piles of stuff around our sacred area. There is, too, a flicker of lights between tent and tent; the Kaffir cry swells up our hill; and tipsy songs ring out from time to time with astounding distinctness. But this night was very silent; something like expectation hung in the very air. I have little doubt that any strange mob would have been warmly met; for there is little love lost between gay New Rush and the toiling Pan.

[1] 'The Mountain' was the extreme leftist party of the French Revolution.

'In the first place, however, there were two miles and a half of barren veldt between the lawless rioters there and this peaceful camp – a long night march; then, at the head of the movement, was a body of respectable and substantial men, who might be irritated by the thought of wrongs into violence, but have already learned caution. Thanks to these causes, the ill-disposed have been disheartened, and Mr K— all of us, perhaps – have escaped considerable danger. Things were wholly quiet throughout the night, nor do we fear a recurrence of the disorders at present; but when they may be renewed, upon fresh cause given or suspected, no one can predict. There is an ominous talk of the Ballarat[1] riots, which may keep mischief alive. That bad characters are greatly on the increase any store-keeper will prove to you at his cost. One firm here, which was accustomed, under the Free State, to leave half its stock-in-trade beside the street all night, and never lost the value of a penny, suffered two attempts at burglary last week, besides the theft of a couple of wine-casks: other and more successful efforts of housebreaking are reported.

'The police are never to be seen, save in a canteen, drinking. It may not be their fault that they never seem to go on duty, or to have any beat by day or night; but, with shame be it confessed, the acts of our Commissioners, when forced beyond the tether of Sir H. Barkly's masterly proclamation, have been feeble. They have remedied no evil that caused complaint under the *régime* of the Free State; they have allowed to be introduced drunkenness and disorder among the negroes, burglary, highway robbery, and rioting amongst the diggers. These are strong words; but when I say that nine people in ten are inclined to regret, or openly anathematize, the British annexation, I shall be held excused by all loyal subjects for the expression. The riots just over would not have been possible under Free State rule. The authority of Mr Truter was too absolute, resting, as it did, on digger prejudices, and his punishments too swift and stern to allow the cause of them; his police too, scarecrows as they were, patrolled the streets, or, if they did not, their vigilance was not missed. Our guardians are drafted from that fine body of men, the Frontier Mounted Police; they avow their detestation of municipal service, for which they did not enlist. The authorities are aware of the illegality, and their officers share the general indignation. I believe the men to be brave and well disciplined, picked soldiers, in fact; but not of such can be made good policemen, even if willing, which our constables certainly are not. The English have brought hither a great parade of forms – the High Commissioners and their High Court are mighty adornments; but we poor

[1] In Australia; when gold was discovered there in 1851.

residents, whether diggers, koopers, or spectators, would rather have some reasonable guarantee for the good behaviour of the ill-disposed than any forms or precedents.'

Nevertheless, the principles of law, order and justice were not to be ignored by the British Administration, and on 6 January 1872 the diary records the sequel to the New Rush riots. 'Mr Giddy, our new Civil Commissioner and magistrate, has shown himself the determined man wanted here. He does not share that sympathy with "diggers' feelings" that so curiously distinguished his predecessor, Mr Gilfillan. Disregarding the open and published threats of New Rush, and the prudent counsel of his friends, he issued warrants against the three most violent of the rioters: Messrs M—n, M—y, and M—m. And these warrants he has seen executed. The case came on for hearing today at 10 a.m. Before that hour the main street of Dutoitspan was very lively. A large crowd of diggers from New Rush had assembled outside the tiny court-house, talking loudly in knots, and overflowing into the near canteens.

'The intention of rescuing the accused, in case they should be committed, was literally shouted out. Nor do I entertain the smallest doubt that this project would have been effected. As time went on, the mob increased. Every cart from New Rush was crammed with excited visitors, and each well-known face aroused a cheer. The accused received an ovation, as they drove up, surrounded by their friends. At 10.30 a.m. the case was called, and a slight rush ensued. Mr Giddy's court-house, a temporary one, is about 20 feet by 12 feet, built of wood, with a roof of corrugated iron. The prisoners answered to their names, and were provided with seats, passed from hand to hand over the diggers' heads outside, and so through the sunny window; boxes they were with the lids torn off. Nothing is more expensive than a chair at these diggings.

'Then A—, whose canteen had first been burnt, was called, and no outbreak of indignation greeted him. He described himself as a canteen-keeper, but several voices accused him of having lately left the hulks at Capetown. Mr A— has not a prepossessing face, but that is an imperfect justification for burning his tent down. His evidence, descriptive of the attack on his canteen, was received with some hooting. The prisoners, seated on their empty boxes before the magistrate – all so close together in that tiny shed, each could have shaken hands with another, prisoners with prosecutor and magistrate with both – the prisoners behaved with creditable respect and propriety. Only one of the three looked quite like a digger. M—n is a tall and powerful young fellow, in flannel shirt, velveteen trousers, and dirty puggaree. His hands and arms, exposed, are scarred

with ancient wounds; his clothes and face white with the limey dust. M—y
is a little man, who seems to concentrate all his faculties in the effort to
retain his eyeglass in its place. M—m is a watch-maker by business, and an
auctioneer in his idle moments.

'The court grew very hot before any conclusive evidence had been taken.
A— deposed that M—m first entered his tent, and struck him with an
empty bottle rightaway. The blow made him "insensible", but he found
his memory faithful as to many incidents that took place during this state
of coma. Mr Giddy adjourned to the new court-house, not yet quite
finished. This building had the misfortune to stand next door to a canteen.
The day was very hot. As time went on, the proceedings became more and
more boisterous. Men went in and out between bar and court, making a
holiday of it, seeking the regular weekly drink in one building and the
weekly spree in the other. They smoked cigars and pipes, lolled on the
benches, cocked their hats in the awful face of justice, and shouted out
their opinions to one another. The police made no attempt to preserve
respect of court, but lighted their own pipes, and wetted their own
throttles, as bold as any.

'Mr Giddy sat actually alone, the representative of law and justice,
amidst a drunken and angry crowd, without one arm to support him. He
kept his temper and fulfilled his duty in the uproar, but it was a most
undignified position for a magistrate to hold. In the result, M—y and M—n
were bound over in £200 each, and M—m in £100 to appear when called
on by the public prosecutor. When it was asked who would go bail for the
prisoners, the diggers present shouted with one voice, "All Colesberg
Kopje! We'll give New Rush for bail!" Then they were released, and the
crowd snatched up their heroes by leg and arm, and paraded them all down
the street. It was not thought at the time that anything more would be
heard of the prosecution if no further outbreak occurred. But Mr Giddy
proved to be of more obstinate stuff.'

The general belief that no more would be done in the matter proved
mistaken. A few weeks later rumours of an impending re-trial arose, to the
renewed anger of the diggers. The chief difficulty of the court, however,
was to obtain reliable evidence for the prosecution. Of the two thousand
diggers who had witnessed the riot, none would give evidence. Even Mr
A—, whose evidence had made possible the original trial, was no longer
available. Immediately after giving his evidence he himself had been
arrested on a charge of illicit diamond buying, had forfeited his bail
and fled to Jacobsdaal in the Free State. There at the 'hotel' he was
seen. 'In a smoking-cap of the most beautiful colours, and a sort of

dressing gown, he ruled the roast mutton, affably conversing with his neighbours!'

Nevertheless, 'undismayed, the Crown Counsel hold their course. They are assured of efficient support. Our new police have been gradually arriving; a body of forty-eight reached here together on Saturday. These men belong to the same corps as our mutinous, incompetent guardians of the peace, but an important difference between them lies in this: the new-comers are volunteers for municipal duty, whilst the others were drafted here in defiance of their wish, or even of their engagement. On the other hand, the diggers breathe naught but fire and flames. They say, and doubtless believe, that several hundred pounds have been subscribed for hiring carts to Klipdrift on the eventful day, and nothing less than burning of the court-house is to be the penalty of conviction. Nevertheless, I do not anticipate much trouble. The subscriptions to the defence fund only amount to £1 5s.! Ominous for the unfortunate accused. Indeed the fiery spirit of December last burns feebly.' The trial duly occurred, amidst great excitement but without rioting, at the end of March, but was adjourned for lack of evidence and apparently never revived.

Nevertheless, the general dissatisfaction and the spirit of revolt it engendered were by no means appeased. A letter by a resident in Kimberley published in *The Times* on 8 February 1872, and written almost immediately after the annexation and the arrival of British officials at the Fields, very definitely states the particular grievances of the diggers and complains of their lack of satisfaction. 'Under the Free State Government, we complained absolutely of nothing but the drunken blackguards composing their police force; and this was a small grievance, inasmuch as there was a tacit mutual-protection feeling among us which enabled us to ignore their existence. We knew best our own requirements, and elected our governing committee, whose acts were recognized and approved by the Free State Government. When the British flag was hoisted, and Sir H. Barkly's proclamation was read, all British subjects, with their usual loyalty, cheered, but not because they expected better things. The result of British Government has been until now far worse than we could have anticipated. There is an everlasting growl among the diggers about being infinitely worse off than they were before. . . . Among many grievances I will detail but a few . . .'

Chief among these were: only one magistrate on the Fields; no new post offices to replace those of the Free State now withdrawn; increased and additional taxes. Not less serious was the British tacit annulment of the diggers' regulations relating to natives. That which forbade natives to possess diamonds and so to have claims was being ignored, for natives were actually working claims for themselves at Dutoitspan; 'fortunately for the "officials",' added the writer, 'the diggers do not yet know this.' Nor had the new Government been active in punishing those who bought diamonds from natives. Indeed a native had just confessed to the crime before a meeting of the diggers. 'The meeting, condemning the general tepidity of the Government, demanded that the native should lead the way and point out the canteen [whose owner had bought the stones]. In less than five minutes after, I saw it utterly demolished, the ruins in flames, and the owner narrowly escaping with his life. Five other suspected and well known offenders against these two regulations were punished similarly during the afternoon.

'I mention this incident to show you to what a climax the vexatious inaction of the British Government has brought its loyal subjects. It will be a severe lesson to them, and it will be rather difficult to allay the dangerous irritability that exists among us, especially as at least one-third of the digging community consists of educated and thinking men. Let the British Government annex as much territory as they choose, but if they cannot properly govern their loyal subjects, let the loyal subjects govern themselves.'

That the writer was by no means exaggerating the strength of feeling among the diggers became very evident five months later when the 'dangerous irritability' boiled over again into a new riot, more violent and extensive than its predecessor. It also included a more determined attack upon suspected natives. Burnings, floggings and cries of lynch-law were the order of the day for the thousands of excited diggers, marching with a musical accompaniment of amateurs at their head to burn tent after tent while the stocks of brandy and liqueurs were smashed and poured over the burning débris, to intensify the flames. Then, as *The Diamond News* of 20 July 1872 described it, 'Inspector G— arrived, and endeavoured to exert his influence in the interest of order, and if possible prevent further destruction of property, when he was seized, lifted upon the shoulders of some sturdy digger, and threatened with closer proximity to the flames than appeared to be pleasant. After this undignified treatment the gallant officer retired.' Nevertheless, the few police did something to restrain the crowd in various places and, when a march to Dutoitspan was beginning, halted it and turned it back.

At a meeting which Mr Giddy convened the following day, he tactfully induced many of the most important diggers to enrol as special constables to maintain law and order. In the meantime the police had made several arrests, and when the news of this spread through the camp, all the diggers again assembled, demanding their release. By tactfully accepting bail, though of £500, Mr Giddy complied with the general cry for the prisoners' release, and at the same time placated their resentment at the creation of special constables by assuring them that their main duty was to 'increase the means whereby rascally native servants and dishonest diamond buyers may be brought to justice'. Unfortunately, as the crowd in better humour advanced upon the gaol to applaud and welcome the released prisoners, they were met by a force of armed police, who, mistaking their arrival for an attack upon the prison in order to rescue the prisoners, charged the crowd with revolvers and truncheons. Although a general mêlée and more disturbances in other parts of the camp followed as a result, they soon died down, and it was evident that the strengthening of the police was having a good effect upon the mob.

On 18 July the Civil Commissioner, Mr Giddy, issued a notice condemning violence, appealing for more special constables, and suggesting the possibility of changes in the law to meet the diggers' complaints, thus: 'In the past history of the camps, there are a sufficient number of well-known facts to convince the public that where special laws are required to suit their special circumstances, the Government is in no degree averse to making such special provisions as may be required, and that a constitutional reference of any grievance will certainly be followed by an earnest endeavour on the part of the Government to grant redress. If, therefore, the digging community consider that further modifications of the Colonial law, or alterations in the form of government, are required to adapt the administration to the peculiar circumstances of the fields, let them state plainly their grievances, and use the unalienable, but constitutional privilege of Englishmen, by petitioning the Government, and they must be well aware that no reasonable request, *constitutionally* urged, will fail to meet with sympathy and consideration.'

Thereupon another great assembly of diggers took place in circumstances graphically described by a 'Special Correspondent' of the *Friend of the Free State* on 27 July. 'My last letter conveyed the intelligence to your readers that the Diggers' Committee and the Commissioners had met in the public offices to confer upon the modifications demanded by the diggers in the laws as they now stand, and I sent you the "modifications" (as they were called), which were alone to satisfy the diggers. It was not known when the Free State post left this Rush what concessions the Commissioners would make. There was a prevailing idea about that they would make none, and that a repetition of the rioting, and setting fire to tents and canteens, and the destruction of men's stock-in-trade would follow. There are not a few in the camp who would regard a scrimmage as jolly good fun, and tent-burning in the same light they would a bonfire.

'There are some who were elected on the committee, but not many, who talk with more flippancy than wisdom, and who speak of an anticipated rupture with Government, and the ruin of their neighbours, the canteen keepers, in a very gleeful strain. There was a good deal of that style of talk in the best frequented bar-rooms on Monday morning, and there was not very much work done by the rowdy white diggers through the day. Grog and gambling were the order of things. The rowdy part of the diggers who attend mass meetings, industriously circulated a report that nothing would be conceded, and that the Commissioners had resolved to put down the diggers with a high hand. They knew nothing about it, of course, but there are gangs of men in all the camps who set up to be diggers *par excellence* who do nothing but loaf about, join Lynch's crew, drink "smoke" (that vile compound which is rank poison), and "jump" whatever they can come across. They have no claims, are not interested in the right government of the country, and never do a day's digging from "year in to year out". You can see little knots of them at the corner of every street, and in every one there, a likely man to "shout" is to be found. They would drink the Vaal River dry if it could be turned into Cape smoke. It is they who are the loudest; they who in the name of the diggers pounce upon the natives, and talk of grievances most of all.

'I do not mean your readers to infer that there is anything like satisfaction in the camp, even amongst the best men in it. There is not. All men, dealers as well as diggers, feel that Government has not taken that interest in the welfare of the fields that should have been taken in them. I do not say that this is altogether the fault of the Commissioners. I do not think it is. . . . The Commissioners have never worked together as they should have done. . . . The Acting Commissioner, Mr Giddy, lives at New Rush, and the other two are forty miles away from him. . . .'

The Special Correspondent next described the great assembly of diggers called to discuss the Commissioners' concessions. It began with impressive panache contributed by sympathizers from Dutoitspan. 'Early in the morning – soon after breakfast in fact – men commenced to show up from Dutoitspan, and they reported that the *Panners* were coming to the meeting a thousand strong, to back up the New Rush opponents of Government. About half an hour before the meeting, a regiment of about a hundred and fifty Dutoitspan diggers marched into the market-place, headed by a Scotchman carrying a red flag – I suppose intended as the flag

of the fiery Lynchers. By 3 p.m., the hour fixed for the meeting, there were
over three thousand persons packed together in front of the public offices.
A buckwaggon was drawn out into the square, and the leading members of
the committee and the choicest spirits of the mass mounted it. There was
great cheering. . . .'

The meeting followed, of course, the previous pattern of such mass
demonstrations, and, after some had expatiated upon the generosity of the
Government's concessions and others, some of them disappointed place-
seekers, had opposed them, contrasting what they considered the better
conditions under Free State rule with those since annexation, the meeting
broke up in general disorder. In fact the concession forbidding natives to
dig was immediately cancelled by the authorities, and further rioting
followed.

The general irritation, the feeling of unsettlement caused by the changes
of Governments, felt not only by all the diggers, had spread also to the
Boer farmers of the region, and was intensified by the fact that many
natives possessed guns sold to them without any effective prohibition by
the British authorities, as part of the tactics of the annexation campaign.
That this 'dangerous irritability' had by no means died down, was very
evident to James Anthony Froude when two years later he visited the
Fields. 'The irritation was hotter as I approached the Diamond Fields.
Farmers clamoured that there was no safety for life or property. As long
as the frontier was unsettled, there could be neither magistrates nor police.
The chiefs might rise at any moment and burn their houses over their
heads. One English settler whom I met at Christiana told me that he was
ashamed of his country. . . . The diggers were in a state of incipient insurrection when I arrived: they rebelled openly a few months after, and troops
were sent from Cape Town to quiet them. It was the old grievance: with
tens of thousands of natives about them, all with guns in their hands, they
could not protect their property or sleep quietly in their beds. My own
business was to enquire into the circumstances of the annexation. Half
the diggers openly called it robbery, and would have preferred to belong
to the Free State. . . .'

It was the following year, 1875, when this, the worst of all the riots,
occurred, inspired by more or less the same grievances and also by a
number of reckless men who hoped to overthrow the Government's
control of the Fields and either to return them to the Free State or set up
their own 'republic' after the manner of Parker in the past. To this end
they joined and soon dominated the Diggers' Protection Association which
had been formed to voice the miners' complaints. The most conspicuous

of these leaders was a Fenian of many aliases, named – probably correctly in this case – Alfred Aylward, recently imprisoned for wounding a fellow digger in cold blood. According to Sir Garnet Wolseley, then administrator and general commanding in Natal, who knew Aylward, he was 'a most amusing ruffian, full of Irish stories which he tells inimitably'. A few years later, indeed, Aylward wrote and published a book on the Transvaal, which has been authoritatively described as 'the best book of his time' on that subject. One digger asserts that Aylward was for a time editor of one of the Diamond Fields newspapers, and describes him as 'a highly gifted man, a talented writer and fluent speaker, but in everyday life a garrulous character and bombastic braggart'.

Another of the leaders was a German officer who had fought in the Franco-Prussian War with distinction, and a third was an ex-criminal whose chief aim in inciting rebellion, as he later confessed, was to be revenged on a digger who had procured his conviction on the charge of inducing natives to steal diamonds. At the first disturbance, he would shoot this man and then disappear: such was his never realized intention.

The aim of the plotters was to create either an independent 'republic' like Parker's, or, if possible, to return to the easy rule of the Free State, which, they believed, they could always dominate if any dispute with it occurred. The reality of some of the diggers' grievances attracted some respectable adherents to the Diggers' Protection Association, which soon became a powerful influence in the camp. Now, too, additional excitement was caused by a prosecution for seditious libel, brought by the Government against a local newspaper which declared, 'our nefarious rulers are about to attempt another swindling land sale'. In the rising storm Aylward was especially prominent. At a mass meeting at Kimberley he violently exhorted his audience to arm themselves with rifles and revolvers, and soon some 800 rebels had formed themselves into a number of distinct battalions with cavalry squadrons, and openly were marching and drilling in the Market Square, and 'sometimes, when ordered to "right about face", they would, in a menacing and derisive manner, point their rifles at the Government Offices'.

At a meeting held on the night of 18 March 1875 Aylward went so far as to issue ball cartridges to his 'troops', and they then held a moonlight parade. Upon this, responsible citizens of Kimberley, including bankers, merchants and the clergy, became alarmed and warned the Lieutenant-Governor, Richard Southey, that the situation was dangerous. A man named Cowie was discovered to be the source of the importation and distribution of arms, and was thereupon arrested and accused of purchasing rifles without a permit.

Amidst tremendous excitement Cowie appeared in court. To show his contempt for authority and his own supposed power, he kept his hat on his head while in the dock until some official removed it. For the moment he was apparently released on bail, but later, refusing to pay the £50 fine imposed with the alternative of three months' imprisonment, he went to gaol. When the Lieutenant-Governor refused to accept the rebels' demand for the liberation of Cowie and in return ordered them to lay down their arms, the signal of revolt, the black flag, was hoisted on one of the mine dumps.

Their plans were to fire on the Government Offices and Court House, attack the prison and release Cowie and all the other prisoners, who were expected to join the rebels if only in gratitude. So the diggers' freedom would be accomplished either by the creation of their own Diggers' Republic or under the Free State.

But from the very first the revolt was a complete failure, despite the melodramatic enthusiasm of the black-bearded Aylward prancing about on a charger with a black flag in one hand, and an enormous sword dangling at his side. 'I shall never forget on this memorable revolutionary occasion,' wrote one digger who was no admirer of this 'leader', 'being in the Main Street and suddenly seeing a man of Satanic bearing come galloping down, waving a black flag in one hand and shouting valorously as if he were leading a heroic charge of cavalry. By his side a huge sabre dangled, which made a tremendous rattle and appeared to frighten a young horseman who followed in his wake like an unwilling dog pulled by his chain. It was none other than the redoubtable Irish-Fenian, Alfred Aylward on his way to see hoisted the piratical emblem which might have brought murder and chaos to many. Arrived at the signalling post the rebel ruffian threw himself recklessly from his steed, and with absolute head-strong courage ordered the banner to be hoisted – and then ran away to escape his deserts.'

Meanwhile, a scene in complete contrast, the quiet, courageous suppression of the rebellion even before it had begun, was being enacted at the Court House, as the acting magistrate, Mr D'Arcy – who four years later won the V.C. in the Zulu war – went straight up to the leaders. When the German officer, Von Schliechmann, hoping to start the riot, fired his revolver and explained it as an 'accident', D'Arcy quietly took the revolver from him, saying: 'Then we will have no more accidents'; and all was over. None of the rebels' plans was attempted; no seizing of the Lieutenant-

Governor, no destruction of the Kimberley gaol, no liberation of prisoners, no storming of the Government Offices. Aylward, indeed, not only promptly disappeared, but was so fearful of discovery and arrest, that he inserted in a local paper a bogus notice of his death.

The complete collapse of the revolt was partly due to the report that a regiment of Government troops from Cape Town was on its way to the Fields. The same report had largely helped to quell the rioters in 1872; but then, although in fact troops were held ready there, their departure had been cancelled at the last moment, as they were no longer needed. This time, however, troops arrived under the command of Sir Arthur Cunynghame. 'When it was all over and finished and nothing for soldiers to do, Cape Town officials despatched British troops to the scene of the recent rebellion.' Young Lionel Phillips, newly arrived in South Africa, travelled with some of the soldiers in a wagon drawn by fourteen mules from Cape Town to Kimberley. On arrival they camped for the night on a ridge overlooking the town. 'We fully expected a sanguinary assault next day but emissaries were sent out with a flag of truce, the ringleaders surrendered, and the troops were regaled at luncheon on the Market Square. So ended the rebellion. Death sentences were pronounced, but no one was severely punished, and the camp soon forgot all about the trouble.'

So ended the greatest and apparently the last of the diggers' riots. A more pleasant glimpse of Kimberley only two years later, showing, incidentally, how quickly the rebellious mood passed, is given us by General Sir Charles Warren in September 1877. 'Sir Arthur Cunynghame has met with a good reception; he was last at Kimberley when he quelled the rebellion in June 1875.

'We have had a field day with the Volunteers at Dutoitspan. It has opened my eyes as to their capabilities. In England we are inclined to think so little of Volunteers. . . . We had a good show of Volunteers, mounted and foot, Dutoitspan Hussars, Kimberley Light Horse, and Griqualand Infantry, all in resplendent uniform. They performed nothing but parade movements, but their precision was excellent, and when they advanced in line to Sir A. Cunynghame, and gave him a general salute, it was done so well that I felt quite proud of our little Province.'

That night, at a 'grand Masonic Ball' in the theatre in honour of General Cunynghame, when he and Sir Charles Warren were sharing a box together, he told Sir Charles 'again about his notable expedition in 1875 to quell the insurrection in Kimberley, and has been pointing out a few of the most prominent rebels, who are now some of our most loyal people. It is a queer subject this question of rebellion; it is the Colonial Office they have rebelled against, not the Crown. They are loyal enough to the Crown, but they resent that incessant change of policy of our Colonial Office due to party government. When they were attached to the Orange Free State they belonged certainly to a Dutch State, but they were masters of the situation and did what they liked.'

EPILOGUE

The Party is Over

HOWEVER impressive the Kimberley Volunteers and their rekindled patriotism might appear in 1877, the individual and colourful 'democratic' days of the amateur diamond diggers were, in fact, almost over. Even in 1872, as the first rebellion crumbled, some had begun to realize that circumstances were becoming too adverse for their survival. 'Indeed, the fiery spirit of December last burns feebly. The fall in diamonds and the uncertainty of prospects in general, have caused great depression; something like pauperism threatens us. It is no uncommon thing to be solicited by a beggar now-a-days. A few incorrigible scamps and vagabonds we always had, but there is now another class abroad – men who are evidently ashamed to beg, yet cannot live by digging. I fear the palmy days of "pick and shovel" are gone past. A few more months of glutted markets and decreasing values will satisfy all prudent colonists that diamond digging should be left to those who have both capital and time to invest therein.'

Such were the early indications of the not very distant future. Increasing costs and increasing difficulties with collapsing roads and rock-falls, the declining diamond market, which was already beginning to fill the Fields with a new, floating population of discontented, impoverished diggers and beggars, all pointed to the approaching day when the individual digger must be replaced by great trusts and companies rich enough to provide the machinery and organization required for the scientific methods of production and the control of the diamond market, without which the diamond industry must become bankrupt and disappear. All these causes for anxiety and unrest among the diggers had played no small part in creating a rebellious mood which some had fomented for their own disloyal ends.

How early these changes began is shown by the fact that already in 1872 even the river diggings were becoming the target of commercial exploitation. 'I have before me', one digger recorded on 8 July 1872, 'the prospectus of the Klipdrift Mining Company, Ltd., just in process of formation at Klipdrift, for the purpose of working that and other diamondiferous localities on a large scale. The capital is modest, £5,000 in 1,000 shares of

£5 each. The names of the provisional committee and officers are well-known and good names, and I fully believe the enterprise will succeed.'
Already the need for capital beyond what the individual digger could provide was becoming apparent; a need that consistently increased during the next decade, until the diggers were finally forced to quit the Fields. Increasing depth brought increasing flooding and rock-falls to such an extent that soon all the diggers' labour on some claims was absorbed in a vain attempt to clear them of fallen reef.

In these circumstances the need for general co-operation among the diggers became more evident; but their ingrained individualism thwarted all attempts at mutual defensive measures. Those whose claims were central and so in little danger refused to join with others, and all preferred to believe in their own 'luck' rather than face unpleasant facts. This same disunity frustrated even the Diggers' Committee, which consequently gave place in 1874 to a Mining Board which for the same reasons proved similarly ineffective. With but limited funds it bought some machinery and attempted some shaft-sinking of little use, and then abandoned its attempts, leaving the situation worse than before.

Another sign of the new tendencies appeared in the same year as the Mining Board, when the number of claims allowed to miners was raised from two to ten. This new concession inevitably helped to pave the way for the further combinations, consolidations and amalgamations of claims which were to follow. The physical impossibility of working the previous small areas at the depths now reached, was realized as well as the problem created by the division of claims at the New Rush into so many separate properties.

Nor was this all. Even the diggers' rows and riots, partly due to their fear of being dispossessed by the landowners, were creating, at least in one respect, the opposite effect. For in 1875 Sir Henry Barkly, anxious to acquire the Diamond Fields for Britain, seized upon the excuse of the diggers' riots, the prevention of further trouble between diggers and owners, to buy Vooruitzigt for the Government of Griqualand West, so incidentally preparing the way for the later amalgamations. Official sanction came to Sir Henry from Downing Street when the Earl of Carnarvon wrote: 'I am prepared to give my sanction to the arrangement you have made on behalf of the Crown to purchase the Vooruitzigt Farm on which the township of Kimberley, Griqualand West, is situated, for the sum of £100,000. The circumstances which have rendered necessary a step involving the Province in so very heavy expenditure, are greatly to be regretted, but the purchase probably affords the best solution now attainable . . . and I trust your anticipation of the financial results of the operation may be justified.' Had the noble Earl been able to see even but a little way into the future, his letter must have taken a much more optimistic tone.

Meanwhile, ever increasing costs, particularly those due to rock-falls and flooding, increasingly threatened the Mining Board with bankruptcy, which finally occurred in March 1883, when a depth of 400 feet had been reached at Kimberley, and the expense risen from £150,000 for the year 1878 to £650,000 in the last eighteen months. With bankruptcy, reclamation work ceased, and what few diggers still remained were faced with the destruction of their claims. No longer could the necessity for new methods of working be ignored if the mines were to continue. Underground methods must henceforth be employed; shafts must be sunk, far enough from the margin of the open mine not to create rock-falls, and underground tunnels made from the shafts deep into the mine itself. To meet the greatly increased expense of such new methods, a high price for diamonds must be assured by the control of production and of the diamond market. Yet not until after some ten years' struggle was this achieved and a practical monopoly attained with the creation in 1888 of the De Beers Consolidated Mines.

'To the general public,' wrote Sir Percy Fitzpatrick in his *Memoirs*, 'the uniting of the diamond mines in the De Beers Consolidated, was an event of the greatest importance in the business world, and of great and growing importance in the political world; but to those closely concerned it was also a romantic adventure packed full of dramatic incidents and developments of which the outer world knew nothing.' Romantic, certainly; but this was a different kind of romance from that of the early days on the Diamond Fields, although its basic inspiration, the thirst for riches, was the same. Henceforth whatever of romance remained was to be found not on the open claims and in diggers' tents, but in the Company Board Room; not in man's strife with nature, but in the contests of astute minds, while the future beckoned to vast wealth, compared with which the 'finds' of the most fortunate of diggers were beneath contempt.

Amid such changes the scene on the Diamond Fields inevitably and quickly changed, too. In place of the white diggers with their hordes of raw natives crowding the streets, came the much smaller numbers of Whites – mechanics, engineers, managers and business-men – now required, while the natives were increasingly housed in compounds, to both their own and the Company's advantage. 'Rode into Kimberley', wrote one of the early diamond miners at this time, 'and found the place strangely altered. The old-time digger, the farmer digger, had almost disappeared, and in their places had sprung up a mushroom breed of financiers. . . .'

Lord Bryce, visiting Kimberley in 1895, approvingly noted the success of De Beers under Rhodes in completing amalgamation, in eliminating the independent diggers and their ruinous competition, and, so he believed, I.D.B., all of which, combined with the physical difficulties of the mines, had so lowered prices and destroyed profits. The population of Kimberley, he found, was now only some 10,000 persons. As for the town: 'Some of the poorer quarters are almost deserted, the stores and taverns as well as the shanty dwellings, empty and falling to pieces. In the better quarters, however, the old roughness has been replaced by order and comfort. Many of the best villas are embowered in groves of tall Australian gum trees, while the streets and roads are bordered either by gum trees or by hedges of prickly-pear or agave. The streets are wide, and most of the houses are detached and of one storey, built like Indian bungalows; so the town covers an area quite disproportionate to its population, and gives the impression of an extensive city. For the residence of the Europeans employed in the two great mines which the Company works, a suburb called Kenilworth has been built by Mr Rhodes, where neat houses of four, five or six rooms each, stand in handsome avenues planted with Australian trees, the so-called "beef-wood" and the red gum. They are not beautiful trees, but they have the merit of growing very fast, and any shade is welcome.' So much for the new Kimberley in 1895.

Bryce's description is unconsciously but very happily supplemented by that of Lady Sarah Wilson, who visited the town the following year. 'Once humming with speculation, business and movement,' it was now 'the essence of a sleepy respectability and visible prosperity. The cause of this change was the gradual amalgamation of the diamond mines and conflicting interests, which was absolutely necessary to limit the output of diamonds. As a result, the stranger soon perceives that the whole community revolves on one axis, and is centred, so to speak, in one authority. "De Beers" is the moving spirit, the generous employer, and the universal benefactor.'

There were, she found, 7,000 white and black employees in the mines, with 'skilled mechanics receiving as much as £6 a week'. She also noted the model village built for the white workmen by the Company, the orchard with 7,000 fruit trees, and a stud farm for improving the breed of horses in South Africa. 'If I asked the profession of any of the smart young men who frequented the house where we were staying, for games of croquet, it amused me always to receive the same answer: "He is something in De

Beers".' And somewhat mournfully she observed that although Kimberley had many good and large buildings, their roofs were without exception of corrugated iron.

Lady Sarah, like Lord Bryce, had looked upon Kimberley with practical and penetrative eyes; but four years earlier, Lord Randolph Churchill on seeing the town, struck a reflective, valedictory note. 'The story of the diamond mines wins our interest not so much because of the element of the marvellous which surrounds the commencement of the industry – the weird situation, the strange origin, the chance discovery – but because of the difficulties which beset its development. . . . The lesson of Kimberley is the value of effort. There was no high motive to elicit this effort. At first sight scarcely a useful purpose was subserved, for the value of a gem is of all values the most artificial, its beauty is of all beautiful objects least securely founded upon utility. But the digger and the capitalists sought not diamonds but wealth: a few were successful, far more were unsuccessful; but South Africa has reaped the benefit of their efforts. . . . The yield of twenty years' search in the Kimberley mines has been exchanged for sixty-five millions of money. This exchange has been a factor of supreme importance in the history of South Africa. The interest of the mother-country was awakened, the railway system of the Cape Colony was developed, and, above all, an energetic and wealthy community was created in the heart of South Africa. What ultimate developments, political and commercial, will follow the era of gold discovery we cannot tell, but of this at least we may be certain, that the present quickened life of South Africa is the direct outcome of the experience, the energy, and the resources which were concentrated there by the search for diamonds – that Johannesburg and Fort Salisbury are alike the offspring of Kimberley.' Romance and reality! That typically Victorian utterance leaves nothing more to be said.

Select Bibliography

ALGAR, F., *The Diamond Fields*. London, 1872.

ANGOVE, J., *In the Early Days*. Kimberley and Johannesburg, 1910.

BEET, G., *The Grand Old Days of the Diamond Fields*. Cape Town, 1931.

BOYLE, F., *To the Cape for Diamonds*. London, 1873.

BRYCE, J., *Impressions of South Africa*. London, 1897. 3rd edition, 1899.

CHILVERS, H. A., *The Seven Wonders of South Africa*. Johannesburg, 1929.

—— *The Story of De Beers*. London, 1939.

CHURCHILL, Lord RANDOLPH, *Men, Mines and Animals in South Africa*. London, 1892.

COHEN, L., *Reminiscences of Kimberley*. London, 1911.

DU VAL, C., *With a Show through Southern Africa*. London, 1884.

EMDEN, P. H., *Randlords*. London, 1935.

FITZPATRICK, SIR JAMES, *South African Memories*. London, 1932.

FORT, G. S., *The Life of Sir Leander Starr Jameson*. London, 1908.

'FOSSOR', *Twelve Months at the South African Diamond Fields*. London, 1872.

FROUDE, JAMES ANTHONY, *Two Lectures on South Africa*. London, 1880. New edition, 1900.

HARRIS, SIR DAVID, *Pioneer, Soldier, Politician*. Cape Town, 1931.

HUTCHINSON, G., *Frank Rhodes: A Memoir*. Printed for Private Publication, 1908.

INGRAM, J. F., *The Land of Gold and Diamonds*. London, 1889.

JOEL, S., *Ace of Diamonds: The Story of Solomon Barnato Joel*. London, 1958.

KLEIN, H., *Stage Coach Dust. Pioneer Days in South Africa*. London, 1937.

LEWINSOHN, R., *Barney Barnato*. London, 1937.

MASSOT, M., *Au Pays de L'Or et du Diamant*. Paris, 1932.

MORTON, W. J., *South African Diamond Fields*. New York, 1877.

MURRAY, R. W., *South African Reminiscences*. Cape Town, 1894.

PAYTON, Sir CHARLES A., *The Diamond Diggings of South Africa*. London, 1872.

—— *Facts from the Diamond Fields*, By 'Sarcelle'. Reprinted from the *Field*, 19 August 1871.

PHILLIPS, Lady FLORENCE, *Some South African Recollections*. London, 1899.

PHILLIPS, Sir LIONEL, *Some Reminiscences*. London, 1924.

RAYMOND, H., *B. I. Barnato: A Memoir*. London, 1897.

REUNERT, A. T., *Diamonds and Gold in South Africa*. Cape Town, 1893.
SAUER, H., *Ex Africa*. London, 1937.
SCULLY, WILLIAM CHARLES, *Reminiscences of a South African Pioneer*. London, 1913.
—— *Further Reminiscences*. London, 1913.
STRUBEN, H. W., *Recollections and Adventures*. Cape Town, 1920.
TAYLOR, W. P., *African Treasures*. London, 1932.
TILBY, A. W., *South Africa*. London, 1914.
TROLLOPE, A., *South Africa*. 2 vols. London, 1878. Abridged edition. London, 1938.
WARREN, Sir CHARLES, *On the Veldt in the Seventies*. London, 1902.
WEINTHAL, L., *Memories, Mines and Millions: The Life of Sir J. B. Robinson*. London, 1929.
WILLIAMS, A. F., *Some Dreams Come True*. Cape Town, 1948.
WILLIAMS, G. F., *The Diamond Mines of South Africa*. London, 1902.
WILMOT, A., *The Life and Times of Sir Robert Southey*. London and Cape Town, 1904.
WILSON, Lady SARAH, *South African Memories*. London, 1909.
WORSFOLD, W. B., *South Africa*. London, 1895.

NOVELS

BELGRAVE, D. J., *Luck at the Diamond Fields*. London, 1887.
COUPER, J. R., *Mixed Humanity*. London and Cape Town, 1892.
WALKER, ERIC A., *A History of Southern Africa*. 3rd edition. London, 1957.